D1478746

ECHOES FROM THE DEAD ZONE

ECHOES FROM THE DEAD ZONE

ACROSS THE CYPRUS DIVIDE

YIANNIS PAPADAKIS

I.B. TAURIS

LONDON · NEW YORK

Reprinted in 2010 by I.B.Tauris & Co Ltd
6 Salem Road, London W2 4BU
175 Fifth Avenue, New York NY 10010
www.ibtauris.com

In the United States of America and in Canada distributed by
Palgrave Macmillan, a division of St. Martin's Press
175 Fifth Avenue, New York NY 10010

Published in 2005 by I.B.Tauris & Co Ltd
Reprinted in 2006, 2008
Copyright © Yiannis Papadakis, 2005

ISBN 978 1 85043 428 3

A full CIP record for this book is available from the British Library
A full CIP record for this book is available from the Library of Congress

Library of Congress catalog card: available

Typeset in Palatino Linotype by Steve Tribe, Andover
Printed and bound in India by Replika Press Pvt. Ltd.

CONTENTS

Acknowledgements   vii

Prelude   xiii

One   Constantinople   (June–August 1990)   1

Two   Lefkosia   (October 1990–February 1991)   45

Three   Lefkosha   (March 1991)   75

Four   Lefkosha/Lefkosia (April 1991–January 1992)   137

Five   Istanbul   (July–September 1992)   185

Six   Pyla/Pile   (September 1994–September 1995)   207

Postscript   239

Main Sources and Suggestions for Further Reading   253

ACKNOWLEDGEMENTS

My debt is enormous to all the people of Cyprus who were willing to spend time with me, talk and help in many different ways. Various names and personal details have been changed, to ensure anonymity as far as possible. My family provided the support and encouragement that made everything much easier. I would like to thank Paul Sant Cassia and Peter Loizos, who adopted me as their supervisee for my Ph.D. and became good friends. The Department of Social Anthropology at Cambridge provided a stimulating environment where many of the ideas were discussed, and a Bodossakis Research Fellowship at Churchill College gave me the opportunity to read more. Keith Hart's lectures provided some ideas and references that later proved to be invaluable. Our conversations, in various forms, with Michael Herzfeld provided a further source of productive questioning.

For their help and guidance from early on I thank Paschalis Kitromilides and Halil Berktay. For their comments on various drafts I thank Ruth Keshishian, Vangelis Calotychos, Sevina Zesimou, Firdevs Robinson, Yiorgos Syrimis, Costas Constantinou, Stathis Papadakis, Peter Loizos, Yiorgos Agelopoulos, Laura Liguori, Iradj Bagherzade and Keith Hart. I thank Toby Macklin for his help with editing and Steve Tribe for copy-editing. All errors are entirely my own.

I would also like to thank Suniti Namjoshi for permission to quote an excerpt from her poem.

Nepheli's arrival in my life was an added reason to complete this. I thank her for her patience. I can not thank Photini enough for her understanding, help and support during this journey.

To Nini, Stathis and Olivia

And all the little monsters said in a chorus:
You must kiss us.
What! You who are evil,
Ugly and uncivil.
You who are cruel,
Afraid and needy,
Uncouth and seedy.

Yes, moody and greedy.
Yes, you must bless us.

But the evil you do,
The endless ado.
Why bless you?
You are composed of such shameful stuff.

Because, said the monsters, beginning to laugh,
Because, they said, cheering up.
You might as well. You are part of us.

Suniti Namjoshi

PRELUDE

The largest single human-made structure is a wall, the Great Wall of China. This wall separated those who made it from the threatening forces lurking outside. In Nicosia, the capital of Cyprus, walls appear abruptly in the middle of the road. A Dead Zone cuts it in two. Only the excrement in the sewers beneath Nicosia has gained the unquestionable right of free movement.

Cyprus is a place where the dead have been left huddled together underground. They remain there unburied, as cemeteries all round are buried. A place inhabited by the phantoms of lost people, phantoms that own property, receive salaries and are married. A place, like most in fact, where the dead are said to speak louder than the living; where only the dead are allowed to speak and where the living should bow down, listen attentively and obey their commands.

All of us in Cyprus, Greek Cypriots on one side of the Dead Zone, Turkish Cypriots on the other, are obsessed by one question. *Who is to blame*? Our border is also known as the Green Line, because it was first drawn in green. Was it first drawn with pen or pencil? Did the foreign hand that drew it plan this to be a permanent line? When I, like many others, decided to try and find out, I did not know that to find answers I would have to travel back to a place where the dead lived. I did not know that the Dead Zone was to draw me in and eventually capture me.

How did this journey begin? Beginnings are always difficult to choose. Birth is always a likely one, but I had not yet become aware that I was marked by my birth in 1964. I search my memory for the answer. But, which one? For hadn't I changed so much on the way? The answer to who I am now, or who I was then?

CHAPTER ONE
CONSTANTINOPLE
JUNE–AUGUST 1990

DEPARTURE

On the plane, I was fairly confident that I wouldn't be slaughtered upon arrival. But my stomach was churning. Dark thoughts flooded my mind, as we approached Turkey. What was I, a Greek Cypriot, doing on that plane? As everyone knew, in 1974 Turkey had invaded Cyprus and divided my country, leaving a barbed wire gash in between: the Attila Line, as they called it. And yet, there I was heading to Turkey of my own volition. I had worked hard to make that trip happen. I had prepared myself well. I had read so much about Turkey that I felt I had reached an impartial understanding. I was even prepared to accept that they might not be barbarians. Now I pondered. How did I end up on that flight from London to Turkey?

> Cyprus, island of Aphrodite, the island of beauty and love, so the legend goes. But Cyprus has also been a place of conflict and animosity. Since 1974 it has been divided, one side being inhabited by Greeks and the other by Turks. Divided, the island is united by mutual fear and mistrust...

So began a proposal I had written in 1988, two years earlier, while studying in the USA. I had recently read a book by Edward Said called

Orientalism, on how the West had created an image of the East as its opposite. The West stood for democracy, civilization, freedom and intellect and the East for barbarism, despotism, oppression and bodily passion. That sounded so familiar. Just like Greeks and Turks. At the University of California, Santa Cruz where I was studying, I applied to enter a Ph.D. programme to examine Cyprus, where once Greeks had lived together with Turks. Actually, my main motivation then was more related to trying to find a way to extend my stay there. But, later, I was to discover the secret of my birth and would forget those mundane impulses. Even though the applications board rejected my proposal, as I began to read more I became more interested. A year later I managed to gain acceptance for a Ph.D. in the UK.

I entered the department of Social Anthropology at Cambridge to do a comparative study of the two sides of Cyprus: how people thought about each other and the past. Perhaps, I thought, this kind of study could identify the problems and help us come together again in a unified Cyprus. As I read more, I came to suspect that our history in Cyprus was not as simple as I had once thought. Studying social anthropology also made me more suspicious of Greek supremacy. The history of social anthropology turned out to be a struggle against claims of one's own superiority and others' inferiority – 'the West and the rest'. I learned that the last headhunters in Europe were the Greeks and their opponents during the Balkan Wars. Still, during my stays abroad in the West, I had been so proud to note how much the contribution of the Greeks to civilization was appreciated. During parties, I had found it much more advantageous to declare myself a Greek than a Cypriot. Such grandeur in the first; the second rhymed so badly. I was not aware then of how the history of Greece had certain parallels to my own personal history, including the choice to become Greek in order to be favourably accepted in the West. Nor that I had embarked on a journey as a certain kind of Greek that would end with some people trying to impose a different identity on me, the opposite of what I once thought Greek stood for: the barbarian.

Gradually, my research project evolved into a comparative study of nationalism in the two sides of divided Cyprus. This was an island that first emerged as an independent republic in 1960 with a population of 448,000 Greek Cypriots (seventy-seven per cent) and 104,000 Turkish Cypriots (eighteen per cent). Since I wanted to do research with Turkish Cypriots, I thought it would be a good idea to spend a few months in Turkey studying the language. This would also give me an opportunity to learn something about the country that featured so prominently, and so negatively, in our schoolbooks and daily discussions on history and politics. I began to read about Turkey and made some Turkish friends at Cambridge, in order to correct possible biases I might have. In my mind, I was confident that I had succeeded. I even managed to obtain a visa. Before leaving for Turkey, I phoned to ask some Turkish friends to meet me at the airport when I arrived. 'Just to be on the safe side,' I thought. I was unable to reach anyone. I was to land there, a Greek Cypriot, all alone!

ARRIVAL

On the plane my stomach took over. What would happen once I arrived? Would I be taken for interrogation? That much I had to be realistically prepared for. Would I be put behind bars for a few days until they checked things out? Perhaps I would disappear into a prison.

I had told my parents in Cyprus where I was going. I was very pleased that they did not create a huge fuss when I told them. They were very worried, naturally. I expected them to try to dissuade me. I was almost shocked by how understanding they were and how much they trusted me. There was no talk of the film *Midnight Express*, no mention of Turkish atrocities.

If only I could strike up a conversation with some Turk on the plane and befriend him, then perhaps I could ask him to wait for me outside the passport control and somehow also hint that he should raise the alarm if I did not appear. This last part seemed difficult. I would not want him to entertain any wrong ideas that Greeks were paranoid about Turks or that we thought they were barbarians. I looked around at people's faces. Most of them did not look like Turks anyway. They were probably foreigners.

The time of judgement came. I was next in line at passport control. The man in front of me moved on. So smoothly. I handed over my passport. I scrutinized the man at the desk, ready to observe the tiniest muscle move on his face. He opened the passport to the page with the visa, stamped it and handed it back. He didn't even look at me to check if the photo matched.

Immediately, I became suspicious. Perhaps it was a plot. Perhaps they would arrest me later, alone, away from the eyes of western tourists. I went to collect my baggage. I waited and waited. It was lost. Could this be a coincidence? Surely not. Now I would have to go to some quiet office to pick it up and then they would get me. When I finally summoned the courage to go to the lost luggage desk, fortunately there were other people there too. Perhaps I had been prejudiced. I should have known it was just typical Turkish inefficiency. I got my bags a few days later.

AGIA SOPHIA

I saw her from the taxi as we were approaching the city centre. The tall dome was visible from far away. I recognized Agia Sophia, the legendary church of Constantinople, from the photographs I had seen in our schoolbooks. An unwelcome shiver ran through me at the sight of the symbol of the Byzantine Empire, now lying in Turkish hands. Despite my intention to arrive in Istanbul, I would first find myself in legendary Constantinople. At the sight of Agia Sophia, the jewel of Constantinople, memories came back to me of the history lessons I thought I had left behind.

We had grown up in Cyprus as the proudest of Greeks. As everyone knew, ancient Greeks were the original creators of civilization, the people who gave its light to the West. Ancient Greece and Rome, then Europe and the Enlightenment: that was the story of civilization. We had learned at school that our dialect, the Greek dialect of Cyprus, was etymologically much closer to ancient Greek than any other dialect of Greece. The other reason we were the truest Greeks, of course, was that we had suffered so much throughout history at the hands of the Turk. Our small island was centre stage for the eternal confrontation between the forces of good and evil, Greeks and Turks, civilization and barbarism. Our cultural and historic centrality was even confirmed by nature. After all we lived in the Mediterranean, meaning 'centre of the earth'.

The fact that we lived in Cyprus, which according to contemporary borders was an independent state not part of Greece, was of no importance. Everyone knew that historically Cyprus had always been a Greek island. My own father had come from Greece. My mother had been arrested by the British when she was still in high school for distributing leaflets in support of the Union of Cyprus with Greece. In the end ENOSIS, the Union, did not come about. But that was a sad aberration of history – a historical injustice. In my own case, I had once found consolation in the fact that I, at least, was the product of a happy union between Greek and Cypriot.

Even the fact that we did not really like the Greeks of Greece – the *kalamarades*, as we called them, originally meaning scribblers – was of no significance whatsoever. Athens for us stood for the Parthenon, not for the people who now happened to live around it. Everyone knew they were an untrustworthy lot who had betrayed their own brothers in Cyprus and opened the gates to the hordes of Attila, as we called the Turks. In 1974, the colonels of the American-supported junta in Greece had staged a coup in Cyprus against our president, which in turn brought the Turkish calamity upon us. The Greeks lived in a Third World country, unorganized and corrupt, whereas we lived in a developed, western country – well run, good roads, everyone knew English, proper western toilets everywhere, not those Turkish-type holes in the ground still found in Greece. We were proud of being the truest Greeks. Modern Greeks did not matter, the ancients did. Everyone knew that the traditions and heritage of Cyprus were closer to those of the ancient Greeks than those of Greece itself.

We had also learned so much about the Turks. Everyone knew how Turkey invaded Cyprus in 1974, out of the blue, ostensibly to protect a small Turkish minority there, grabbing forty per cent of its territory and tearing away one third of its population from their ancestral lands, turning them into refugees; everyone knew about the killings, the rapes, and the 1,619 persons still missing and unaccounted for. And all this, we knew, was part of a plan hatched by the foreign powers, with Americans in the lead. Even if westerners were so aware of their huge historical debt to us, they had betrayed us by siding with the Turks for political reasons.

Throughout history there had been so many massacres, so many helpless women and children killed by the Turks in bloodbaths. From pictures all over our classrooms the slain Greek heroes always watched us, with their thick moustaches, their traditional head-covers and their stern, proud looks. Sometimes we became them. In our school plays we re-enacted scenes from the Greek Revolution against the Turks, wore their clothes, talked and suffered like them.

We had grown up knowing four dates: 1453, 1821, 1922, 1974.

1453: The Fall of Constantinople to the Turks. Before they came, the Byzantine Empire was a glorious civilization. At its peak, it had taken civilization to the whole of Asia Minor, parts of the Middle East and even Egypt. I still remembered the map of the Byzantine Empire we used at school showing all those lands in the same colour. How proud it made us, and how sad for what had later become of us. Those were the historic lands of the Byzantine Empire, our lands that the Turks gradually took away. Another map was round and had Constantinople in the centre, the centre of the then known world. There were great kings too, eager to spread the light of civilization and the true faith of Christianity to the infidel barbarians living in darkness. Glorious kings like Constantine, known as the Great for so many reasons. The first reason, as we had learned, was his preference for Christianity over pagan and other mistaken faiths. Ours was the Orthodox religion, meaning the correct faith. Basilios the Second was another noble king. We proudly called him *Basilios Boulgaroktonos*, the Slayer of Bulgarians. We were taught how considerate he was in setting captives free, leaving one man out of each hundred with one eye to guide the blind safely home. Many threats had been heroically thwarted during the course of the glorious Empire. Until the galloping arrival of the war-hungry, barbaric hordes of the Turks.

The Turks were nomads, people with no civilization, people of the horse and the sword, descendants of the Mongols, infidels, people of no real religion. People of the Koran, Muslim fanatics who had vowed to spread Islam by the force of fire and the sword. They were told that they were fighting a Holy War and that those who died would become martyrs for the faith. We were told how they were made to believe that their deaths would be handsomely rewarded in the afterlife when they went to paradise, where mountains of rice, rivers of milk and plenty of *houris*, lovely female angels, were waiting for them. All virgins! And they believed it.

We learned how the borders of our Byzantine Empire were heroically defended against infidel attacks by the *Akrites*, meaning the ones living at the edges. I did not know then that, during my later research in Cyprus, I would come to live with another kind of *Akrites*, the people living next to our current border with the Turks in Lefkosia, the divided capital of Cyprus.

The Fall of Constantinople was actually the work of a traitor, we learned. A Byzantine had opened a secret door, the *Kerkoporta*, and the Turks came in, murder and plunder in their eyes, their swords gleaming. Soon they were not gleaming, they were dripping. It was on a Tuesday, and ever since Tuesday has been considered an unlucky day for Hellenism. And it was all the work of a traitor. Just like the 300 brave men of Leonidas, when the Spartans were fighting the Persians. They fought against thousands of Persians. The name of the traitor on that occasion was Efialtis ('Nightmare'). Had there been no traitor, would

Constantinople have fallen? We had also learned about the abduction of children to turn them into janissaries, fighters for the Turks. Torn from their mothers' embraces they became, without knowing it, traitors. The janissaries were the bravest warriors the Turks had. They became the bravest Turkish warriors because their blood was Greek, even if they did not know it. If the janissaries, who were really Greek, had not helped them, would the Turks have accomplished what they did? The Turks were also helped by the West, of course. The Catholics had ransacked, plundered and weakened the Empire during the Crusades, thus making it easier for the Turks to do the deed. The last reason for the defeat was disunity, the Greek disease, our greatest vice. 'Five Greeks, six parties,' the saying went. And what were traitors anyway but an expression of disunity? Of course, we also learned there was some honour in disunity. Because we were by nature the most democratic people, the inventors of democracy, we were bound to disagree with each other.

The Ottoman period was presented as the bleak middle ages in the history of Greece. As the rest of the world went on through Enlightenment to rediscover freedom and democracy – a Greek invention and a Greek word – we were stuck under the yoke of the Turks. 'The Sick Man of Europe' was how the Ottoman Empire was described. I had found that name biased and unfair. Since when did the Turks belong in Europe?

But the sickness was clearly contagious. Take cheating, for example, that was said to be the national vice of the Greeks. We all admitted this. We were cheating in queues, cheating to get a government job, cheating the tax inspector, cheating the state in every way we could. And we knew where it came from, whose fault it was. The generic word for corruption in Greek was *rousfeti*; etymologically, this was not a Greek word but Turkish. Even the cribs we used for cheating at school, that came especially handy during the ancient Greek lessons, had a Turkish name, *kettapes*. So, it was clearly all the Turks' fault. At the same time we took some historical pride in our cheating. For 400 years we were enslaved under the brutal and oppressive regime of the Ottoman Empire, a barbaric regime that laid waste our previously glorious, refined and tolerant Byzantine civilization. What could we do under such conditions? The only way to survive was to cheat, to cheat against the authorities. And old, historic – a Greek word too – habits died hard.

Even under the oppression of backward Turkish rule, we did not lose our courage and hope. Our legends spoke of the resurrection of our empire, of the fall of the oppressor. What if Constantinople was named Istanbul? Even the name the Turks took from us. The Greek phrase *eis tin Polin*, meaning 'to the city', became Istanbul. Even if it was Greek, we never used it. It was the name our enemies used for the City. Only traitors would refer to the historically Greek Constantinople as Istanbul. For Greeks it always was, and always would be, Constantinople. Legends spoke of how one day Constantine, the last emperor, would be resurrected to liberate Constantinople, chase the Turks away and 'there will be such a bloodbath that the cattle will have to swim in blood.' We knew whose blood it would be.

1821: The Greek Revolution against the Turks finally began. Men, and even women, fought bravely. Words could not describe the atrocities committed against them. The Greeks preferred to kill themselves than fall alive into the hands of the Turks. Our heroes had proud names like Nikitaras the *Tourkofagos*, the Turk-eater. Finally, after 400 years, freedom came. A small kingdom of Greece was first created, tiny in comparison to what historically belonged to Greece. But it was expanding. The *Megali Idea*, the Great Idea, was to re-establish a state covering the lands that rightfully belonged to the Greeks, those of the Byzantine Empire. In 1919 the Greeks, with the support and encouragement of the Great Powers, launched the Asia Minor Campaign to recapture what belonged to them and to liberate the people from the decaying, miserly 'Sick Man of Europe'. The Greeks were winning but then internal divisions and the treachery of the Great Powers, who suddenly abandoned them, led to defeat in 1922.

1922: The Catastrophe, as it has since come to be called. The Turkish army once more committed untold atrocities and Greeks were expelled from their historic homelands in Asia Minor, millions of them coming to Greece as refugees. Among the lucky ones who came to Greece having survived the massacres was a small child called Maria. She was my grandmother.

1974: The Attila Invasion in Cyprus. Once more Turkish barbarism was unleashed, this time in Cyprus, my own birthplace. I was a child of ten then, more or less my grandmother's age when she was torn away from her home. Once more there were refugees, once more there were atrocities when the Turkish army invaded, tearing our island apart. Tents sprang up all around. Long convoys arrived in the south where I lived, unloading people with darkness in their eyes. Many people were lost. Abortion was made legal because so many women had been raped by Turks.

Every important date in our history as Greeks bespoke our encounters with Turkish barbarism. And I was a product of this history.

WAITING FOR THE BARBARIANS

When I saw them approaching, staring at me intensely, I realized I was treading on their turf. I prepared for the confrontation.

I had only just moved there, after spending a couple of hours sitting mesmerized at Beyazit, a central square in Constantinople where the university's administration was housed. The sun had just risen and a light mist was still hanging in the air. The square was large, with spectacular Ottoman buildings. The city was still sleepy. Gradually people had begun to appear. First, long lines of workers emerged from the bus station, heading to their jobs. Then various sellers appeared, mostly old men peddling seeds, and children with plastic baskets. I had never been so fascinated by people. There was nothing extraordinary about them at all. That was the most extraordinary thing. That people in Turkey looked like... well, like people. There were people in Turkey, not just men, or warriors, all kinds of people. Sitting there I felt numbed by the force of that discovery. It was not the first time I had seen Turks. I had Turkish friends back at the university. But somehow they did not seem quite real. They did not seem like Turks, or Turk enough perhaps. Somehow, I had regarded them as exceptions.

After enrolling for the language course at the university, I sat outside to wait for the first class. That was when I saw them approaching. I realized that I had taken their spot. They outnumbered me, but I was not scared. They were sellers, carrying their wares in tiny baskets. Inside the plastic baskets were packets of chewing gum and biscuits; others carried brushes and the usual paraphernalia of shoe shiners. The boys had dark vivid eyes and short hair, the girls had long wild hair. All were thin and full of energy, around eight to ten years old. It did not take long to break the ice. They began to laugh at me unashamedly, from the first instance that I tried to talk to them in my stumbling Turkish. They were very curious and excited to meet a foreigner who tried to speak Turkish. From then on, my day would start with a visit outside the mosque where, faithful to our early morning date, we would meet, talk and laugh. That became my daily lesson in Turkish before going to the classes. After our first meeting, they stopped trying to sell me things, but pressed free chewing gum and biscuits on me instead. My shoes, like it or not, were shined. Later I managed to cheat on them by appearing with sandals. They looked just like the kids back home but I had never been that moved by children before.

THE COMPATRIOT

The time came to go to my Turkish language class. All my classmates were foreigners, Italian, French and German, apart from Alkiviades, who was from Greece. I was glad to find one of my own people there. He was shocked. 'You are from Cyprus? Do you realize that you are in a high-risk group here?'

He was slim, with nervous dark eyes, constantly darting from myself to our surroundings in the cafeteria, sometimes turning back to check as he spoke. 'I can't believe you did this. You, a Cypriot, coming to Turkey! How did you manage this? How come they allowed you? How come you haven't been detained yet? Do you know you are being followed?' I was alarmed. He came closer and lowered his voice even though there was no one near our table:

> I don't see anyone right now who might be following you, but I can guarantee that the police are checking your every step. They may do something to you any time. Someone else might do it, but the police or the security or the government will have given the order. Or some crazy guy may attack you just like that if you tell anyone you are from Cyprus. There are such fanatics here you will not believe. I've been here longer than you. I know what I'm talking about. Imagine this, I come to Turkey and here I meet a compatriot from Cyprus for the first time.

I asked him if anything had happened to him. Nothing so far but he was always on guard. 'I come from the Peloponnese,' he explained. 'You know where it is?' I couldn't hide feeling offended. 'Of course,' I replied, 'we all know where the Peloponnese is.' 'OK, yes you do, of course you must know down there,' he said:

> I hope to go to university here. After I learn the language well, I hope to enter university here and study Ottoman civilization. Pfff, civilization, what did they have? Nothing, and what they had they took from us. I know what I'm talking about. That's how they learned to build their mosques, by copying our churches. They were just savages before they came here riding on their horses. Take music, which I know well. Do you know that all the music

they have, what they call their real, authentic, traditional music, Ottoman music, they took from us? I want to prove that they took it all from us, everything. Even this drink they call *raki* that they present to poor tourists who don't know any better, they call it their national drink. Well, it is exactly like our ouzo but they don't know that they took it from us. Do you see what I mean?

I wasn't sure that I agreed and he may have sensed it. One reason I was mistrustful was that he was a Greek from Greece and we didn't trust them much. They didn't like us much either. Still, in the beginning we stuck together a lot even if 'there was always something between us', as we would say back home. His remarks about my safety though hit right on target. For a while I used all the tricks I had seen in spy movies to check if anyone was following me. I used shop windows as mirrors to check behind me, I bent down to redo my shoelaces and threw brief glances behind. Whenever I went into a coffee shop I checked who else came in. After a few days of doing this, I began to feel important. Was the Turkish government so concerned about me that they had to pay people to tail me all the time? I must have been a real drain on their poor resources. Then in the spy movies there was always a gorgeous woman who would try to find out about you by various not so tortuous means. After a couple of weeks of checking behind my back and waiting, hoping rather, for her to make her move, I began to feel just a little foolish. But Alkiviades had been right after all. As I would soon realize, someone was watching me most of the time, sometimes in uniform, sometimes in civilian clothes, and he was no ordinary man.

A GUARDIAN SAINT

My personal guardian angel appeared when I went to the all-male student hostel in Majka. The registration desk was swarming with students, all pushing and putting forward various forms. I tried to push my way through. But in Cyprus we were not as skilled in such matters as the *kalamarades* in Greece. That was when he appeared. He asked if I was a foreigner. I explained, and he took my forms without commenting on where I came from. As he walked towards the desk, I noticed that he moved with a pronounced limp. As he entered into the swarm, it seemed to open up in front of him, like Moses parting the waters. Clearly, he was well known and respected. In no time, all was arranged. He then accompanied me to my room and from that moment we became friends. He told me his name was Veli, meaning guardian or saint. With him and his friends I felt more comfortable about exploring the city.

ORAL HYGIENE AND MOUTH LIBERATION

When it came to speaking Turkish, I had a clear advantage over my other European classmates and Alkiviades because I was able to easily pronounce most Turkish sounds. Speaking Turkish felt like a welcome liberation to my mouth. It often felt more comfortable than speaking Greek. In Cyprus, we mostly spoke the local Greek dialect. I now realized that it was full of sounds similar to the sounds of Turkish, ones that the Greeks from Greece had real trouble with, as I confirmed with a touch of malicious glee, seeing Alkiviades struggle. Back in Cyprus, we had been for years scolded and punished at school for using our dialect. The sounds of our dialect that resembled Turkish sounds, sounds like *sh*, *ch* and *j*, were said to be wrong and vulgar. That was how peasants spoke. My teachers in Cyprus had been very keen on oral hygiene. We were told endlessly that we should speak 'cleanly', meaning that we should speak like Greeks in Greece, and that we should not put 'dirty' words in our mouths, meaning, as I was coming to realize, that we should not use many words of Turkish origin. Many of our swear words came from Turkish. Their vulgar sound accentuated their content.

Take the word for homosexual, for example. Homosexuality was often said to be another corrupting influence from the Turks who ruled Greece for 400 years. The act itself was sometimes called in Greek *Othomaniko*, meaning the Ottoman way. Didn't the Ottoman rulers like to keep a plump, young boy at their side for entertainment of various sorts? There was even a special word in Greek for the Turkish boy in that position: *yiousoufaki*. The word for homosexual in Greek was *poushtis*. This was a Turkish word, not a Greek one, and etymology, as we all knew, provided conclusive proof with regards to origins.

But we had many more words in common, as I now realized while eating with my friends. With our beers we ordered various titbits to nibble, called *meze* in Greece and Cyprus, and the same in Turkey. Everything that arrived on the table was food I knew and whose Turkish name I already knew: *keftes, taramas, tzatziki, ttavas*, all traditional food served in tourist restaurants all over Greece and Cyprus. The same with sweets: *loukkoumi, soutzoukos, paklavas, kourabies*. The problem was that they regarded them as typically Turkish while I regarded them as typically Greek. Fortunately, etymology could settle the issue.

Unfortunately, they were right. All the words were Turkish. So all the food we served to unsuspecting tourists was not authentic Greek or Cypriot food, but Turkish.

A couple of evenings after my arrival, a small group gathered in the yard of the hostel. Musical instruments were produced, along with a couple of bottles of Turkish *raki*. When I asked how come Muslims drank alcohol they laughed. First, they were not believers. Second, even those who were drank anyway. A couple of friends joined us and Veli introduced them as Kurds. They were surprised and pleased to meet me. 'You are Greek from Cyprus? We are brothers then,' they commented in low voices and we shook hands warmly. 'They say there are no Kurds in Turkey. That we are some kind of mountain Turks. That we speak a dialect of Turkish.' They started singing, but I could not understand the words. After each song, I asked what it was about. The answer was always the same: Freedom. Then came the time for dancing. 'What kinds of things do you dance?' they asked. 'Well,' I replied, '*karshilamas*, *chifteteli*, *zeymbekiko*, these are our traditional dances.' They roared with laughter for they too knew the names of the dances, and all the names came from Turkish.

Etymology had become a problem, but gradually it turned into a source of welcome self-revelation. Learning Turkish was an exploration deep into the subconscious of the Greek language. An exploration of denial and suppression. There were so many things I knew and did not know at the same time; so many words we used whose origins were found in Turkish; so many words that were dear and intimate but were also regarded as barbaric and vulgar. Not just swear words, or words for sweets and food, but words expressing intimate feelings too, such as *kefi*, *glenti*, *nazi* or *marazi*: joy, partying, coyness, sadness. And so many expressions: in Greek, as in Turkish, we would 'drink' a cigarette; to get beaten up was 'to eat wood'; proverbs like 'Do the good deed and throw it into the sea' (don't ask anything in return); endings of words in Greek such as those for professions in '-tzi' (*taxitzis*). These I now encountered as I was learning Turkish.

The dialect we spoke in Cyprus, as I came to realize, contained many more such words than the Greek we learned at school. When I learned the numbers in Turkish I realized that I had already known them in a way. I had used them so often while playing backgammon – *tavli* in Greek, *tavla* in Turkish – but did not really know what they meant. A dice score of two-one we called *kibiros* but I did not know that it was *iki-bir* (two-one) in Turkish. Double four was *tortja* (in Turkish four was *dort*), double five was *toubeshi* (in Turkish five was *besh*). We knew that certain sounds distinguished our dialect from 'proper' Greek, all sounds I found in Turkish. In Cyprus we had even borrowed whole grammatical structures. In Turkish one made an inferential statement ('It is said that…') by adding *-mish* at the end of a sentence. In Cyprus too, though not in Greece, we used *-imish* or *-mishimou* in the same way. In Cyprus we sometimes called to God in Turkish, to Allah, and in perfect Turkish accent too: *mashalla* ('may God bless you'), *inshalla* ('let God's will be done'). We used the name of the devil in Turkish too – of course: *sheyttanis*.

When it came to other sensual pleasures beyond food, we even shared the same dream. My friends felt that Turkish society was too oppressive. In Turkey, a man was expected to provide a significant dowry to have a good chance in marriage. Fortunately, I thought, in Cyprus, such unfair and oppressive measures did not exist. In Cyprus, the woman was expected to provide the dowry. Like us, they dreamt of going to the West, where getting sex was easy. At least, we realized, we shared the same anthropological fantasy. We all hoped to one day discover a society where foreign men would be as desirable as foreign women were in our own.

GLORIOUS EMPIRES

Initially, as if by unspoken agreement, we avoided talking about history and politics. I think that we all doubted if we would be able to remain friends if we did. One day, finally, almost to my relief, Veli asked me to tell him about the history we had learned at school. I told him everything exactly as we had been told. How the Turks had attacked our glorious, civilized, tolerant and cosmopolitan Byzantine Empire reducing it to the current small Greek state. How historically they were always the aggressors and we the victims. How they had always been expansionist against us. How they even tried to grab Cyprus with the invasion of 1974, the final proof of their historical expansionism. Veli and his friends were speechless, shocked by the propaganda we had learned. I asked what they had learned at school. They told me all about their cosmopolitan, tolerant Ottoman Empire; how the Greeks had a privileged role there and how, instead of showing appreciation, they stabbed the Turks in the back by being the first to revolt; of the atrocities the Turks had suffered at the hands of the Greeks; how the Greeks were the first to grow at their Empire's expense, reducing it to the current

small state of Turkey; how Greek expansionism led to the invasion of
Turkey in the 1920s; how Greeks proved their expansionism once more
by staging the coup in Cyprus in 1974 in order to unite Cyprus with
Greece, forcing Turkey to intervene. I was numbed by the propaganda
they had learned.

We spoke for a long time. Something was wrong. Someone had been
cheated. The more we talked the more we realized that probably both
of us had.

A SCARRED MARXIST

I met Erkin at one of the cafés near the sea at Ortakoy. I approached the
table where he was reading amidst a pile of books to ask if I could have
a look at one of them. Soon we were talking amicably. Erkin told me
that his real passion was Marxism. ('Erkin', by the way, meant free or
independent.) Even though he was younger than me he had read a lot,
much more widely and deeply than I had ever ventured. He explained
that he liked reading but people here in Turkey did not. 'When they see
me read at a bus stop or in the bus they sometimes push me on purpose,'
he complained. 'They think that anyone who reads is a reactionary.
But even we Marxists are not much better. You see this scar here?' He
pointed to his forehead. 'The Freudian Marxists did it to me when I
went to one of their meetings and disagreed with them.' He pointed out
various other scars: 'This one is from the Leninist Marxists, the other
one from the nationalist Marxists, this one from Islamic Marxists, and
this from postmodern Marxists.'

He explained how Marxism had been outlawed in Turkey and
the jails had until recently been full of Marxists, who were treated as
national traitors. But it was beginning to be tolerated and to re-emerge.
He also told me about the secret police:

> In the university, they say that one in ten is secret police or working
> for them. There is this organization that controls the universities,
> itself controlled by the army. You can pick out these secret policemen
> easily. First of all, usually everyone knows who they are. Often,
> they pretend they are Marxists too but, of course, they have a very
> shallow knowledge of Marxism. This always gives them away.

From that day, whenever we met a Marxist he knew but did not like he
told me the same thing: 'Pfff, even the secret police know more about
Marxism than him.'

A few days later he took me to a 'Marxist conference', which he explained was 'half underground'. It was given a less threatening gloss by presenting it as a 'workers' conference'. He pointed out the man videotaping the proceedings: 'You see him? He is a secret policeman.' Then pointed to the photographers: 'You see them? They are policemen too.'

One day he came to our meeting laughing, eager to tell me of his recent encounter with a Turkish Cypriot:

> You won't believe what happened to me as I was coming. I took a taxi and from the accent of the taxi driver I knew he came from Cyprus. We can tell them at once when they open their mouths. Anyway, I told him I was going to meet with a Greek Cypriot, just to see his reaction, and he started on the story of his life. 'Ah, I had a good job back in Cyprus, a sweet life but I had to leave. The Greeks forced me out.' So I asked him what he did. 'I was a *pezevenk*.' You know what *pezevenk* means, don't you? [Of course. It was one of those words.] It is the man who sells women, usually a swear word. 'You see,' the driver said, 'I was selling Turkish women but the Greeks were able to sell both Greek and Turkish women, so I could not compete with them. I'll tell you my theory about men and women. Greek women are more active in bed while the Turkish are more reserved, except when the man is unable to continue and then they become very active. The bed is like a battleground, you see, between the man and the woman. Men who were sure of themselves went for Greek women, those who were not so sure went for Turkish women. But I could not offer a choice. So I came here to practise my profession, but it was no good. The market here is controlled by the Armenians, and so I ended up as a taxi driver.'

We also spoke about other important aspects of history. Erkin did not trust the Turkish version of history. Nor the Greek one, for exactly the same reasons. Both took huge empires at their peak as their starting points, making both people now feel that history had been totally unjust given their current smaller states. Both accused the other of expansionism for exactly the same reason: because each regarded the lands of their past Empire as historically theirs. Both hid the atrocities that were committed against the others, making each side feel that only they had been victimized. 'The trick is simple,' he said. 'Both histories lie using the truth. That is always the best way to lie. When they talk about their own empires, it is all about the kings and the glory of

Empire. When they talk about others' empires, it is all about the people and how they were oppressed.' Erkin explained that for the mass of the population, the shifts of Empires did not necessarily make much difference. For the emperors yes, but for the common people very little, if any. Yet that was how we learned history: as a procession of Empires. 'How do you think Agia Sophia was built?' he asked:

> How do you think all those enormous Ottoman mosques were created? The emperors commissioned them. Think of all those people who built them working like slaves at the whim of an emperor who just wanted to build a monument as testimony to his own glory. How can we admire those monuments today? Shouldn't we cry when we see the pyramids of the pharaohs? Think of the thousands of slaves who toiled and died building them. The pharaoh could just as easily have lain in an ordinary one by two piece of land like the rest of us.

A TOUR OF CONSTANTINOPLE

'Come with me,' Alkiviades said one day at the end of our classes. 'I'll show you Constantinople.' First stop was Agia Sophia. I could have guessed as much. I protested that I had been there already, but Alkiviades thought we should see it again. So, we strolled around Agia Sophia. Alkiviades reminded me how the greatest symbol of Hellenism had been turned into a mosque, and pointed out how badly preserved it was. His eyes got stuck on the enormous round inscriptions from the Koran on the ceiling. 'You see how they desecrated the greatest symbol of Byzantium by turning it into a mosque and placing those ugly Arabic banners inside? So how do you feel now?'

Then we went to the Patriarchate. Here was another symbol of Hellenism under the Turkish yoke. We had lunch with the priests. They spoke in Turkish among themselves. I was surprised. In the heart of Orthodoxy, in the heart of Hellenism, the priests spoke Turkish! 'It's not strange,' Alkiviades explained. 'Most of them were born here in Turkey. Anyway, how do you feel now after our visit to the Patriarchate?'

After the Patriarchate we walked around the area where the Phanariotes, the Greek nobles of the Ottoman Empire used to live. We walked for a long time along the old Byzantine walls of Constantinople, pausing to read Greek inscriptions. Alkiviades took me to the ruins of the Byzantine Palace, the residence of Emperor Constantine until 'it fell into foreign, barbaric hands', as he put it. Then we visited the place where he was staying. We met a gardener there, a Greek born in Turkey. He was angry. 'You are Cypriot? Well, it's because of you we got all this,' he muttered and left. 'Don't misunderstand him,' Alkiviades said. He explained how in the 1950s, riots erupted in Turkey against the Greeks living there, sparked off by the political troubles in Cyprus. 'You saw the deep scar in his cheek? Well he got it here during the events in Cyprus. The mob attacked him and he barely managed to escape.'

On our way back, we were tired and solemn. Turning a corner, we were surprised by some pigeons taking off in front of us. 'Stupid Turkish pigeons,' muttered Alkiviades. Then a group of kids who were playing almost ran into us. 'Silly Turks,' he exclaimed. When we sat down to eat, Alkiviades exploded. 'You see what they did to us? You see what they took from us? You see how all Turkey is really Greek, how Hellenism painfully encounters you at every step here? It's not a bad place this Turkey you see, but the pity is that the Turks live here.' We sat in silence. I thought he wanted me to add something to express my disgust too, but I didn't feel like it. I felt under pressure though, because I knew that Greeks had doubts about us in Cyprus and I did not want to confirm them. Finally, I came up with something. 'Yes, the problem is that here there is no price...' I started, intending to describe how I had just gone to a film shop and there were no prices on the films so I had to bargain, and that no price here was ever fixed. But the word for price in Greek was the same as for honour: *timi*. Alkiviades cut me short. 'Yes, well put, there is no *timi* here, one day they pretend to be your friend, next day they stab you in the back, no sense of honour at all.'

Our rice had just arrived. It was deliciously spiced with pine kernels and sultanas. I tried to change the subject. 'This rice is really good, isn't it?' I suggested meekly. 'Yes it is,' he replied. 'It's Byzantine rice of course, that's how the Byzantines used to cook it. They even stole our rice. Well, how do you feel now after our tour?'

I felt angry, but I didn't tell him. That question had been getting on my nerves. It was as if he doubted me, as if he doubted the patriotism of people from Cyprus. I knew that he did not approve of my Turkish friends. He had told me that he didn't expect a Greek, especially one from Cyprus, he underlined, to behave here in Turkey in that way. The fact that it was a Greek from Greece who dared doubt our patriotism made me angrier. I wanted to tell him that it was all their fault, with that bloody coup that they staged in Cyprus. All that talk about Constantinople this, Constantinople that, was getting on my nerves too. I had begun to make friends here, and this was their city. Lately, I had begun feeling less that I was in Constantinople and more that I was in Istanbul.

The more I lived there, learning the language, eating and drinking, doing ordinary things, the more difficult it became to hate the Turks as I once did. I was glad to see that Turks were nowhere near as bad as we had made them out to be and to see that we had many things in common. I thought that all this was very good news for Cyprus. Surely Greek Cypriots and Turkish Cypriots had even more in common and so perhaps it would be possible for us to live together some day.

REJECTION

I was very interested in meeting the Greeks who still lived in Turkey. I decided to visit the Islands, as they were called, four small islands close to Istanbul, where Jews, Armenians and Greeks still lived. In part I was in search of my own personal history: to find my grandmother's holiday home, where she used to go as a child before she left Turkey, and maybe discover a relative of hers. Cars were banned there, turning the islands with their imposing wooden houses into green oases of calm and beauty.

Mr Kostas, the first local Greek I met there, was a gentle old man who operated a small grocery shop. His face darkened when I told him where I came from. 'Cyprus!' he said. 'You know things happened here because of you, and as for that Makarios, I really don't know what to say.' That was all he said. My presence clearly made him feel uncomfortable and so I left. The man he mentioned, Makarios, was the Archbishop of Cyprus, one of the leaders of the EOKA movement, who in 1960 became the first President of Cyprus.

I tried to find my grandmother's summer house. It was almost seventy years since she had left but she vaguely remembered having been there as a child. 'It is the last house on the way to the hill where the monastery is,' she had told me on the phone. But many new houses had since been built. I found the oldest looking one and took photos to show her later.

As I was asking around for the house, someone pointed me to a Greek woman living there who might remember. I met the old woman sitting at her doorstep. When I said where I came from, she twitched in discomfort. This time it was of a different kind – as if a cloud of fear suddenly engulfed her. She lowered her voice as she greeted me and looked around her. Once again I left without talking more. She did not try to stop me. She seemed relieved to see me leave.

A few days later, I became friends with a Greek who had grown up and lived in Istanbul. Nearhos, a well educated man in his fifties, told me about the tragic links in our histories. Before the start of the Greek Cypriot EOKA struggle for ENOSIS, relations between Greece and Turkey were in one of their most positive stages. The Greek minority in Turkey was enjoying a time of security and prosperity. Things rapidly deteriorated with the start of EOKA in 1955. Pressure was placed on the Greeks in Turkey to denounce EOKA. Most people tried to remain neutral in the Cyprus dispute, refraining from either condemning the Greek Cypriots as the Turkish press demanded, or enthusiastically supporting them as Greeks in Greece and Cyprus expected. Some distinguished Greeks there said that the status quo of British colonialism in Cyprus should continue. Even the Patriarch, the spiritual leader of Hellenism, appeared to favour the continuation of the colonial status quo. He made critical remarks about Archbishop Makarios. One eminent member of the Greek community there, a member of the Democratic Party of Turkey, went as far as to say that Cyprus should be handed over to Turkey.

On 6 and 7 September 1955, soon after the struggle for ENOSIS in Cyprus had begun, widespread rioting broke out in Istanbul against the Greek minority. Hundreds of buildings, including churches, shops, schools and houses were looted in one night and many Greeks were killed. The Turkish government used this opportunity to strike at its own enemies, the communists, alleging that the rioting was part of a communist plot. These events triggered by the EOKA struggle, events within living memory, led to the persecution of the Greek minority and a sharp decline in their fortunes and numbers. They came to associate Cyprus with their persecution and downfall. Nearhos said that his mother never uttered the name of Makarios without cursing.

Things did not go well with people from Greece I got to meet in Istanbul either. When I met a group of tourists from Greece and introduced myself in Greek to a couple they looked at me curiously. They were surprised. But not for the reason I thought. 'You are Greek Cypriot really? So you actually speak Greek down there?' What did they think we spoke in Cyprus? Turkish? Soon, there would be consolation of sorts, when I found out that Turkish Cypriots were equally misunderstood.

WHO AM I?

My friends gave me an easy book of stories by a contemporary Turkish writer they liked. His surname was Nesin, meaning 'What are you?' He had chosen this surname in order to have this philosophical question posed each time he was addressed. I didn't need to go to such lengths since I was asked all the time. What are you? Where are you from? The answer was always difficult. I had to choose carefully. The reactions were even more problematic: either I was not loved, or not hated enough. Or else, I was totally misunderstood.

At first, I thought it would be safer to introduce myself as 'Greek' when I met someone on my own, outside of my circle of friends. Reactions ranged from indifference to intensity, the latter especially from young people. 'We should be friends you know. We, the people have nothing to fight about. It's all the politicians' fault.' I was to hear this last sentiment so often in Turkey. Sometimes, people came up with pieces of our overlapping, torn-apart past. 'My grandfather came from Crete, he spoke fluent Greek,' said one, referring, I learned, to the 1922 population exchanges after the war. A taxi driver who was taking me back to the hostel had stronger views: 'You hate us, don't you? The Greeks hate the Turks, they want war with us.' During a dinner, one of the guests described his holiday to the Greek islands. 'I was on the boat doing a tour of the islands with some European tourists. At every island, the guide would tell us about the history. "Here the Turks killed so many thousands, at the other island so many hundreds were slaughtered by the Turks..." and on and on.'

At some point, I was rather disappointed that they did not seem to hate Greeks as much as I had thought. I was disappointed because one of the reasons I had felt we were justified in hating them was that they hated us more and that they started hating us first. Perhaps they were just being polite, and not showing their true feelings. One thing I came to be certain of was that they did not bother as much with Greece, as we did about Turkey. In the media, there was little mention of Greece, whereas Turkey was always prominent in Greece and Cyprus. The Turks had other more pressing problems. Economic and social issues, along with the Kurdish problem, dominated the media. Perhaps they did not feel threatened by Greece. After all, they were the stronger state.

Gradually I felt confident enough to take the next step. Come out with a truer truth: 'I am from Cyprus.' This caused problems and soon I had to stop, at least when I spoke in Turkish. 'Oh, from the babyland (*yavru-vatan*)! Welcome to the motherland (*anavatan*),' a street-vendor exclaimed. 'Babyland' was what Turks called Cyprus: Turkey was the 'motherland'. The vendor had mistaken me for a Turkish Cypriot. I explained that I was a Greek Cypriot, but he was not convinced. 'You look just like a Turk,' he protested. Looks would always be a problem. I often caught myself thinking in such terms: 'Doesn't he look like my friend Kostas from Limassol?' or 'Isn't she just like Maria?' It took time to understand these reactions. We had been brought up to believe that we were so different, like day and night, black and white, humans and monsters.

I thought that my bad Turkish would make it obvious that I could not be Turkish Cypriot. Things worked the other way round. Some people seemed to believe that Turkish Cypriots could not speak good Turkish anyway. After my experience with the Greek tourists, I was quite pleased to hear that Turkish Cypriots were similarly misunderstood.

In the end I learned from my friends how best to describe myself. In Turkish I was *Kibrisli Rum*. *Kibrisli* meant Cypriot, no problem, but *Rum*? Where did that come from? I knew that during the Ottoman Empire, the Greeks called themselves *Romii*, meaning Romans, the people of the Eastern Roman Empire, as the Byzantine Empire was also known. The Ottomans called them *Rum*. The Greeks still living in Turkey were called *Rum* by Turks, while those in Greece were *Yunanli*. I did not like the implication of this, that we living in Cyprus were regarded as ex-Ottoman subjects.

Like it or not, if I wanted to explain who I was in Turkish it would have to be *Kibrisli Rum*. Even then, I didn't get much reaction. People didn't seem to care or know much about Cyprus. Perhaps, I thought, the issue was closed for them, over and done with. For us it was still an open wound.

In the hostel, someone moved into my room right after me. He gave me the creeps and was the one person I suspected of being a spy. One day he started a conversation on Cyprus. In contrast to others, he knew some names and dates like 1960, the year of independence, and 1963, when some troubles took place. He knew names too. Makarios, everyone knew, but he had also heard of Grivas, an army officer who, along with Makarios, became the second leader of the EOKA struggle. 'How do you feel about the Turkish Cypriots?' he asked. I said that I had nothing against them. 'Yes,' he responded, 'but you used to kill them before, and now they want Turkish guarantees for their safety. It's only natural, isn't it?' I thought of what Erkin had told me about people who possessed a shallow knowledge of a topic.

I did have one more option available, one I cherished for special occasions: *gavur*, infidel. Say I was introduced to a woman I wanted to strike a chord with. Then I would nonchalantly reply: 'Oh, I am just an infidel (*gavur*), you know.' She would laugh with embarrassment and apologize. 'Please, don't use that word. It was only used in the past for your people but it was wrong and one shouldn't use it any more.' What a great opening line! It immediately drew attention, created interest and put the other on the defensive. I was kind of hoping it would then lead to an attempt to demonstrate in practice how much they liked us.

The reactions to my presence in Turkey were not what I had anticipated. All rather disappointing, especially as I had gone there thinking I was doing something heroic and dangerous. And I had no problems with the secret police as far as I knew. As I began to feel more comfortable there and less worried about my safety, a different fear took over. What would I tell people back in Cyprus about my visit? What would I say when they asked how I was treated as a Greek Cypriot in Turkey? It would all sound so suspicious. In fact, the problems with the secret police would only begin when I got back home.

THE BIRTH OF THE FATHER

How should one go about finding out who someone is? Where I came from, I learnt that the first thing was to find out about their family; which really meant their father. In the case of Turkey nothing could be easier. Everyone knew him. He was Ataturk, his name meaning 'Father Turk'.

He watched me sternly everywhere I went, as if he had grave doubts about this intrusion in his own home. In the towns it was impossible to escape the hardness of those eyes looking down on me as I strolled around museums, government buildings, shops and restaurants. In the open squares, a shiver down my back made me twist abruptly round with the certainty of being watched. In the countryside, he followed me from the highest hills. But he was not there to watch me, of course. He was there to watch over his children. His deep frown, lingering between severity and disapproval, anticipated what every father knew was inevitable and, at the same time, deep down hoped would not happen. That one day his children would rise up against him, that revolt was part of the process of growing up. Most of the time there was something curious about his eyes. In his commonest presence – his face set as a golden mask – his eyes were strangely absent. Sometimes it seemed they had turned introspectively inwards. He always appeared so thoughtful. Was his frown caused by doubts he entertained about himself? His children did not appear as happy as their father would have hoped for. His home was full of squabbles, fighting and poverty. So many of his children seemed to want to abandon the home he had created for them. From the hardness of bronze and the coldness of marble emanated an air of sadness.

His words still echoed all around me. So many phrases, directives, orders and advice to his children. At the Ministry of Agriculture, his thoughts on agriculture appeared under a marble stem of wheat. At the Ministry of Transport, his thoughts on the necessity of building roads were inscribed under a statue of a bridge. The words of the Father appeared in capital letters on statues, and in small letters on countless stickers which people stuck wherever they fancied. Even then, it felt as if they had been written in capitals: fatherly injunctions from the past for the living to obey. Ataturk was the man who was credited with the invention of 'Turkey' and the 'Turks', neither of which had existed before.

If this was the man who made Turkey, who made him then? How was he born?

It was – so historians appeared to agree – the actions of the Greeks that caused the birth of the Father of the Turks. The Greek assault provided the spark leading to a resurgence of popular feeling in favour of the Turkish nationalist followers of Mustafa Kemal, as he was known before he became the Father. As Ataturk was to say later, if the Greeks had not attacked, the nation would have continued its slumber. Four days after the Greek assault, Mustafa Kemal landed in Samsun. That date now stood for the Turks as the beginning of the War for Independence. For his ultimate victory against the Greeks, Mustafa was given the title of *Gazi*, meaning victor in the holy war. Pasha was an older military honorific title. When Gazi Mustafa or Kemal Pasha passed a law making surnames compulsory, his children adopted him as their father through an act of congress, baptizing him as their one and only 'Father Turk'. No one else was allowed this surname.

A MAN OF MANY NAMES AND HATS

Ataturk was depicted in many different ways, a man of many uniforms, hats and names. He sought the unity of the people of Turkey but was not even able to accomplish the unity of his own image.

The commonest and, to my eyes, the most striking depiction was the mask. This was a three-dimensional depiction of Ataturk showing the front of his face in shiny bronze with the eyes absent. It was a hard and austere face, always looking from high up. The style, like the man, was modernist. In this depiction, he became the symbol of the state and the fatherland: the austere father whose gaze would always hover above his children. In Turkish, the state was often called *devlet baba*, father state. Another word that came to be widely used was *anavatan*. *Ana* for mother while *vatan* became, under the influence of French revolution, the equivalent of *patrie*, the fatherland. *Anavatan* then stood for 'mother-fatherland' in Turkish. The exact equivalent of the Greek *mitera patrida*.

The mask symbolized the relationship between the state and the people: the father-state stood above the people, supervising the children. A tradition of strong central state control, known as statism, developed in Turkey with the aim of modernizing society. Ataturk's style of rule was seen by many commentators as bordering on authoritarianism. The state was supposed to monitor everything: the economy, the faith and the body politic; how people spoke, how they dressed, what hats they should wear. State monitoring extended to Ataturk's own images. The state was given the legal right to prohibit those it considered distasteful and to sue their creator for defamation.

Another depiction of Ataturk showed him as a general wearing his army hat and uniform and climbing pensively up a hill. The military establishment in Turkey liked this one. Leftists preferred an image of Ataturk taken before he came to power, wearing what looked like a Bolshevik hat, symbolizing frugality and revolutionary ideals untainted by power.

The image that came closest to realism, to presenting him as he really was, was the Father as the European gentleman. Here Ataturk appeared dressed in a tuxedo. He was a great believer in westernization, which became a powerful driving force in Turkey. This Father-in-tails often came in added colour in order to emphasize his blue eyes and blonde hair. How much more European could one be?

In order to carry Turkey over to the West where it properly belonged, or 'to catch up with contemporary civilization' as he often said, he initiated a number of drastic reforms. First of all, the creation of a brand new state necessitated a break with the old regime. Ataturk went about it with steely determination. Everything would have to change, from the state itself, to how people wrote and thought, even what they wore. He transformed the state from an imperial religious regime to a secular western-style state. He set out to eradicate religion. One morning, instead of dawning as 1 January 1342, dawned as 1 January 1926. Time now began from Christ's birth, not Muhammad's flight from Mecca. Ataturk attempted what, in a deeply religious society, was unthinkable: to dethrone the Creator, the Father, putting a new supreme Father in his place. 'It is a disgrace for civilized society to appeal for help to the dead,' he said, referring to the shrines of Muslim saints where people went for support and guidance. That saying was to stay with me throughout my research. Yet the attempt to change this aspect of society proved to be his biggest failure.

Ataturk changed the way people dressed. The fez, the round late-Ottoman hat, was prohibited. Western hats were compulsory. When I was there, I only saw ice cream sellers in tourist areas still wearing the fez, as part of a 'traditional' Turkish attire. He also launched a successful attack against the veil, but was not able to beat the head-cover. He abandoned his old army uniform and changed into civilian clothes. The Republic was to become a true civilian republic and the army was to become subservient to the civilian authorities. He stopped using Pasha or Gazi, the military and religious titles that his children had honoured him with. The dinner jacket became his favourite attire. Tails and top hats were decreed for ceremonial occasions.

Ataturk's new state required a new name. It adopted the western-derived name 'Turkey' with a Greek ending, becoming 'Turkiye' in Turkish. He changed the capital from Istanbul to Ankara, in the heart of Anatolia. This was a capital to be constructed from scratch, according to state directives, just as the recently discovered age-old Turkish nation would have to be created anew by the state. Ankara was proclaimed the ancestral heartland of the new eternal nation: the Turks. Istanbul was associated with the previous Ottoman regime, and was thought to be too multi-ethnic, too untidy, and too decadent. Ankara would gradually emerge as a carefully planned city, tidy, and full of straight roads and square squares, as any self-respecting western city ought to be. Road names were carefully chosen as space was being baptized, given form and identity, with appellations alluding to the new age-old Turkish history. Ankara was to have no new mosques. It was to be full of universities, theatres, opera houses, sports centres and other modern buildings.

Reverence for the West and for the state were to be the twin pillars of the new faith. Ankara became its centre, the destination for the annual pilgrimage, where the Turkish nation would congregate to pay their respects and seek advice from their dead Father and Prophet. Even in death, Ataturk emphasized the significance of Ankara by choosing to be laid to rest there: the creator at the heart of his own creation. He died in Istanbul in 1938, but was later placed in a mausoleum in Ankara, where even from the grave he could oversee his creation. It was built in an austere, modernist German style, bearing resemblance to the Parthenon. But the Ankara I saw when I went there was not one that Ataturk would have liked. Sacrilege had been committed. A large mosque built during the 1970s now competed with Ataturk's mausoleum on the skyline of Ankara.

Ataturk also changed the Turkish language, liberating it, he said, 'from the yoke of foreign tongues'. He changed the alphabet from the Arabic of the Koran to the Latin alphabet of Europe. At the stroke of a pen, Turks were cut off from the languages of Islam written in the Arabic script. But, the Father pointed out, this made learning of the civilized languages much easier. Others objected strongly. Did he mean that the people should use the script of infidel westerners to prove that they were patriotic Turks?

The Ottoman language was a mixture of mostly Turkish with Arabic and Persian. Turkish was closer to the popular spoken language. The new language was called *Ozturkce*, pure Turkish. Ataturk created a powerful committee in charge of linguistic purification and reform to clean it from what were now regarded as corrupting foreign influences from the East. But meddling with the language proved to be a risky enterprise. The first thing the committee had to do in its second meeting was to follow the directives it had laid down during the first: this meant removing the Arabic words in the committee's own name. Exceptions were made however. The letter Q, for example, did not make it into the Turkish alphabet, because Kemal Ataturk did not like the look of his name spelled with a Q instead of a K.

THE MAN WHO CHANGED HISTORY

Writing or teaching history would never be the same after Ataturk's reforms. The first step towards creating a new future was to create a new past. In order to create a new people – a new identity – one began with the creation of a new history.

During the early nineteenth century, history in the Ottoman Empire meant two specific things. First, the mission of the Prophet Muhammad and the rise of Islam. Second, the rise of the Ottoman Empire. The beginning of history for the Ottomans was traced right back to Muhammad and his successors. During the nineteenth century, two revolutionary concepts emerged: the idea of Turkey and the idea of the Turks. Turkey was a western term. The word 'Turk' existed during the Ottoman Empire as an insult to describe an uneducated, rough peasant, a barbarian of sorts. Then certain groups that came under western influence began to employ the notions of a Turkish people distinct from the Ottomans and of a land called Turkey. Among them were a group of intellectuals and army officers calling themselves the Young Turks, who were to launch an ideological revolution. For the Young Turks, history meant the history of Turkey and of the Turks, rather than the history of a dynasty, the Ottoman Empire and of a religion, the faith of Islam. It was from this ground that Ataturk was to emerge. 'How happy is one who says I am a Turk,' he would eventually proclaim in what became his best-known saying.

The reformists, with Ataturk in the lead, despised the Ottoman past because of its connection with religion and the older regime. It also fell into the western historical category of the *dark* Middle Ages. The Ottoman Empire was now regarded as an irrational, religious and barbaric regime, based – in the Father's words – on 'the enslavement of the nation'. This was a view very close to the Greek view of the Ottomans. Ataturk also wanted to put an end to any consideration of military expansion and adventurism. He accused the Ottomans of having initiated a number of wars that proved disastrous for their people.

The new official history of Turkey was proclaimed during 1928–1930 as the Turkish Thesis of History. It was simple, but a lot of interesting conclusions derived from it:

- The Turks are a white, Aryan people originating in Central Asia, the cradle of all civilization, from where they migrated in all directions around 7,000 BC for strictly climatic reasons.
- Therefore, the civilization of all people – Indians, Chinese, Greeks too! – originated with the Turks who migrated from Central Asia.
- Therefore, the pioneers of Middle Eastern civilization were really Turkish people.
- Therefore, Anatolia, which had been settled by them a long time ago had been a Turkish land since antiquity and a second centre of Turkish civilization,

This reminded me of another history I knew well. But who could believe such things? What people could be so vain as to claim themselves as the origin of civilization? In fact, as I gradually realized, in one way or another, many people did. The Turks too had set themselves as the one and original beginning: as the Big Bang of civilization, whence it expanded in all directions, eventually creating the universe of human civilization.

In order to join the West, Ataturk simply added one chapter, a new beginning, in the West's history of civilization. How could the West now exclude those who had given it civilization? Behind such grandiose pronouncements, there was a tone of defensiveness and pleading. One story has it that Ataturk was shown a European book which contained the statement that the Turks were a yellow-skinned race regarded by Europeans as inferior. As the Turks were struggling to gain acceptance in the civilized West that they so admired, they also felt betrayed. They saw that the word 'Turk' was used as an insult in many European languages. They realized that they were regarded as the last great historical enemy of the West; its opposite even. They were living in a land known in the West as Anatolia, the name they themselves adopted for their beloved mother-fatherland. It came from Greek. And it meant the East.

There were various reasons why Ataturk stressed the notion of Anatolia as the mother-fatherland since the dawn of history, beyond the Greek historical claims. It was important to persuade Turks that this land dotted with various pre-Ottoman monuments had been theirs all along. So if, say, the Hittites who were the first people to create a civilization in Anatolia were in fact Turks, then they had been there all along. The Turkish Thesis of History served further functions. Ataturk was trying to create a democratic society – eventually, at least – and the imperial order of the Ottomans was a bad example. The egalitarian tribal democracies of Central Asia could serve as a much better example. A pre-Islamic beginning could also side step the association with Islam.

The Turkish Thesis of History was accompanied by a theory of language. The Sun-Language Theory calmly stated that scientific research had objectively proved Turkish to be the mother of all languages and the most aristocratic of all. (This sounded familiar too.) Eventually the Sun-Language Theory was employed to limit the expulsion of foreign words from Turkish since – so the logical argument went – if all languages were originally derived from Turkish as etymologists amply demonstrated, then it could be said that all words, including foreign ones, were originally Turkish.

Just as Ataturk reinvented history, he also had to reinvent himself. In the beginning he was just Mustafa. That was the name he was given according to custom as his umbilical cord was cut, one chosen from among the titles of the Prophet – Mustafa, 'the Chosen'. Then he acquired Kemal, 'the Perfect One'. He explained that during preparatory school he was so good at mathematics that he surpassed his teacher, who was also called Mustafa and who gave his brilliant student an appropriate second name so that the two could be told apart. Others thought it more likely that Ataturk adopted the second name in honour of Namik Kemal, one of the favourite poets of the Young Turks. In any case, he later dropped Mustafa, which sounded too Arabic, and for a short while he tried to replace Kemal, which also sounded Arabic, with the more Turkish sounding Kamal. He preferred Ataturk.

Did his children respect his wishes? What did they call Gazi Mustafa Kemal Pasha Ataturk – the Holy Warrior-the Chosen one-the Perfect one-the Master-the Father of the Turks?

Many simply called him Ata, Father or Ancestor. Religious people chose Gazi, even if many would rather not say his name at all. Those who saw Turkey's future in the East used Mustafa. The militarily inclined chose Pasha. Turkish nationalists or westernizers, his true heirs, called him Ataturk. Others also called him Ataturk, albeit in a manner he would have disliked. These were people who espoused the ideology of Pan-Turkism, seeking the union of all Turkic peoples, which he fervently disapproved of during his life.

Ataturk even chose his own beginning, his own birth. He chose 19 May as his birthday to coincide with the birth of his nation. This was the date when Ataturk landed in Samsun, commemorated in Turkey as the beginning of the War of Independence. This choice made his life course appear as a higher act of destiny. It is difficult to know his real birth date since no such records were kept in 1880/1 when he was born. His mother told others he was born in winter, whereas he said that he heard her say he was born in spring, adding that in his view it was probably in May. When his mother's surviving friends were asked, they agreed with Ataturk. By then, who could question the word of the Father?

ARMY MUSEUM

The thick plastic moustaches of the fierce Ottoman warriors proudly walking in front of me were shining in the sun. A horde of them in full Ottoman uniform still paraded daily to the sound of drums, all for the benefit of visitors to the Army Museum in Istanbul. This was a very large museum, as befitted the role of the army in Turkey.

The last section in the museum was dedicated to Cyprus, presumably as the scene of the last grand feat of the Turkish army. The section presented the '1974 Peace Operation' as they called the barbaric invasion. A display featured large butcher's knives that were allegedly used by Greek Cypriots during the period 1963–1967 'to butcher Turkish Cypriots'. (Later, I was to encounter the same knives in another museum elsewhere, with the accusation reversed.) A map showed the northern Turkish-occupied part of Cyprus in full detail. The south, the free part of the Republic of Cyprus, was left blank. This was the opposite of our normal maps, which showed the free south in full detail, while the occupied north was blank apart from the words 'Occupied Areas of Cyprus'. On closer inspection, I noticed that the map did include all Muslim monuments in Cyprus, including those in the south. No other monuments – Greek, Byzantine, Venetian – were shown. The map spoke loud and clear: Cyprus is historically Turkish and nothing but Turkish – all of it. It was a troubling map for many reasons. For one, I had never known there were so many Turkish or Ottoman monuments in Cyprus. I also wondered how come the Ottomans were now so glorified in this museum where, as usual, Ataturk sternly looked down on the visitor upon entering.

The Army Museum was opposite one of the city's arts centres, the Istanbul Concert Hall. Outside was a long line of cannons of various ages and sizes. All were pointing directly at the concert hall opposite, poised, I thought, as a warning. I thought of the artists and intellectuals jailed in Turkish prisons.

ZORBA THE TURK?

'Karagoz is not Greek or Byzantine as some claim, but a Turk.' This was stated in the first display of Bursa's Ethnographic Museum. The Greek Karagiozis, as distinct from the Turkish Karagoz, was someone I had grown up with. He was not just any someone. He was an emblem of what it meant to be Greek. So, it came as a surprise to learn that the Turks knew him too, and with the same name, which was in fact a Turkish name – Kara-goz, Black-eye. Whereas, I had known Karagiozis as the quintessential Greek, as Greek as mousakka, tzatziki and doner kebab.

Karagiozis, as I knew him, was the star of shadow theatre, a traditional form of art that as a child I never missed on TV. Karagiozis was a strange kind of hero, more of an anti-hero really. He always made a fool of himself, and of everyone around him. The setting usually showed

Karagiozis' poor hut on one side and the tall, imposing palace of the Ottoman ruler on the other. He was the embodiment of the cunning, insubordinate Greek, who constantly 'played the fool' in front of the Ottoman Pasha, and who made a fool of the Pasha without the latter realizing it. He never really achieved what he set out to do, but had a good laugh on the way. He stood for the real Greek, what Greeks knew themselves to be but would not admit to others, the Greek whom harsh Ottoman rule had made cunning, devious and insubordinate. He was the mirror that allowed Greeks to laugh at their own reflection. And he was a Turk!

Why did these count as extraordinary revelations? What could have been more natural than the two peoples influencing each other? Perhaps so, but that was not how we grew up to think. We grew up thinking that Greeks and Turks were opposites; they had nothing in common. A frightful no man's land separated them. That was what made them opposites. A no woman's land too, though this never seemed worth mentioning. And all the time, Turkish was hidden in our own names.

An English friend had once joked that the most famous Greek was Anthony Quinn. He was referring to the film *Zorba the Greek*, based on a book by the author Kazantzakis. Quinn played Zorba, the hero. Actually, my friend had it all wrong. In fact, Zorba was a Turkish name, meaning bully or brute. The Cretan author's surname too came from Turkish, from *kazan*, for cooking pot, a word still used in Greek. How about the names of the two most famous Greek poets, Kavafis and Seferis? One day I should check.

Even my own name began to feel rather less Greco-Orthodox than I had once thought. Yiannis, the colloquial version of Ioannis: a Greek name, taken from the Christian Orthodox tradition; Papadakis, from 'Papa' meaning a priest as in 'father' and 'Dakis' – endings in *-akis* were typical of Crete, another island, like Cyprus, historically renowned for its Greekness, its ancient monuments, the insubordination of its people against all foreign conquerors, its heroic fighters against the Turks, and the bloodshed the Turks caused there. Once, I had been proud that the two components of Greek identity – the Hellenic-Christian Ideals – were present in my own name. But now it sounded more on the Greco-Turkish, or Greco-Islamic side. The word for father in Greece was *mpampas*, one that we Cypriots pronounced as *papas*. Could this derive from the Turkish *baba*, meaning father, or Muslim saint? In any case, had things been unfair in the other direction I would have taken my mother's surname: Hajitsagari. 'Haji' was taken from the Turkish *haji*, an appellation for those who had made the pilgrimage to Mecca, which Christians later adopted for those who went to Jerusalem. By now it did not feel strange to discover this. It was simply one more of history's touches, a history present even in our identity cards; a common history violently torn apart. A common history that could surely help to bring us closer together in Cyprus, but that had become invisible because we had been denied knowledge of it; we had been betrayed.

INVISIBLE PEOPLE

The trouble with some of my Turkish friends was that either they did not officially exist or they preferred to be invisible. Some existed only now and then, others did not exist at all, others were to officially exist only much later. Kurds, for example, did not exist. They were said to be 'mountain Turks' speaking 'a dialect of Turkish'. My friend Veli said he was an Alevi, a member of a 'heterodox' Islamic sect. In theory, that is, because he did not worship. The existence of Alevis, a sect different from the orthodox Sunnis, was only grudgingly admitted, to a degree that depended on the prevailing political climate. Marxists could not openly exist either. If they did, then they could not exist as Turks, for 'a real Turk cannot be a communist.' Many had chosen to make themselves invisible. Or else, those who openly existed were hidden away in jails. Much of this was a legacy of Ataturkism. He was trying to create a nation, which meant a united nation. Those who pointed out class divisions, as Marxists did, were branded 'Subversives', and those who pointed out ethnic divisions, as the Kurds did, were called 'Dividers': heretics of the faith and traitors to the nation. The problem was that there were too many people around who did not exist. Everyone knew someone who did not exist.

This had serious consequences. It created a land of unbelievers, though not as Ataturk had hoped for. It created, so I thought, a culture of disbelief: 'It's in our school textbooks? So it must be wrong.' Or 'Tell us, what really happened in Cyprus? We only learn about it from television and the radio.' Some of the people I knew were Marxists, Alevis, or Kurds but others, my 'normal' Turkish friends, were equally sceptical. Perhaps this was because my friends were young, many of them students or intellectuals; and perhaps it took an infidel to befriend a Greek Cypriot.

But maybe they too were products of Ataturk. He wanted people to believe in the modern secular state and abandon belief in God. The father-state was to replace the all-knowing, all-encompassing Father, and would guide its children towards the promised land of westernization. But people seemed not to believe in the state, and religion did not disappear either. The promised destination seemed as distant as ever, and what emerged was accompanied by much pain, misery and social disruption. Westernization, modernization, whatever one chose to call it, came at a heavy cost. Harsh realities came nowhere close to the grand dreams. People felt betrayed and betrayal created traitors. The father-state was unable to deliver. If the saviour-state never fulfilled its promise, the children were bound to seek other saviours. And didn't all children eventually revolt against the father?

Ataturk also wanted to bring about democracy. But democracy was all about the expression of difference and disagreement. And it was about the state obeying the people – not the other way round. Perhaps the plan was flawed from the beginning. The effort to instil admiration for the West and democracy was so successful that now everyone I met wanted to leave Turkey for the West. Many people I met felt lonely, abandoned and misunderstood in a poor land scattered with sad embers of past glory, visible enough to heighten the agony. It was a feeling I understood well because I too had once felt that way as a Greek. 'We resemble only ourselves,' Ataturk had said. 'A Turk has no friend but the Turk,' the saying went. 'We are a nation without brothers,' echoed the Greeks.

THE LAST COMPATRIOT

We met as I was wandering about a bazaar a few days before I left Turkey. As often happened, I struck up a conversation with one of the sellers. 'Come,' he gesticulated, 'there is someone from Greece inside.' He pointed and I peeked inside his stall. A man was sitting there, lying back, smoking and laughing as he sipped his *chay*. The seller explained in English that I was from Cyprus. His smile vanished. His body tensed as he sat stiffly upright. 'Oh, so you are Greek from Cyprus?' he asked in Greek. I nodded. He was a Greek sailor. Embarrassed, he drew a puff from his cigarette, as if I had caught him red-handed, simply by being there, having a tea and laughing. In order to break the awkward silence I explained that I had come to learn the language. I asked if this was the first time he had been here. He replied that he often came to Turkey on his ship. He was still measuring me up. 'So what do you think of the country, the people, then?' His voice had a tone of urgency.

'Well,' I replied cautiously, 'I think some parts of the country are so beautiful. I've met a lot of people. To be honest, I've never had any real problems here.' His whole body relaxed and the smile returned to his face. 'I think so too,' he agreed:

> These are some of my good friends here. I see them every time I come and we have become like brothers. You know, I even brought my son along a couple of times. In the beginning he didn't want to come. No way. But in the end, when he came he was so surprised. 'Dad,' he said, 'I like the people here. They are people too, human beings. Not at all like we learn about the Turks in our schoolbooks. Why do they lie to us? Why do they make us hate them so much?'

We spent the evening with the Turkish sellers. But it was each other's company that we enjoyed most, as if an unspoken bond had developed between us. We were joined by a common guilt for not hating the Turks. I was sure we both felt like traitors for this. I was sure we also felt betrayed.

A SHORT GUIDE TO WATCHING HISTORICAL FILMS FOR NON-TURKISH SPEAKERS

During the late 1980s, historical films set during the Ottoman Empire were still in fashion. The plot was simple: Ottomans vs. Byzantines. Because I spoke little Turkish I developed other methods to understand these films, methods now made available for the general benefit of non-Turkish speakers.

How to identify the Turkish men:

1) They're the good looking ones, dressed in shades of red, appearing in parades with identical long moustaches made of black plastic.

2) They have decent table manners.

3) They win battles even when outnumbered by 20 to 1.

4) They win such battles unarmed, wounded, and after they have been deviously captured by the Byzantines in a trap where they are swung by their feet.

5) They get tortured.

6) They rush at their opponents in a series of forward somersaults, and escape with a number of backward somersaults.

7) They are masters of the following fighting techniques:

    i) Medieval swordsmanship.

ii) Japanese karate where opponents pause and scream in between blows.

iii) Western cowboy skills, such as riding at the side of the horse, so it looks like it has no rider.

iv) American Indian skills involving the use of bow and arrows, such as firing two arrows at the same time, both of which hit their separate targets and cut the ropes by which two Ottoman men have just been hanged.

v) American show wrestling, where one guy takes on a number of opponents simultaneously.

8) They make love, and women fall in love with them.

9) They have authentic Turkish names.

10) They win in the end.

How to identify the Byzantine men:

1) They're the ugly ones with big crosses. Bald, bearded and ugly is a Byzantine torturer.

2) They appear on sets that have 2 by 3 metre crosses as interior decoration.

3) They have appalling table manners and dribble while they eat the meat they just tore from the roast with their own dirty hands.

4) They lose battles where they outnumber their opponents 20 to 1.

5) They even lose when their opponent is wounded, unarmed, and hanging upside down by his feet.

6) They deviously stab their outnumbered opponent in the back, and ruthlessly kill women and children.

7) They torture people.

8) They stand still in amazement when their opponent approaches them with a number of forward somersaults.

9) They have no established traditional fighting skills.

10) They do not make love and women do not fall in love with them. They rape instead.

11) They have names that are commonly found among the current Greek minority in Turkey.

12) They lose.

How to spot the Turkish women:

1) Good looking, no make-up, girl-from-the-village type.

2) Non-prominent and well-covered breasts.

3) Conservatively dressed.

4) Chaste.

5) They get raped, and are sometimes saved by a handsome Turk.

6) They never offer anyone poisoned wine.

How to spot the Byzantine women:

1) Good looking, lots of make-up, prostitute-from-the-town type.

2) Well-developed breasts always highly visible.

3) Usually dressed in a sexy, revealing manner, except when having or are about to have sex. The parts of Byzantine women are played by soft-porn actresses.

4) They have sex:

> i) in order to turn a Turkish fighter into a spy, make him convert to Christianity, or get him to reveal military secrets.
>
> ii) because they have been overwhelmed by his looks and character, and have fallen in love with him, despite the knowledge that he is a Turk.

5) They are never raped but make love of their own volition.

6) They offer Turks poisoned wine as a toast on occasions such as the recently signed peace treaty with the Byzantines.

On first sight, these methods are complicated by the films where the same man dressed in different clothes appears to fight sometimes against the Byzantines and sometimes against the Turks. The puzzle is solved once we realize that the story involves a set of Turkish twins, one of whom was torn from the (well-covered) bosom of his wailing mother and raised as a Byzantine. His brother meanwhile is raised as a Turk. Since the same brave Turkish blood runs in the veins of both, they both become heroes, the one despite his upbringing among the cowardly Byzantines.

Exciting as these films were to watch – provided one adored the Ottomans, hated the Byzantines and liked Westerns, wrestling and karate – there were serious problems with them. For one, when I was living in Turkey almost no one watched them any more. Or those who watched them did so for the wrong reasons – to laugh. The young people I saw watching them were mainly interested in spotting the director's mistakes. A plane flying in the distance as the hero galloped across the screen, or telephone lines behind the rushing chariot, or a watch on the hero's wrist as he raised his sword for the final blow.

But those were not the main problems in my view. What really troubled me was something that my Turkish friends seemed oblivious to (which troubled me more). How come, after Ataturk, films were made glorifying the Ottomans? But this was no longer an issue because my friends had grown up in a society that had come to regard the once despised Ottomans not only as glorious, but as their own ancestors.

BACK TO THE ZONE OF THE DEAD

Before leaving Turkey, I wanted to work out how things had changed since Ataturk. The Turkish Thesis of History appeared to have been abandoned. The Turks no longer agreed with the Greeks about the evil Ottomans. The Ottomans had made a galloping comeback to the stage of history. Even the Sun-Language Theory was now ridiculed as people laughed at etymologies like Amazon (from the Turkish *amma-uzun*) and OK (*ok-ay*). How had this come about? I would have to look at history, and at the history of history to understand how the history books had changed.

Turkey's history after Ataturk continued to be one of upheaval and unrest. As some statues of Ataturk were defaced, his personal myth was disputed and some of his radical reforms were challenged. I too gradually came to understand that he was not necessarily the sole beginning since many of the reforms credited to him had begun earlier. The fighting in Turkey had not ended with the Independence War against the foreigners. Turkey remained in a state of war, this time against insiders: religion, Kurds and later Marxists. It was losing badly on all fronts. Religion persisted, so the state tried to make the best of it. Religious extremists were sometimes tolerated and given a free hand to combat the unbelievers, the Marxists. Sometimes religion was also seen as a solution to the Kurdish problem: all were Muslim brothers after all. Some felt that too much democracy was the real problem. Turkey went through three military coups, at the start of each decade from the 1960s. Inonu, Ataturk's successor, expressed a liking for the emerging German fascist model and was called *Milli Shef*, National Leader, an exact translation of 'Fuehrer'.

The historian Koprulu had disagreed with Ataturk's Turkish Thesis of History that all civilization was derived from the Turks. For this, he was viciously accused of harbouring 'pro-Greek' sentiments. He too tried to legitimate the Turkish possession of Anatolia. But instead of arguing that the Hittites were 'proto-Turks' he brought the focus of historical enquiry 3,000 years forward. He proposed a 'Turco-Islamic synthesis' that explained how Ottoman institutions gradually evolved during the first half of the second millennium in the footsteps of previous Islamic-Turkish dynasties. The Ottoman Empire, then, was a true Turkish creation and not simply a long list of institutions borrowed from Byzantium, as westerners, plus the Greeks, claimed in the 'Byzance après Byzance' thesis. Koprulu sometimes went to the other extreme. Instead of the Ottoman Empire being a poor copy of Byzantium, it was now said to have borrowed almost nothing from Byzantium.

But Koprulu did not idealize the Ottomans as a superior race or dynasty arguing that their rise was a historical accident. They simply happened to be closest to Byzantium during the period of its internal crisis. The idealization came later during the period of authoritarian one-party rule in Turkey after Ataturk's death. The model of tribal democracy no longer seemed appropriate. Instead, the Ottoman Empire came to be revered as an indigenous Turkish example of the beneficial influence of a strong – authoritarian? – state. And it was Muslim too. No longer 'cruel and despotic' as the Father had called it, it was now described as a regime where 'all worked for the state and the state for all', where the subjection of the peasants was for their own good, since their taxes paid for the soldiers to protect them from the far worse feudal autocracies that threatened the empire. So, the Ottomans did not conquer: they liberated and civilized. They liberated enslaved people from harsh regimes like corrupt Byzantium. The Ottomans, being a superior race, had created a cosmopolitan, multi-ethnic, tolerant state, rather like the Byzantine Empire as presented by the Greeks.

Under this new model of history, Greeks became enemies twice over – for having been the first to revolt, 'the first to stab their own benefactors in the back' despite their privileged position and, second, for the Asia Minor campaign of the 1920s. Turkish history too became a search for an explanation of how the Turks were reduced from a vast empire – the tyranny of school maps – to the small state of Turkey. Greece was seen as pursuing an aggressive, expansionist policy against the Turks. The effort to take Cyprus in 1974 was seen as the final proof of this. Long gone was Ataturk's peace and friendship protocol with Venizelos – the very man who had launched the first wave of Greek attacks against Anatolia – a protocol which was supposed to herald a new era of friendship between the two states so soon after their bloody confrontation. Venizelos even proposed Ataturk for the Nobel Peace Prize. Things were going well until Cyprus entered into the picture.

The era of rapprochement ended with the beginning in 1955 of the EOKA (National Organization of Cypriot Fighters) struggle in Cyprus for Union with Greece: ENOSIS. Turkish Cypriots opposed this, asking for the partition – TAKSIM – of Cyprus, and set up their own fighter's organization called TMT (Turkish Resistance Organization). Events in

Cyprus had negative repercussions on the life of the Greek minority in Turkey and the Turkish minority in Greece. They were even said to have caused the return of the Wolves. A man from Cyprus spearheaded the rise of this extreme right Pan-Turkist movement in Turkey, which Ataturk had opposed. Their symbol was the Grey Wolf of the steppe, a powerful figure in ancient Turkic folk tradition. Their leader was a Cypriot who, like so many others, did not want to be one: *Turkesh*, 'the Spouse of the Turk'. His first name was Alparslan, 'the Brave Lion'. He came from the babyland to the live in the bosom of the mother-fatherland, rising to prominence in a movement that took pride in its racism, screening members for racial purity and demanding the union of the superior Turkish race under one state. Rumours of the alleged slaughter of Turks in Cyprus gave the Pan-Turkist movement a great boost and fuelled their belief that 'Cyprus is Turkish'. Pan-Turkism never became official ideology, nor was it able to gain control of political power. Even if officially their views were not endorsed, the Pan-Turkists were often given a free hand in the internal fight against communists, killing left-wing students and fighting the communists of the Kurdish PKK. Pan-Turkists later went to Cyprus to fight in defence of their Turkish co-racers there.

APHRODITE

My time was over. I travelled from Istanbul to Izmir, which was also called Smirni when my grandmother lived there as a child. I wanted to see it and then catch a boat from a nearby port to Rhodes, where my grandmother lived, and then on to Cyprus. At a trade fair in Izmir I noticed the kiosk of the 'Turkish Republic of Northern Cyprus', the self-declared Turkish Cypriot 'state' in northern Cyprus that remained unrecognized by the rest of the world, except Turkey. Because it did not officially exist, it was always placed in quotation marks.

There I encountered the familiar naked form of Aphrodite on a poster despite the attempt to disguise her under a different name. 'Cyprus the Island of Venus' proclaimed this poster. So, they were using her as a symbol of Cyprus as well. They were capitalizing on the indisputable appeal of Aphrodite while using her Roman name, instead of her original Greek one that would show Cyprus as Greek.

As I got ready to leave Turkey I started to worry again. Would I be allowed out? Once again things worked fairly smoothly, almost disappointingly so. But not all the way.

DEPARTURE

'How dare you travel to Turkey? You should be ashamed of yourself.' The veins on the man's neck were protruding as he looked at my passport, screaming at me in Greek. This was my welcome reception in what I had once considered my mother-fatherland. I had just disembarked in Rhodes to see my relatives there. It was getting to be quite a fashion for Greeks to go to Turkey for cheap shopping, and the boat was filled with Greeks on their way home.

Clearly, this was the first time the official had come across a case like mine. 'You, you have a Cypriot passport, you are a Cypriot, and you went to Turkey? After what the Turks have done to us, after what they did to Cyprus, you have the nerve to go there? What for? Shopping, tourism?' I wasn't going to stand for this. Especially from a Greek. I lost my temper. I screamed back. 'Who do you think you are questioning me like this? Why should I give you a list of the reasons why I went to Turkey?' Then came the grand blow. I did not even need to shout this. 'And who is to blame for what happened to Cyprus? It was not our fault, it's yours. It's you Greeks who made the coup. Who brought the Turks upon us. And now you have the nerve to shout at me?'

After the incident at the port, I went to see my grandmother in Rhodes. She was my father's mother and after my trip to Turkey I was eager to meet her. We had occasionally spoken about our family past, but now I wanted to find out more. I knew that she came from a wealthy family. She had left in the population exchanges after the war ended in 1922. From Smirni, they moved to an area in Athens that they called New Smirni. Later, she met my grandfather, who had come from Cyprus to work in Greece, and eventually they settled in Rhodes.

I was still upset from my recent encounter at customs when I saw her. As usual, I found her sitting in her special chair – 'the royal chair' as my cousins and I used to call it. She understood something was wrong and so I explained. 'Don't be upset,' she said:

> These people here, the Greeks, have no culture or manners. Us refugees from Asia Minor taught them everything. We were civilized, we knew how to read and about the arts. We were in touch with the civilized world when they were just backward peasants. Greece would never have become a civilized country – if it ever did – were it not for us. And do you know how they called us then, these peasants? They called us *Tourkosporoi* ['seed of the Turks'] because of where we came from and because many of us did not speak Greek. And it was them, the Greeks, who ruined us with all

their petty politics, all the grand ideas of recreating Byzantium, all their internal political bickering and petty disagreements. But we paid the real costs, we became refugees, we came into exile in this backward country.

It had not taken much to get her started. In fact, she had already told me all this a few times. Previously, I had dismissed it but now I listened attentively. I began to understand better why she was such a lonely woman, why she had almost no friends, why she looked down on Greeks and why she had this haughty air that made my cousins and I call her 'the Queen'. Her story – and my family history – was one of hardship, dislocation, discrimination and tragedy, all caused by the lofty political ambitions of the Greeks. She told me the horrible names that refugees had been called when they arrived in Greece; how going to Greece was not a return to the mother-fatherland as we had learnt at school but harsh exile; of the atrocities that the Greeks committed during the campaign in Anatolia. I heard it as a story of historic discrimination by Greeks against my own family, who became refugees and found themselves unwanted and ridiculed in the new country where they were forced to settle.

I asked her for the first time what her family name had been before she married. '*Kiourtzi*,' she replied. It came from the Turkish word *kurkju*, meaning a fur trader. 'Let me show you something,' she said and came back with a large photograph of an old man with a short white beard and moustache. He was wearing a fez, baggy trousers, a black leather vest, and tall shiny leather boots. In his hand was a set of black worry beads, and around his neck were thick animal tails. 'This was my grandfather, the fur trader,' she explained. I asked if she would give me the photograph. 'Well,' she said, 'none of your cousins expressed any interest, so it is yours.' I took it back to Cyprus and gave him a prominent place on the centre shelf of my library. Later, I would often work under the gaze of my newly discovered ancestor, as I was writing about my research in Cyprus.

In turn I showed her the photo of a house in the Islands that I had found following her sparse recollections of her childhood holiday home, but I was disappointed. She did not think it was the right one. Later, after her death, I would find out that she was wrong. Her memory had failed her, as memory often did. By then it was too late to show her the photo again that would fill a gap in her memory. By then she only existed as a memory.

I called my parents in Cyprus, to let them know that I had made it out of Turkey, that I was fine and was on my way home. For the first time they openly expressed relief. They told me that the police had been to see them a few times, because of the calls they had been making and receiving from Turkey. 'It's natural,' my father said. 'They thought we could be some kind of spies or traitors for calling Turkey. But they were polite and seemed to understand when we explained.'

On the plane from Rhodes to Cyprus I was overwhelmed by sadness as I contemplated my stay in Turkey. I felt different. I had never before returned home with such a sense of fear – of dread. Usually I was glad. Now it was all sadness and weight. The baggage I was carrying with me – not my suitcases – seemed to weigh insufferably. I did not know then that this feeling would later accompany me in other crossings. I was carrying gifts from my friends, friendship and what they taught me. I was carrying my great grandfather's photograph. These things felt like a heavy burden. What should I tell people when they asked about Turkey? Who should I betray? My friends in Turkey, or those in Cyprus?

'Imagine if one day we meet having to shoot each other from opposite trenches,' Erkin had mused sadly as a way to say goodbye. But one thing I knew clearly: I could not hate the Turks. They no longer felt like opposites. I had seen how intermingled the cultures and histories of Greece and Turkey were. They had also made Cyprus, and Cyprus had made them.

I was going back to Cyprus to start my real research, on nationalism, identity and history. I hoped this research would involve Turkish Cypriots. I thought my trip to Turkey had made it impossible for me to remain a Greek: for one thing – and there were many more – I did not hate the Turks. And that was what being Greek meant, or so my schoolbooks had taught me. Things were shown to us in contrasts: Greek or Turk, with us or with them, here or there. There was no other place left.

But perhaps after all there was a place that was both Greek and Turkish. There were even flights to it and I was on one. There was still hope then, hope for something else.

CHAPTER TWO
LEFKOSIA
OCTOBER 1990–FEBRUARY 1991

THE BEGINNING

It was 1 October 1990 and I was ready to begin my research in Cyprus. Since October was the month that term began at Cambridge, I thought this would be a good time to start. I was in the house I had rented in Lefkosia, the divided capital, full of hope and apprehension.

At this time of day, the streets would be busy. I stepped outside. All quiet. No was one around. I turned round, went back in, and closed the door behind me. I collapsed on a chair. So much for my triumphant beginning. I turned on the radio. It was a national holiday, the anniversary of the independence of Cyprus in 1960. How could I possibly not have known this?

On reflection, I felt sure that when I was growing up in Cyprus, the anniversary did not exist. I left Cyprus when I was nineteen to study abroad. Now coming back, aged twenty-six, there it was on the TV, celebrated in all its glory with flags, parades, music and crowds. In my absence an anniversary had been born.

The odd thing was that Cyprus actually began its independence on 16 August 1960 – the end of an era and the beginning of another. But today was 1 October! So we were triumphantly celebrating our anniversary on the wrong date. Outside, the main roads were full of flags – not just our state flag, the flag of the Republic of Cyprus. The flag of another state, Greece, was hanging next to ours. Another national anthem was playing, the Greek one. Ours was nowhere to be heard. Come to think of it, that was because we didn't have one. And this was supposed to be the anniversary of the *independence* of Cyprus. We forgot the anniversary of our birth for many years, then about 30 years later we remembered it. But by then the island was divided. Even so, we celebrated the independence of a state which we claimed extended over all Cyprus – but it did not because there was another state there that did not officially exist, the 'Turkish Republic of Northern Cyprus', boasting its very own 'President', Denktash. Clearly, there was a lot of work to do.

I had chosen to live in the old town of Lefkosia, which was surrounded by massive circular Venetian walls. The Dead Zone (*Nekri Zoni*) – as Greek Cypriots called the dividing line – passed right through the walled city, cutting it in two. The line was known by various other names too: Green Line, line of shame, and Attila Line. As everyone knew, the last name was what the Turks themselves called the line they created by force of arms. Greek Cypriots too, were particularly fond of this name, which brought to mind the deeds of the infamous 'Attila the Hun', and often used it to let the rest of the world know of the situation in Cyprus.

My designated research area comprised three neighbourhoods, each named after the local church or mosque: Chrysaliniotissa and Agios Kassianos, each with its own church, and Tahtakallas where the mosque was. Turkish Cypriots used to live in the neighbourhood around the mosque and they left, I thought, when the island was divided in 1974.

The whole area, all three neighbourhoods together, was known by various names: Lower Parishes, Tahtakallas and Akritic Parishes. Locals were particularly fond of Tahtakallas for the general area. When I had walked around the area before people had seemed friendly and willing to talk to me. Now I planned to spend a year there hoping that people would gradually get to know me and trust me enough to talk honestly about the past. But I wondered about my honesty too. Should I tell people that I had been to Turkey? I was worried that if I told people about going to Turkey, they would not want to talk to me any more. Especially if they asked me what I thought about it. That would end my research right there. I decided that I would tell them eventually, but only after they got to know me. But it was not to be as simple as that. I expected them to be truthful but would lie to them each and every time we spoke, not by what I said, but by what I failed to say.

A LOCAL TURKISH CYPRIOT

Once I'd got over the failure of my initial foray into Tahtakallas, I ventured out again and gradually got to know people. The grocery shop around the corner was run by two tiny old ladies, Mrs Hara, meaning Joy, and Mrs Elpida, Hope. They welcomed me to the neighbourhood and suggested I should sit around their shop in order to meet everyone. The grocery shop was a great place for this. The only problem was that, for my own small needs, I had to shop from all four grocery shops there, in order to hang around. I bought bread from one and then took it home so as not to appear with a bag of groceries in the next one. Then on to the next shop to buy milk, back home, on to the third one for eggs and so on. But it was all worth it.

In Mrs Hara's and Mrs Elpida's shop I made a real discovery. A Turkish Cypriot man was a frequent customer of theirs. Kadir, his real name, was pronounced as Katiris by Greek Cypriots. Kadir meant mighty or powerful. When I met him he appeared the opposite: old, frail and virtually blind. His presence though was exciting news for me because it would give me the chance to see how Greek Cypriots treated a Turkish Cypriot now living among them. They seemed to adore him. Before I met him, Mrs Hara had told me his story:

> Listen Yiannaki, he was living in the occupied north, in Kerinia. Just after the invasion he tried to help some Greek Cypriots. He tried to prevent some Turks from killing them. The army officer, who was a Turk from Turkey, a *yiouroukkis*, took out one of his eyes as punishment for this. You will see when you meet him that one of his eyes is damaged, blind. Anyway, he could not live there any more. He likes us so much you see, so he came over here. He is very poor and can't work, so he gets money from our social security services. And you know what he does? When he receives his cheque, he brings it here and tells me 'Mrs Hara, may God bless you, can you please deduct what I owe you this month and then give me the rest of the money?' He is always polite, well mannered and everyone around likes him. You'll see for yourself Yiannaki.

Yiouroukkis was a name often used for people from Turkey, meaning rough, uncivilized peasants. Regarding my name, for some reason, as if by quiet conspiracy, everyone in Tahtakallas had chosen to call me 'Yiannaki', even though I always introduced myself as 'Yiannis' and was twenty-six years old. 'Yiannakis', the diminutive of 'Yiannis', meant 'little Yiannis'. Perhaps this was because they were much older than me. Perhaps they wanted to make clear who was going to learn from whom.

THE CRUCIAL QUESTION

Mrs Marianna was known in Tahtakallas as the expert in the area's history and folklore. She was a gentle woman in her sixties who had written a lot of things on the subject, as everyone told me. She was one of the first people I got to know well and we became good friends. During our first meeting Mrs Marianna suggested that I draw up a list of questions to ask. 'The most important one is how we used to live together. What were our relations with the Turks?' She was right. This was what I was interested in. And what everyone wanted to talk to me about.

Mrs Marianna was honest and straightforward with me. I was neither. From the start she made her position clear:

> I am hyper-nationally conscious, I love Hellenism, my nation and anything to do with it moves me greatly. This is my personal passion. The Turks by contrast are simply barbarians. Tell me what relation whatsoever they have with civilization. We, by contrast… well, everyone knows that we created civilization. But our Turks were different. The Turks who are from Cyprus, our own Turks, the Cypriot Turks I mean. They were very nice, and I know this first-hand because I used to live with them right here. I still remember their *hoja*, you know, *hoja* is their priest. He was such a kind-looking man, wise too, and every morning I looked forward to meeting him in the street. He would always greet me in perfect Greek. 'Good morning, madam, may God be with you.' I miss him now that he's gone. You see, this is how well we got on together! These are the kinds of things you should try to find out about, Yiannaki.

As she spoke, I nodded and kept an impassive face. I never expressed disagreement.

THE SPY

'Oh, it's you. I thought you were a spy,' Mrs Eleni said matter-of-factly when I first went to her kiosk for a newspaper. I explained that I had just rented a house there. I also told her why I was there.

Yes, you are the one who has been going around with a backpack, aren't you? You appeared here all of a sudden and when I asked no one knew you, so I got worried that perhaps you were a spy. I even told my husband, who is a policeman. You don't seem like a bad person now that we meet. What did you say your name is? Yiannis, eh? Well, pleased to meet you Yiannaki. What do you expect people to think when you just appear like this? You know, especially here, next to the Dead Zone, in such a sensitive area, full of army posts. You know that taking photos is prohibited around here, eh? How long do you intend to stay? A year? My God, that's a long time. And how will you live? Will you work?

I explained that I had a grant from the university to do research, which should be enough.

Which university? Oh, I see, it's from England... So they are the ones who are paying you then? And will they allow you to write the truth? The English have their arms dirty up to here with the Cyprus Problem. They are the ones who started it anyway and they are always on the side of the Turks. They are the ones we fought against. They hung our fighters; they were just children. And now you hope that they will let you write about this? Since they pay you, they must control what you write.

Everyone asked me questions like this when I first appeared in Tahtakallas. They did not know me, I was interested in anything and everything, I kept asking questions and taking notes, I had a camera and tape recorder in my backpack, and I was paid by the English. I hoped that as they got to know me better these problems would disappear. After all, that was why we anthropologists tried to spend long periods in one place. To get close to the people, to obtain first-hand, intimate knowledge of their lives – to become an insider. But weren't spies in the same profession? Trying to obtain inside knowledge? These thoughts occurred to me even before the formal approaches were made. Early on, I decided that for a while it would be best not to use the tape recorder so that people could speak more openly. I became rather good, I hoped, at jotting down things as we spoke and then reproducing the dialogue and people's reactions from memory. But the suspicion that I was a spy had already begun to follow me like a shadow.

CHURCH BELLS AND THE HOJA'S CALL
Tahtakallas was so close to the Dead Zone that one often heard sounds from occupied Lefkosia. In the late afternoons it was common to hear the church bells on our side, together with the *hoja's* calling on the other. A battle was being waged over who would dominate the soundscape. Churches had loudspeakers pointing to the occupied north and the mosques had them pointing towards the free south.

Mrs Evdokia, another grocer, heard the voice of the *hoja* from the occupied side as we were talking. 'Oh, welcome to the truth,' she suddenly exclaimed. Sensing my surprise, she explained:

> You don't know what this means, do you? No? Well, when we hear the sound of the *hoja*, this is what we say: Welcome to the truth. Same thing when we hear the sound of our church bells. It means that what you say at that moment is true. They have their religion, you see, and we have ours. That is their truth and we have ours. What's the problem with this? The *hoja* is only doing his duty. We don't hate them because they are Turks. Ah, it was so nice when we lived together. They used to cook the sweetest food, I tell you this for a fact. I know, I lived it myself. Do you know that many of the Turks of Cyprus ate pork and drank alcohol? Then there were the people who sold *ayrani* in the street. It was the most refreshing drink in this heat, made with water, milk, salt and mint. They taught us these things and still we can't do them as well as they did. I still remember what the *ayrani*-sellers used to shout. I shiver now that I am saying this, I can almost hear it in my ears. They walked outside my shop here and would shout '*ayran buz gibi*', it means cold like ice. But how can you know these things, you are too young, Yiannaki. How I miss those days! Sometimes, when I'm here alone, I say to myself, I wish I could hear the voice of the *ayrani*-seller once more before I die.

Of course, I knew what *ayran buz gibi* meant.

MILK-MOTHERS AND OTHERS
'Did you know, Yiannaki, that we had milk-mothers before?' Mrs Katinou asked me:

> Sometimes a woman who gave birth didn't have enough milk so another woman who had also just given birth would breastfeed her

child. The two children who had drunk milk from the same mother became something like brothers, and the woman became like a mother to the child who drank from her breast, a milk-mother. The Turks, our Turks, did exactly the same. They had a name for this... oh, how does it go? I haven't spoken Turkish for so long that I'm losing it. No one speaks Turkish any more, you young ones have no idea. Ah, it's just here on my lips... wait, here it comes: *sut-ana*. 'Sut' means milk, and 'ana' mother. But how would you know this kind of thing?

I nodded and she continued.

So, they had the same custom like us, I tell you. But what am I saying? The Turks of Cyprus were just like us, there was no difference. Those days you didn't say, 'They are Turks and we are Greeks.' All that started later. Anyway, this house where you are now, this house where I live belongs to Mustafa, a Turk. I used to rent it from him, and I stayed here after they left. I'll never forget the day, their tears, the way they said goodbye and held on to us because they didn't want to leave us. But they had to. Their leaders, that monster Denktash, forced them to go, otherwise they would have stayed here with us. You want me to tell you how well we lived? Look, you see my son eating inside. Well, when I gave birth to him I was ill afterwards and couldn't feed him, so you know what happened one day? Zehra, Mustafa's wife, we were like this with her [she made a gesture with two fingers pressed together]. She comes, I did not ask her anything, she sits down, just like you are sitting now there and tells me: '*Be kkomshu,*' it means neighbour, 'you not enough milk, me a lot. I give Savvakis.' So I said, 'Yes, may Allah guard you, Zehra.' She was glad. 'And God, bless you too,' she said to me.

She took a sip from her coffee, and stared upwards to the ceiling.

Her daughters were lovely, both so white and beautiful, Pembe, it means pink, and Havva, it is our Eva. I still remember Pembe when she got married, with all her jewels and gold coins. We were invited of course, we always went to their weddings and they all came to ours. And when they had a *bayrami*, it means religious holiday, they would invite us and offer us the special food they prepared for the occasion. Us too, always, always, when we had a religious celebration, we would take them our special sweets. You know that they believed in our saints too? How would you, you are too young, Yiannaki. Well, they did, their Havva was our Eva, our Maria they called Meyrem-Anne, our Abraham was their Ibrahim. When we went on pilgrimage to the monastery of Apostle Andreas that is now occupied, they would come with us. Who knows, perhaps they were Christians once and had to convert. I tell you that Zehra, when she opened her heart to me, would tell me that she was jealous of us because we held onto our religion, while they were losing theirs. Who knows what they are doing now? Who knows if they are even alive? This is what bothers me, that she may be dead and I did not even have the chance to go and cry at her funeral. Probably she won't come to mine either.

Her hand trembled slightly as she brought the coffee cup to her lips again.

You know that for years after they left, my husband saved the money for the rent in the bank? He felt bad that we were living in Mustafa's house and not paying the rent. I remember that a few years after the invasion – may God one day punish those who divided our country – he tried to see if he could find a way to send him the money. But others told him that it wouldn't be a good idea. Perhaps the Turks from Turkey, those savages, would not like it if Mustafa got money from a Greek Cypriot. Or if those TMT fanatics, like that Denktash, found out they would punish him. So he saved it in the bank, waiting for the day when Mustafa would return. I think he stopped doing it a few years ago. But if God blesses us and Mustafa and Zehra return one day, then I swear on the bones of my mother that we will pay them every last pound.

Her eyes darkened as her thoughts carried her elsewhere. She clenched her hand and placed it on the table.

But who created all this? It's them, the foreigners, the Great Powers. It was all in their plans to divide us. The Americans. And the English, they created all this, it's called Divide and Rule, they did it everywhere in the colonies. India too. Ah, but we were to blame too, not us really, but those wretched Greeks, the *kalamarades* who staged the coup in 1974 and brought the Turks here. It's strange isn't it? We were once fighting to unite with them and then they destroyed us. They betrayed us just like that. Our own mother betrayed us. Well, perhaps it was for the best. Who would want

to unite with them now? If it weren't for those savage Turks of
Turkey, those *yiouroukkides*, and those *kalamarades*, we would have
been living like in the past with our Turks. I went on holiday to
Athens once, only once – if only God would make that a holiday.
You go there and they treat you like a foreigner, the taxi driver is all
smooth talk 'our brothers from Cyprus' and all that and then they
cheat you on the fare. That's all they are good for, smooth talk and
cheating. Their country is so disorganized. They are lazy and big
talkers and that's why they are so poor. We are more European than
them. They have that way of talking that fools you, they speak such
clear and beautiful Greek but it's all empty, just glitter, and then they
stab you in the back. Like they did to us in 1974. I remember how
we used to admire the Greek army officers before, how proud and
tall they looked, how we were impressed by their noble uniforms,
how we loved to hear them talk. It was the dream of every mother
for her daughter to marry one. It took us time to really understand
them. So they took advantage of us, you know how innocent and
well meaning we Cypriots are. They would come and get engaged
to a young Cypriot girl and then abandon her when the time came
to leave. In the meantime they had destroyed her, they had slept
with her. Who would want to marry a used girl any more? After
1974, I told my daughter never to think about marrying a *kalamara*
and to avoid even meeting them. Better an Arab, I told her, than a
kalamara.

LOWER PARISHES

Maria was a sculptress. She had, along with several other artists, chosen
to set up her workshop in Tahtakallas. The Dead Zone drew artists too.
They liked the traditional-old-houses-winding-narrow-streets look of
the area. Some felt that the area made them more keenly aware of the
political problems of Cyprus and this inspired their work. Others came
because they felt a strong presence of history in the old town; and for
all the rent was low.

Mrs Frosou, who lived next door, was Maria's elderly landlady. Even
though Maria, in her early thirties, had rented the house, Mrs Frosou
kept a key of her own, entering and exiting at will. She had done this
all her life and she could not understand why the presence of a tenant
should change things. Mrs Frosou lived alone with a brown cat that
she adored. Maria told me how she had complimented Mrs Frosou

over Riris, her cat, only to be slightly corrected. Using a word meaning neighbourhood, Maria had said: 'Riris is the king of the *gitonia*.' Mrs Frosou corrected her with a different word: 'You mean Riris is the king of the *mahallas*.'

Gitonia and *mahallas*: two words that meant the same but did not feel the same. The first was the Greek word, while the second came from Turkish. The first was generic, proper and cold in comparison to the second, which was intimate, warm and personal ('our own special neighbourhood'). *Gitonia* could be any place, while *mahallas* evoked memories of a place where Alexandros used to live 'just there in that house next door', where 'under the shade of this tree Olgou used to sit every afternoon making thin pasta – God rest her soul', where 'in this doorway Ahmetoui waved at us "Good afternoon ladies" as we passed by.' It evoked the presences of those who had passed on into the zone of the dead, and of others who had moved just a small step across the Dead Zone; relations, feelings, friendships made and broken, smells, tastes, gossip, fights.

Locals often called the area Lower *Mahallades* rather than Lower *Enories* (Parishes). Outsiders referred to it only as Lower *Enories*. The young people living there could not know that *mahallas* was a Turkish word, but then again few of them used the word anyway. They considered it a kind of local Cypriot word, a word of the dialect or perhaps an outdated Greek word. It was gradually being replaced by the clean and proper Greek *gitonia*. Perhaps the feeling of living in a *mahallas* was not there for them. They longed for real, modern life. The Turkish Cypriots of Tahtakallas did not exist for them either. They only lived in the memories of the elders. Quite a few of the elders knew that it was Turkish since their Turkish neighbours used the word.

'All languages are good to know, even Turkish,' said Mr Andreas rather defensively, after mentioning that he spoke Turkish. He pointed out many words and expressions we used that came from Turkish. 'How would you know this, Yiannaki? You are too young, and the young ones don't speak a word of Turkish,' he added regretfully.

> Why, many of you do not even speak our own language. You don't speak Cypriot any more. But my Turkish is nothing in comparison to how well my father spoke. You could not tell him apart from the Turks when he spoke. You know, I still remember how when he really wanted to express himself, when he got emotional, he sometimes spoke in Turkish. And you know what else? When we lived together

our television sometimes showed Turkish films. People preferred their love stories to ours. They were just so moving.

When I was in Turkey I had noted the similarities between Turkish and Greek love stories. Blonde, rich girl loves poor, dark, handsome boy. Her father wants her to marry a rich fat businessman. The couple meet secretly and often dance to the sound of a hidden orchestra. Passers-by join in; they know all the steps. And finally, just in the nick of time, they marry. The only difference in the story was that in Turkish films the poor, handsome boy had to also support a blind sister.

Since some people there knew Turkish, and to my surprise seemed proud of it, I felt I could now come out and say that I too had been learning Turkish and I was still studying it. Both things were true. But I was still afraid to say where I had first learnt it.

TAHTAKALLAS

'Watch out, Yiannaki,' I was warned when I told people I intended to spend a year there. 'Whoever drinks the cool water of Tahtakallas stays here for ever.' Tahtakallas was the name of the mosque and the Turkish Cypriot neighbourhood, also used for all three neighbourhoods together instead of Lower Parishes. I read that it derived from Ottoman Turkish: *Taht-el-Kale* or *Tahta Kale*. In Turkish it meant 'wooden fortress' but only a couple of the old Greek Cypriots who lived there knew this meaning. Some said that the name referred to Famagusta Gate, the large wooden gate on the walls. I remembered a neighbourhood in Istanbul with the same name.

Of the three names by which the area was known – Lower Parishes, Akritic Parishes, and Tahtakallas – Tahtakallas was the name people most often used when they spoke about themselves among themselves. They called themselves Tahtakallites, good and honest people, people who 'speak from the heart', brave, if sometimes rowdy and even a bit crazy. When old people spoke about the Tahtakallites, they meant everyone who used to live there, including the Turkish Cypriots, who were said to share the same qualities. Old women prided themselves that Tahtakallas was renowned for a traditional local dish. This was called *kaourmas* and was prepared at Easter. It was lamb cooked in the oven with olive oil and tomatoes, and took the place of the usual Easter skewered lamb. I was aware that the name of the dish came from Turkish, from *kavurmak*, meaning to roast. I had come across a dish with this name in Turkey.

So Tahtakallas, like *mahallas*, brought a certain sweetness to the mouth for many. The fact that elderly locals liked the Turkish name of the area so much was in itself confirmation of past good relations. To younger people who came to live there later, however, the taste was bitter. When it was spoken, their faces squirmed as if they had just eaten a large mouthful of lemon. They hated the name and tried to get the government to change it.

AKRITIC PARISHES

'We are the present day Akrites,' Mrs Eleni, a local community leader, always told journalists. Journalists, local and foreign, came here a lot because of the Dead Zone; it pulled them in too. Everyone knew who the Akrites were: the heroic guardians of the Byzantine borders against infidel attacks. Their descendants – or those who adopted them as their forefathers – were now living in the area where I had chosen to do research. *Akrites* meant living on the edge, the border. It fitted well with Tahtakallas' own sad circumstances, I thought at the time, because after 1974 this place found itself right on the edge of the Dead Zone.

Mrs Eleni would then continue with the words she had often repeated:

> It is because of us that the rest of Lefkosia can sleep peacefully. It is because of us that the Turks did not invade the rest of Lefkosia. During 1974 we stayed put here and the presence of people around made it more difficult for the Turkish troops to advance. Had they found the area empty, do you think there is any chance that this ground would not now be part of the occupied areas? And if we did not decide to stay here, still suffering the hardships, fears and uncertainties of life so near the Dead Zone, the Turks might easily take it one day. We decided to stay here for reasons of national security and national interest. So, the state has both a moral and national duty to help us live here. Many things are badly needed here. You may not know that this used to be a mixed area. Turkish Cypriots lived with us here. We were neighbours and I should tell you that we lived well with each other. You should write this too, it is very important and I can say this because I know first-hand.

These beliefs were widely shared and many people told me similar things. One thing puzzled me, though it took me months to notice it. When Tahtakallites spoke among themselves, they always lived in Tahtakallas; when they spoke to others, especially journalists or officials, they lived in the heroic Akritic Parishes.

ARMY MEMORIES

Achilleas was a carpenter living in Tahtakallas. When he said that he was in the army in 1974, I asked more. I wanted to find out about the war but he did not say much about it. He chose to speak about other things:

> You really want to know how it was? Hell, that's how it was. It was the time of the Greek junta you see and all our officers here were junta people. They were true *kalamarades*, just scum, they came here thinking we were backward peasants. They had that attitude, you know, we come from the metropolis and you are just peasants here. All they were interested in was what they would take back to Greece. They knew all the brands of televisions, washing machines, stereos. Their true passion was cars. All of them wanted a BMW to take back to Greece and show off. They got double salary, you see, when they came to Cyprus plus they could buy things duty-free. But I doubt they even knew how to use the stereo. They could not even read the manuals in English. Our commander had to ask me, an eighteen-year-old, to read the manual and explain it. Can you imagine it? He was forty-five and didn't speak a word of English. But why am I going so far back? Look at them today. You went to the army. Did they talk about anything beyond the differences between this or that model of BMW?

I nodded, this time with earnest agreement. He continued:

> Anyway, then at the time of the junta the only other thing that interested them was to find out who was left-wing. They hated communists, more than they hated the Turks. Well, my father was left-wing, he supported the communists, the AKEL party, and they found out as soon as I went into the army. Back then I was not that interested in politics and didn't know a lot about it. But I learned quickly that being a communist, a 'red' as they called us, was the biggest crime. They had files on all of us, 'files of beliefs' was what they called them. So from the first day I was a 'red'. I still remember how the *kalamaras* officer 'baptized' me. In front of everyone, everyone I tell you, and I was only a child then, eighteen. 'Achilleas? What kind of name is that? They give you, a communist, a glorious Greek name? From today you are to be called Red.' They

were into all that junta shit that a communist atheist can not be Greek, and 'Greece of Greek Orthodox Christians'.

His hand moved over his unshaven chin and the two fingers removed the burning cigarette from his lips.

> And then hell started. Who is going to clean the toilet? The Red. Who is going to scrub the charred cooking pans? The Red. Oh, and I forgot the 'jokes'. 'Red go and get me a glass of water from the other side of the camp. Run. Get me another one, I'm still thirsty. Oh, silly me, look I spilled it. Oh you brought it, well actually I am not that thirsty after all.' And on and on. 'Show us your dick, let's see what colour it is. Come on boy, that's an order. Oh, look, it's red, even your dick is red.'

He paused to draw a breath. For a few of seconds, his mouth remained twisted in the position he used while imitating the accent of the *kalamarades*. 'Telling you all this, I can hear their voices in my ears. Even now when I hear anyone from Greece, my stomach twists into a knot and it all comes back.'

He paused once more to compose himself.

> Then 1974 came. They sent me to the mountains at Kerinia. The idea was that we would decimate the Turks if they came. We had really good fortified posts that even bombs could not destroy and a clear view of the coast. If the Turks dared to land, they'd be dead the moment they stepped on the ground. It was that easy. But we didn't know that there were other plans. When the Turks did invade, first our *kalamarades* officers left. They left, I tell you, just like that and ordered us to stay behind. Then, when we tried the machine guns, none of them worked. It was betrayal, pure betrayal. They had arranged it all so that we would not be able to stop the Turks and left us there to be slaughtered.

A BICYCLE NOT FOR SALE

Mr Kostas was a very old man. His white hair was turning the yellow of his cigarette-stained fingers. 'He drinks too much,' people said, 'his heart is broken. He will die from alcohol one day.' His small old shop was dark, untidy and cluttered, the plaster on the walls falling apart, spider webs hanging on the windows instead of curtains.

I was looking for a bicycle to make my daily rounds in Tahtakallas when I saw one in the corner of his shop. It was a beautiful old bicycle, a kind one could not find any more. It was silver, always polished, shining like a beacon in that grim shop. Mr Kostas never used it. It was always sitting there. I asked Mr Andreas, his close friend, whether I should ask to buy it. 'No, many people have already asked, it's not for sale. He'll never sell it. It belongs to his son who is missing.' His son was one of the 1,619 persons still missing after the Turkish invasion, people who were considered alive until proven otherwise, who still legally existed, owned their property and whose wives were still married to them.

NOT GOING TO THE BEACH
Marilena told me of her mother's broken promise:

> When we were children, in the summer, we used to go to the beach near Ammohostos. We loved it so much that we always wanted to stay more. The day before – how could we know that would become 'the day before?' – my mother had real trouble getting us out of the water. 'Look,' she said, 'we have to go now, but I promise that tomorrow you can stay as long as you like.' I looked forward to the next day so much, but we never ever went back again. Next day they invaded.

Like Marilena, many refugees remembered the day before the invasion vividly. Many grown-ups feared that Turkey might react to the coup, but they dared not take their fears seriously enough to make preparations. So when it happened, they were unprepared. A woman had just made some preserved fruit. 'All that hassle for nothing.' A man had just finished repainting his house. Everyone talked about what they would have done, what they would have taken with them, had they known. They also spoke of what they would never have been able to take with them. Often this was about the trees in their garden, which they or their parents had planted. The trees that they had cared for over many years, watching them grow and bear fruit, enjoying the scent of their blossom each spring.

PREPARING SUITCASES FOR THE RETURN
TO A GHOST TOWN
Ammohostos, a seaside city known for its sandy beaches, was one of the

last places that the Turkish army captured. The name meant 'covered with sand'. In English it was known as Famagusta. After 1974, another name was used: the Ghost Town. A large part of the town, the Greek Cypriot part including an area where the hotels were still standing, charred and gutted from the bombings of the Turkish planes, was left empty. It was sealed off by the Turkish authorities. Because it had been left uninhabited, it was presumed that this would be the first place Turkey might return. And since this was one of the last places to be occupied, they had the chance to prepare their suitcases and take with them what was most precious.

How does one do this? The parents, the children, and often the elderly grandparents? How do you pack the whole family's life into one car? What do you take? The practical things – clothes, utensils, blankets, tools? Or things that mean more: photos, old gifts, mementos? The records of your past selves, the photographs reminding you how you and your children were once different people. And what about the children's toys? This is what the people of Ammohostos, those lucky ones who were given the chance, had to decide. 'Only a refugee can understand a refugee,' they told me. 'Can you understand, Yiannaki, what it means for your life to be cut?' Mr Constantinos tried to explain. 'Cut just like that, like with a pair of scissors. Do you understand what it means for all your dreams to be cut like that? No, you can't. You are from Lemesos, you were not refugees.'

After the 1974 war, the refugees moved into the free areas in the south with nothing but their suitcases. Then negotiations began. Every time there were new hopes, new rumours. Everyone said that Ammohostos would be the first place Greek Cypriots would return to, if things went well. 'When Carter got elected in the USA, we thought he would be good for Cyprus,' Mrs Anna said.

> The church bells rang with joy all over Cyprus. We started packing our suitcases once more. In the beginning, after the invasion, many of us, like myself, had kept our suitcases ready all the time under our bed. Gradually some started to unpack them, but they still left them under the bed and if things seemed to be going really well, we would think about packing them again. Until two years ago, I still had them under the bed. Then I put them away.

People from Ammohostos were left waiting. Mr Herakles' eyes dampened as he remembered. 'We were living in the refugee camps for years then. In the tents. Waiting and waiting. Like animals in a cage.

They fed us and watered us but we had nothing to do in the meantime. No life to live.'

I DON'T FORGET

Two issues were clear from my research so far. They were often repeated as I was telling people that I would try to cross over in order to talk with Turkish Cypriots. The first was how much refugees wanted to return to their homes; how much they insisted that their memories of their villages should be kept alive. If they were lost, so would be the desire to return.

'I Don't Forget.' These words were a symbol found everywhere in Cyprus. They were on school exercise books and on photos of villages under occupation. Children saw them every day they went to school, every time they had to write. Every night, before the main evening news, the photo of an occupied village was shown with 'I Don't Forget' underneath. What should not be forgotten was so clear that there was no need to say more. 'The memories of our occupied villages, our ancestral hearths, our graveyards, our occupied churches, our occupied homes, our gardens, our orchards…'

The second was how much people remembered, and in such intricate detail, about how well we had lived with Turkish Cypriots. One thing began to puzzle me, though, when it came to what should be remembered. Most people, including refugees, were so keen to talk to me about their memories of harmonious coexistence with Turkish Cypriots. How come these memories did not earn their own symbol?

BACK TO THE ZONE OF THE DEAD

The old people of Tahtakallas had taken me back to the past many times in their memories. They had spoken at great length about how well we used to live with Turkish Cypriots and about the harmful involvement of the Greeks. Now I wanted to see what the professionals, the historians, had to say.

When I had learned about the history of Turkey, I had come to doubt many things about the history of Greece. Now, with what I had been learning about the good relations with our ex-neighbours, the Turkish Cypriots, I had cause to doubt even more. Especially given the things I had heard about the Greeks, the *kalamarades*. I had to deal with the ex-brothers first, those who lived in mainland Greece – as if we Cypriots lived in a provincial, not-so-main-land. The question was straightforward: if here we had been living so well with Turkish Cypriots, who was to blame for what happened? The answer seemed as clear. Since we had no problems between us in Cyprus, it must have been outsiders who caused the tragedy. The Greeks, who staged the coup and brought the Turks here; and the Turks, who used the excuse the Greeks had given them. The two so-called arch-enemies had cooperated to ruin us in Cyprus.

The Greeks had much more in common with the Turks. As I read how Greece came to be what it now was, the similarities with Turkey were striking: changing capitals, cleansing the language, adopting new ancestors and histories, changing clothes, and desperately striving to become western by moving away from the East. Who discovered Greece anyhow? The Greece that now mattered was discovered by the West during the Enlightenment, as westerners turned for inspiration to ancient Greece. This was good news for Greeks who lived and had been educated in the West. For, if Greece was the cradle of civilization how could modern Greeks be allowed to live under the arch-enemy and opposite of the West, the Ottomans? The first calls to liberate the Greeks – who, by the way, did not yet know that they were Greek – came from such western Greeks, along with the Philhellenes. The *Philhellenes*! Such a noble sounding word in Greek; a European who was cultured and fair and so would naturally side with the Greeks. This in contrast to *Turkophile*; a horrible word in Greek meaning someone evil and biased, a word that rhymed with certain other bad words. But the romantic Philhellenes, who loved Greece from afar, were gravely disappointed when they actually met real *modern* Greeks. So much so that some became Turkophiles.

From Nafplion, a city with a certain prestige, the capital moved to what was then a small, squalid town. *Athens*. Not just a name, so much more besides. It gradually came to acquire its own academy, parliament, palace and other public buildings modelled upon glorious classical Athens.

Trying to fit into the mould of Greece made in the West and to be accepted as western necessitated strict demarcation from the East. The Herculean task of clearing the Ottoman 'stench' commenced. Language was cleansed of toxic Turkish pollutants. A new language was created, made fit for the children of the ancient Greeks by borrowing from the ancient Attic dialect. It was called *katharevousa*, 'the clean one'. That the new ancient language was one people neither spoke nor understood well was immaterial. A Greek word, *diglossia*, was later to emerge in linguistics to describe this problematic situation in Greece and elsewhere.

The landscape, like the clothes, suddenly didn't fit. Mosques were turned into ruins and buried in the ground, as ancient Greek ruins were unburied, their columns made to stand majestically once more. The mosque on the Acropolis disappeared. A mosque at the symbol of modern-ancient Greece? The symbol of all civilization! Wouldn't look too good on tourist postcards. Gone were the palm trees in Athens' central Omonia (Unity) Square. Too oriental! Later, with the rise in the 1960s of the Colonel's junta that destroyed the people of Cyprus, the name of the coffee people drank was officially changed from 'Turkish' to 'Greek'. Houses received new neoclassical façades, though the interiors usually remained unchanged, as Greeks also shed their traditional attire in favour of western clothes. As new forefathers were born, newborns were baptized in their names. The place was soon crawling with little Socrates, Heracles, Pericles, Persephones, and Aphrodites.

There was just one minor difficulty with all this: the people had to learn that they were Greek. 'The nation has to be awoken.' When a Philhellene spoke to one of the Greek chieftains of 'the heroic Achilles' he received a blank stare: 'Who is this Achilles? Did he shoot a lot of enemies with his gun?' People simply did not know that they were Greeks. Many had only heard the name *Hellenes* in fairy tales. These Hellenes were a mythical race with superhuman powers that used to live thereabout. In one version, the real reason they became extinct was that they were exterminated by mosquitoes. The inhabitants of the newly created Greek state did not feel that those Hellenes had anything to do with *them*. They called themselves *Romii*, Romans. They regarded themselves as descendants of the Byzantine Empire. This was an Empire that traced its origins back to Rome, not Athens. During the reign of the Empire, the name Hellenes was reserved for pagans, the heathen, barbarians. Muslim inhabitants of Syria could be called 'Hellenes', but not the Christians of the Empire. But there was nothing that a strong dose of education and the army could not fix.

During the early nineteenth century when the Greek state was first created, Byzantium did not fare well. Neither did Alexander the Great for that matter. Byzantium was regarded by the new historians as a dark period of barbaric oppression. And was it not Alexander the Not-So-Terribly Great who destroyed classical Greece? Greek historians posited classical Greece as the glorious beginning. From there history descended into a prolonged dark age, including Alexander and the Byzantines, only to re-emerge now with the glory of the new state. A beginning and an end, but no middle. Becoming European also meant adopting a European outlook on history. The Byzantine Empire fell inside the western historical category of the 'dark Middle Ages', a rather unpleasant period.

By the middle of the nineteenth century, Greek politicians had begun looking towards Asia Minor with expansion in their eyes. There was a need to link the 'unredeemed brothers' still living in Asia Minor with the citizens of the recently created Greek kingdom. As the Greek state started to look eastwards, towards the crumbling Ottoman Empire, the need for a bridge emerged. Ideological bridges were to be built first, if the military bridgeheads were to follow. Thus the Byzantines and Alexander were gradually adopted as new ancestors. Didn't the Byzantine Empire cover Asia Minor? Did Alexander the Great not create a vast empire towards the East? A new historian – Paparigopoulos – emerged with a new history, providing the bridge. Greek history eventually settled into three periods: ancient, Byzantine, and modern.

The new history provided the historical rationale for the military implementation of the Great Idea. Since Asia Minor historically belonged to the Greeks, Greece should extend its borders there, eventually incorporating – 'reincorporating' – the 'unredeemed brothers', and sisters too of course. But the campaign for the Great Idea culminated in the Catastrophe, the 1922 defeat of the Greeks by the 'Turks', who were in fact to become Turks as a result of these events. The two had created each other as they fought out their wars of independence against each other. And both of them together created this mess that was Cyprus, my home.

As far as Cyprus was concerned, the important question was: had we really lived so well together? When I read the recent Greek Cypriot historical research, it confirmed what people had been telling me all along. The historians had even coined a new term: 'peaceful coexistence'. I did not remember us being taught anything like this when I was at school but then our books came from Greece and we learned very little about the history of Cyprus. I now learned some new historical facts. How sometimes the Christian and Muslim peasants revolted together, either against the oppression of the Ottoman authorities, or against the oppression of the Orthodox Church in Cyprus, which was an equally ruthless oppressor. The historians had documented how people visited each others' houses and coffee shops, how they exchanged gifts or sweets on religious days. We had used religious differences to unite, not divide us. There were cases of intermarriage and of people of one religion worshipping at the others' sacred places. That was how much we respected each other and how well we had lived together. We were different from the Greeks and Turks, who had been enemies for centuries.

If we had been living so well, how did the problems emerge? Once again, the answer Greek Cypriot historians gave was clear: foreign influences and outside interferences. First, the two 'mother-fatherlands' exported their education systems to Cyprus along with the venomous messages of their nationalisms. They gradually divided the people and spread the seeds of hatred. No longer accommodating Orthodox and Muslim peasants, they were turning into educated Greeks and Turks who hated each other. Even so, people did not buy wholesale into the poisonous messages of the two educational systems and still lived together well until the 1950s. Until the British introduced their tried and trusted 'Divide and Rule' schemes. They started to employ Turkish Cypriot policemen against the Greek Cypriot EOKA fighters, which was bound to lead to conflict between us. That was the whole plan after all. The first ever violent confrontation between us took place under the British in 1956. Even after independence the two 'mother-fatherlands' continued to interfere in our politics. Other foreign powers interfered too, including the USA. Our democratically elected president after independence, Archbishop Makarios, was seen by Americans as 'the Castro of the Mediterranean' on account of the support he received from the communists here. There had been some minor incidents of inter-ethnic strife during the time of the EOKA insurrection in the late 1950s, and later in the 1960s, but they were unimportant. Those before 1960 were orchestrated by the British, and the ones during independence by the nationalist agitators for the 'mother-fatherlands'. But 400 years of peaceful coexistence could not be written off by minor incidents during the past 30 years. They were the exceptions that proved the rule, and they had been provoked by outsiders.

Just like Cyprus, my own past, my birth even, had been influenced by the fighting between the two 'mother-fatherlands'. It forced Maria my grandmother to move into exile, where she married Yiannis, my grandfather and gave birth to my father. My origins were Cypriot through and through. My mother was Cypriot, born and raised here. My father was born and grew up in Greece but his father was a Cypriot who went to Greece for work. My father eventually, wisely, returned to

Cyprus, gave up his Greek passport, acquired a Cypriot one, married a woman from Cyprus and settled here for good.

I searched my own memories of life in Cyprus with the Turkish Cypriots. I was only ten in 1974, when they too had to leave their homes next to ours. Even so, I vividly remembered contacts and coexistence in my hometown, Lemesos. I remembered how we sometimes ate at a Turkish restaurant in the Turkish neighbourhood. We often went there with my father to buy things. We always bought our yogurt and watermelons there. Had I only been older, I would have remembered much more of our peaceful past.

APHRODITE

During my readings I often came across Aphrodite. She would turn out to be a most insightful guide throughout this journey. The Goddess of Love was such an appropriate symbol for Cyprus, a place where we had lived harmoniously together. As I learned more about Aphrodite, the whole historical situation of Cyprus became clearer. There was a pattern in stories involving Aphrodite. She had a talent for causing *children* to fall in love with their *parents*, with *disastrous* consequences. She caused Myrha to fall in love with her father, King Kinyras. Adonis was their forbidden fruit. She made Phaedra fall in love with her step-son, Hippolytus, a tragedy ending with the death of both. Wasn't this what the Dead Zone was all about? Children falling in love with parents, with disastrous consequences? Then there was her birth. She was born of an act of insubordination of a son, Cronus, against a father, Uranus.

At school we Cypriots learned that Aphrodite was a goddess of the Greek Pantheon, and we always thought that she had come to Cyprus from Greece. But, from what I now read, it was actually the other way around. Aphrodite was a transformation of the Near Eastern goddess Ishtar or Astarte. Even the ancient Greeks knew that Aphrodite had Asiatic origins. Herodotus described her as a Phoenician goddess whose worship spread to Greece via Cyprus. Assyrians called her Milytta, Arabians called her Alilat, for Persians she was Mitra and for Scythians Argimpasa. In short, Aphrodite was a mixture of cultures of the East and the West. Cyprus too was a mixture of eastern and western civilizations, a mixture that produced something unique like Aphrodite. Cyprus was a mixture but also something unique and different from all its components. This kind of mixing made even my name sound different. I discovered that it originated from Ea, the Sumerian Water

God, becoming in Greek Oannes, in Latin Johannes, in Hebrew Yohanan and in English John. As for Aphrodite, some linguists argued that her name apparently did not derive from the Greek *aphros* for foam but from the Egyptian fertility goddess *Pr-Wedyt*.

There were yet more revealing aspects of Aphrodite. Her cult in Cyprus revolved around sacred prostitution. Before they could marry, women entered Aphrodite's temple and were made available to visitors to the temple. Lively rituals, the Aphrodisia, had been dedicated to the Goddess, during which mass orgies took place under her blessing. Some authors argued that the practice of temple prostitution moved from Cyprus towards the East, all the way to India, as others also pointed out that 'Asia' derived from Al-asia, an ancient name of Cyprus. Somehow, these contributions to world civilization had been left out of our schoolbooks. We never even learnt that during the last day of the Aphrodisia, rituals took place during which, as one theory proposed, the emblems of the Goddess – salt and the phallus – were used in certain ways. Our old customs and traditions were said to have so scandalized early Christian writers that they thought the people of Cyprus descended from demons.

Aphrodite, the goddess of prostitutes. Hadn't I heard Cyprus described as the 'prostitute of the Mediterranean'? She was ruthlessly used by others throughout history: Arabs, Venetians, Byzantines, Ottomans, British, Greeks and Turks, all outsiders who used us for their own satisfaction and interests and then abandoned us to bear the bitter fruits of our encounters.

Did the ancient Greeks really consider us as one of them? Aeschylus spoke of the 'Cypriot type' as something alien. In one of his poems, Cypriot women were grouped with other alien races such as the Egyptians and the Indians. What of our name, Kypros? Was this Greek? Etymologists argued that our name could derive from *zubar*, the Sumerian word for copper, for which Cyprus was renowned.

Perhaps the ancient Cypriots knew better. What did Kinyras, the Cypriot priest-king do when Odysseus requested, demanded rather, his help in the Trojan War? He was afraid to refuse because the Greek forces were overwhelming, so he promised forty ships. But he was in a difficult spot since the goddess he served, Aphrodite – our symbol, our goddess – did not side with the Greeks but with the Trojans. How did he escape this dreadful situation? He outcrafted even the crafty Greek Odysseus. He kept his promise by sending the Greeks one ship with thirty-nine tiny replica ships on board.

PERMISSION REQUESTED

In the meantime, I was trying to find a way to do research in the occupied areas with Turkish Cypriots. Ideally, I wanted to spend at least eight months to learn as much as I could from Turkish Cypriots, especially those who had previously lived in Tahtakallas. Using a special telephone line, I was able to talk to a Turkish Cypriot 'official' of the 'Turkish Republic of Northern Cyprus'. The pseudo-official said he would meet me at the Ledra Palace checkpoint in 'Lefkosha'. Lefkosha was what they called Lefkosia. The checkpoint was named after the once magnificent Ledra Palace Hotel now lying in the Dead Zone and used as UN barracks. From there, foreign tourists could cross for visits to the occupied areas, but they had to come back the same afternoon because we did not want them to spend the night in our occupied hotels. Our journalists who were sometimes permitted to cross for the day complained that the Turkish Cypriot 'authorities' forced them to fill in and sign a form, like an airport arrival form to another country. This had caused a lot of discussion, because it was deemed to mean the political recognition of an illegal regime.

I went there with 'my heart in my mouth', as we Cypriots would say. The future of my research depended on it. Our meeting was brief. He listened carefully and did not speak much as I explained myself:

> I am doing my Ph.D. research in Cambridge on how people in Cyprus think of the past. I am also learning Turkish, and I visited Istanbul for this, because I want to use Turkish and Turkish Cypriot sources and talk to Turkish Cypriot people. For this purpose, I would like to come to live in… in Lefkosha. So far other Greek Cypriots who have done this kind of research have only used Greek Cypriot sources and only spoke to Greek Cypriots. But I want to take the Turkish Cypriot perspective into consideration. I think it is impossible to understand what happened otherwise. Will you help me in my effort to understand and document the Turkish Cypriot perspective?

He said that he would pass on my request to the right person and they would contact me.

I did not expect much to happen. Just to be on the safe side, I started casually mentioning to people in Tahtakallas that I had asked for a permit to go to our occupied areas. I did not want to say out of the blue one day, 'Goodbye, I am going to the other side.' I was worried how people would react, especially the refugees who could not go to their homes. But no one paid much attention to this because they all agreed it would never take place. 'It would be good to go over, talk to them and find out how well they lived with us. You would meet our old friends there and you could bring us their news,' people agreed. 'But unfortunately they'll never allow you'.

THE PUBLIC INFORMATION OFFICE

Three weeks after I had spoken with the Turkish Cypriot 'official' I received the call. *Yes.* I could go there for a month from 1 March and then they would see if I could stay longer. I was overjoyed. Then I began to get suspicious. Did they have a hidden agenda? A secret plan?

I decided that it would be good idea to first inform our authorities of my plans to visit the occupied areas. I was concerned whether they would allow me to cross. The person to see was the head of our Public Information Office, the government office engaged in *Diafotisi*, Enlightenment. This meant explaining to anyone interested the truth about the Cyprus Problem. Everyone knew that this was an important job because foreigners were often misinformed by the enormous and costly Turkish propaganda campaign.

The official received me rather informally in his office, lying deep in his chair, the chair tilted back, his feet on the desk in front of him, playing with a set of worry beads. Behind him were photographs of Archbishop Makarios, the first president of the Republic of Cyprus, and of the current president, Vasiliou. He saw no problem with me crossing. He was glad that young people like me who were trying to do objective academic research were interested in the issue of Cyprus, because this would make it easier for our truth to shine forth to the rest of the world. It was the first time that he had come across a Greek Cypriot who had been allowed to go to the so-called 'Turkish Republic of Northern Cyprus' and he only hoped that I could retain my objectivity, seek the truth and nothing but the truth. He warned me not to sign anything as this would mean that I was recognizing their pseudo-state, that no country in the world recognized except Turkey. He cautioned me not to be carried away by their propaganda, something at which, he commented sadly, they were unfortunately much better than us, due to the help they got from Turkey. He knew of cases when they had bought academics, a highly valued resource for propaganda purposes because they were supposed to speak the truth. It was widely known, he added, that all academics that expressed pro-Turkish views were on the payroll of the Turkish government. There was no concrete evidence as such, except in a couple of cases. But if they were real objective academics, why would they express pro-Turkish views?

He was confident of what I would find out there:

> Our job here is to follow what happens on the occupied side. We know their side better than anyone else. We follow their press, their television, everything that comes out. Then we provide translations for our politicians and the media of what is important to know about them. Everything people on this side know about the other comes through us. Whether you will be able to reach the truth will depend on whether they allow you to talk to the people freely. If they do, which I doubt, then I'm sure the ordinary people there will tell you that they want to live together with us. Only some fanatics of Denktash, and of course the Turks from Turkey, those illegal immigrants, may tell you otherwise. Why would the common people not want to live with us? We lived in harmonious coexistence in the past and prospered together. Now they are poor, they have so many problems with the Turkish immigrants, they are oppressed by the pseudo-government of Denktash, and they are oppressed by the Turkish army. These are the messages we get here all the time. Of course some say other things but those are just the propagandists of Denktash and Turkey. They even have an illegal propaganda office in the occupied areas that they also call The Public Information Office.

ADVICE

All that was left was to tell people in Tahtakallas that I was to cross. I was worried it could ruin the good relations I thought I had established with them over the past five months. Would they approve? Would they think that if the Turkish Cypriot 'authorities' liked me enough to allow me to go, that was proof I was on their side? A spy even? I explained that I had been allowed to cross and was now hoping to trace the Turkish Cypriots who had been previously living in Tahtakallas. They were surprised and shocked that I was going to go over. Only some of the older people were unperturbed. They said something like 'We used to go over ourselves in the past.' At the time, I misunderstood what they meant. I thought they meant before 1974. Thankfully, most people were quite positive and encouraged me to go, even as they expressed certain reservations.

Some advice I heard from all. 'Don't do anything that will mean you recognize them.' 'Don't get carried away by their propaganda.' 'Always be on your guard, always be suspicious.' 'Watch out for the Turkish army there, the place is full of them.' 'Don't trust anyone there, the place is full of spies. You'll be followed everywhere, you won't be able to take a step on your own.' 'Take care with what they give you to eat.' 'Try to find our old friends.' An old man applauded my decision for different reasons: 'Yes, it's good to go there and do research. We need to know our enemies.' Many refugees told me the name of their village and asked me to bring back a photograph.

I noticed that some men now treated me differently. One day, Mr Hristoforos asked me not to smoke in his shop because smoking was not allowed there. But I had been there many times and I knew that everyone smoked there. What he was telling me was that he did not want me to go there. So I stopped going. Later when we met in the street, he did not return my greetings and pretended not to have seen me. It was clear that he did not like me. I began to get the same feeling with a couple of friends of his. Eventually, I think I found out why I was unwelcome. But that was when I went to the other side.

'They should have slaughtered your parents here in Cyprus, or your grandparents in Asia Minor somewhere. Then we'd have seen if you were so keen to go there.' This was the worst reaction I got, coming from a young man of my age. He was the most outspoken and proud of being Greek. He kept on shouting angrily at me:

> And you are from Lemesos, aren't you? You never knew what the war meant, you never had to live with the Dead Zone, and you never became refugees. How can you understand what a refugee would feel if he crossed? And now you intend to just go over for a walk, like for tourism, as if you are going to another country not our sacred occupied lands. Or for research as you call it. And what exactly are you going to research? If Turkish barbarism exists? The problem is simple, they killed and slaughtered us in 1974 as they did throughout history. Plus, by going there, either as a Greek of Cyprus or as a British university student, you are giving them international recognition. Of course, what should one expect of a product of British education such as yourself?

I found myself unable to respond or defend myself. I left without a word. But I was deeply worried that others might share his views.

Mrs Marianna, the local folklorist, understood my concerns better than anyone, even though I never discussed them openly with her. 'I'll take care of your reputation while you are away,' she said.

> I know that you must be worried that our people will start to wonder whether you are some kind of spy for them. Already I hear things: Why did they give Yiannaki permission? Why do they like him so much? Could he perhaps be, you know what? But don't you worry about all this. I think what you are doing is great and I'm proud of you. Just send us some news every now and then so that we know you are well.

GOODBYE FROM MY FATHER

Just before leaving the free areas of the Republic of Cyprus, I went to say goodbye to friends, my girlfriend and then my parents. I found them calmer than I expected. My father told me some things he had never told me before:

> Go and find Mr Yusuf Ahmet. We were colleagues, before they had to leave. He worked for the same company here in Lemesos like me and that's how we got to know each other. He was a really nice man and I hope he is well. I'm sure he'll treat you well and help you. If I could have reached him, I would have asked him to look after you. I'll never forget what happened to him in 1974. They gathered the Turkish Cypriots after the invasion and put them in the Lemesos football stadium. One day, I received a message from a friend that Yusuf had to see me. I'll never forget what happened. You see, in those days the Turkish army was landing boats and parachutists and the war was on, so when I went to the stadium and said I want to see this Turkish Cypriot the army officer looked at me like I was scum. All the army officers there were from Greece and I had to walk through them as some shouted obscene things at me. Yusuf… when I saw him he was like another man, aged overnight. Tired, unshaven, soaking wet with perspiration – they had them there under forty degrees – his eyes were empty, like he wanted to tell me: 'Stathi, how did we end up like this?' He told me quickly what he wanted. He had hidden all his life's savings in his home and wanted me to get them and look after it until we found a way to give it back. It was all cash, and if I wanted I could have taken it all for myself. This is how much we trusted each other then. So I waited for dusk and went to his house. I was afraid people would

get suspicious, but his house had already been looted by our people like the other houses around. People were still loading things into vans and no one paid attention to me. I found the money still hidden there and took it. A few months later, he found a way to contact me and I returned it via someone from England. So go, tell him you are my son, send him my regards and I'm sure he'll help and take care of you.

We had placed *Turkish Cypriots* in concentration camps after the invasion? I had never heard that before, only about how well we lived. Then again those were not ordinary days when the war was raging. People had sometimes spoken vaguely about some incidents, but that was all. And how come my own father had not told me such things before?

DEPARTURE FROM THE FREE AREAS

The day came to cross from free Lefkosia into occupied Lefkosia. I was going to cross the Dead Zone at the Ledra Palace Hotel, the only crossing point. The Greek Cypriot policemen at the checkpoint did not create any problems, though one was particularly curious. He was dressed in civilian clothes and belonged to the Secret Police. He openly expressed suspicion that I had been allowed to go over to the occupied area and cautioned me that I should never recognize their illegal regime by signing the entry form. He advised me not to trust anyone because 'the place is full of secret police dressed in civilian clothes.' I was free to go.

I was standing right in front of the Dead Zone. All around me were posters explaining the facts of the Cyprus Problem with numbers and photographs. 'The Deeds of Attila' were presented in black and white photos of the refugees fleeing for their lives in 1974, of atrocities committed by the Turkish troops, and of houses charred by Turkish napalm bombs. On my right, Cyprus was shown crucified on a large cross. On top of the cross was a wreath made with barbed wire, like Jesus' crown of thorns.

ACROSS THE DEAD ZONE

One step brought me inside the Dead Zone. On my left was the imposing Ledra Palace Hotel, still full of bullet holes from the invasion, the UN flag flying on a balcony. The road was slightly winding, with UN guards around. I paused to look back at the free side. The last thing

I saw behind me was a large Greek flag and a wall erected as a barrier, painted in blue and white stripes, echoing those of the Greek flag. Before turning the corner and becoming visible to the Turks, I put my bag down. I did not want to appear tired and dispirited when they first saw me. I picked it up, straightening my body and lifting my head, as I walked down the road towards a state that did not exist.

CHAPTER THREE
LEFKOSHA
MARCH 1991

ACROSS THE DEAD ZONE

I turned the corner past the last UN soldier. Their checkpoint into occupied Lefkosia was in front of me. The first thing I saw was a large Turkish flag. On my right I saw the notice boards. I had never seen those photos. The notice boards were filled with their propaganda: black and white photos of mass graves, of Turkish Cypriot children and women supposedly murdered by Greek Cypriots, of Turkish Cypriot refugees supposedly fleeing their homes, of allegedly looted and burned homes. Actually, I had seen similar black and white pictures on the side I had just left behind.

ARRIVAL IN THE OCCUPIED AREAS OF THE 'TURKISH REPUBLIC OF NORTHERN CYPRUS'

To my surprise, nothing dramatic occurred when I reached their checkpoint. I spoke to the pseudo-policemen, noting a small pseudo-flag of their pseudo-state on their uniforms. They had turned even their uniforms, their own bodies into a vehicle for propaganda. I did not know then that a plan had already been hatched to turn my body too into an instrument of their propaganda campaign. They said that an 'official' was on his way meet me. The apparent calm worried me.

The 'official' soon arrived. He was in his mid forties, tall, thin with blue eyes and short blondish hair. I thought I saw a mischievous spark in his eyes. He welcomed me heartily. 'Welcome Yiannaki. I am Levent Bey and you have been assigned to me. I am glad you came. I was a bit worried that your people in the Greek sector might not let you.' I hated this 'Yiannaki'. Levent was his name, and Bey meant Mr in Turkish. Soon I would find out that I had just been welcomed by my Stepfather.

He spoke Greek like my father did, better in fact. He was a Greek from Greece. Here I was in occupied Cyprus and the man in charge of me was a *kalamaras*! 'You are not Cypriot,' I blurted. He understood what I meant. Initially he tried to evade the issue, but later he explained:

> I am a Turk, of course. But I know what you mean. I speak with a Greek accent, *kalamaristika* is how you Greeks of Cyprus call it. Well yes, I was born and brought up in northern Greece. I was born a Turk but with Greek citizenship. And let me tell you Yiannaki, it is not pleasant to be a Turk living in Greece. As bad, or even worse, as being a Turk living among you, the Greeks, over here in Cyprus. One day I couldn't take it any more and left.

'Just give him the form to fill in,' he said casually, turning to the policeman. What I dreaded was happening. 'I regret but as you may realize, I cannot sign the form you are about to offer me. I hope you will understand and respect my reasons for this. I am an independent scholar and do not wish to get involved in political issues by signing something that amounts to recognition of…' Levent Bey cut me short. 'Who said you have to sign anything? This is just a form for your name, age, etc. If you had even looked at it before you opened your mouth, you would have seen that there isn't even a place for a signature on it.' He put it in my face and I saw he was right.

> But I know all about this signature myth that your journalists propagate in the south. And journalists are supposed to report facts! Do you know that one of them even published a photocopy of this form in your press, saying that no one should sign it? It was in Turkish of course, but still no one noticed that there was no place for a signature. You are so absolutely taken in by your own mythology that even when the truth is in front of you, you cannot see it. From what I see, you too are brainwashed by what they tell you in the Greek sector. Here, give it back to me. I'll just ask your details and fill it in myself.

Embarrassed, I began to fill in the form myself. I was still worried though. It could be a trick. I wondered how many such forms were needed to get a pseudo-state internationally recognized.

ADOPTION
'Anyway, you should know that I'm in charge of you,' he continued.

> You see all these buildings around us? Well, if anything happens to you while you are here they will all fall on my head. This is what my boss, the one high up who assigned me to you, told me. Apart from me I have assigned you to Ahmet, one of my assistants who will be with you in case I'm busy. You'll meet him later. You'll stay for a month and then we'll see. It'll all depend on how well you behave, if I am pleased with you, and what I decide. But now I want to get to know you a little, so let's go for a drive together, just the two of us. I want to help you as much as I can with your work. You know you are the first person from the Greek sector, the 'free areas' as you call them, to stay for a whole month. I hope you are here to do objective research. We need this in Cyprus. I hope you'll see the truth here and that you'll then have the courage to write it. We'll see how 'free' your side is, if they allow you to write what you see here. You are free of course to talk to anyone you want to. We wouldn't want your Greeks to say that a researcher was not free to do his research. But Ahmet or I will have to be around for your own safety. Who knows how an old man whose children you slaughtered will react to you? You understand, don't you? If you don't, you will soon.

We went over to his car. There he explained, in his fluent, sly Greek Greek, what his job was. Later when he spoke Turkish, I noticed that he spoke Turkish Turkish, not how Turkish Cypriots spoke. So he had also lived in Turkey. Soon he would tell me what he was:

> I provide information on your side. Because I grew up in Greece and lived there I know you, the Greeks, better than anyone. I know you because in a way I am Greek myself. I know all about you, your culture, religion, history, how you think about history, even how you swear – you swear a lot in Turkish don't you? I speak Greek, but never forget that first and foremost I am a Turk. Yes, you try to make us forget our Turkish identity in Greece. 'Muslim minority' is what you call us there, never Turks, but we are Turks

and we will always persist in our national identity. I read all your
newspapers, listen to all your news and decide what should be
cut out and translated into Turkish so that our government and
our people can learn about you. I'm in charge of providing all the
information on your side.

We entered the car and drove away. At one point he showed me his
home in occupied Lefkosia. He was listening to one of his tapes of Greek
music. He was right about how Greek he was. His sense of humour
was Greek too. Every time a Mercedes crossed our way, he would say
'What car is this? A Mercedes, right. And you say that we are so poor,
eh [smile]?' He asked this every single time a Mercedes passed (which
I still thought would have been much more often had we been on the
free side), smiling slyly before breaking into laughter when he saw the
exasperation on my face.

We stopped at various shops where he had to run small errands.
Sometimes he just stopped to introduce me to people. 'This is Yiannakis
from the Greek sector. He has come to learn about the Cyprus Problem
from us. You should help him if he asks you. While he is here I am his
Stepfather and he is my adopted son.' Then he would to turn to me and
add: 'OK, my dear stepson? [smile]' He said this to every person we met.
It was the dream of every anthropologist to be adopted by someone in
the society that one studied. This immediately created 'fictive kinship
links' and gave the researcher a circle of 'relatives' and friends who
could be asked for information, give advice and, if needed, provide
protection. But I was adopted and given a new identity against my will,
by the last person I would have wished as a Stepfather: an 'official',
a man of the 'government' and, as I could already see, an extremist.
How would I be able to approach ordinary Turkish Cypriots who were
probably oppressed by this 'government'? Would they talk to me freely
if word spread that Levent Bey was my 'Stepfather'?

THE PUBLIC MISINFORMATION OFFICE
Levent Bey said that he worked at the 'Public Information Office', whose
job was to enlighten outsiders about the truth of the Cyprus Problem. I
knew that this was the centre for the dissemination of their propaganda.
I had even come across some of their publications. Their Public
Misinformation Office was housed in their 'Ministry of Exterior and
Defence'. The 'head' of the Public Misinformation Office was expecting
me. He was sitting deep in his chair, leaning back, playing with a set of

worry beads. Two photographs were hanging on the wall above him: Ataturk in his dinner jacket, and Rauf Denktash, the 'President' of the 'TRNC'. There was something curious about the second photograph. He looked like a nice person. It took me a while to understand why. The head of the Public Misinformation Office welcomed me warmly. He was pleased that I had decided to study the Cyprus Problem because not many knew the truth and there was a real need for objective research. He only hoped that my Greek Cypriot background would not cloud my objectivity.

We occasionally met during my stay there and I soon got to like him, even if I felt uncomfortable about this. He came across as a gentle, thoughtful man. What made him different from many of the other 'officials' I met was that he did not try to persuade me of anything. He seemed genuinely interested in my own views and listened attentively without interrupting to tell me how wrong I was, as many others did. (But was all this a smokescreen to gradually win me over?) He treated me with respect, as an 'expert' who knew more than he did. (Did what I told him during our casual lunches end up in a secret military report?) He was even prepared to accept criticism about his side, if I made a fair argument. (Another trick to win my trust?) After I left the occupied side for good, I heard that he had been 'retired', because it was felt that he was too 'soft' (meaning, I later understood, that he did not hate us enough).

WELCOME LUNCH

Levent Bey wanted me to pass by his office before he would take me out for a welcome lunch. There Ahmet, a medium-built young man with short dark hair and a tidy moustache, came to greet us. He was Turkish Cypriot and spoke Greek with a Cypriot accent. Levent Bey said:

> Remember what I told you before? If anything happens to you, all these buildings will fall on my head. From now on Ahmet or I will always be with you. Even if an accident happens to you in the street, do you know what will then happen? This is what everyone on your side will say: 'A young independent scholar came and they killed him and made it look like an accident.' Your people will use it for propaganda. I know what I am saying because I know you well. You want to talk to people, that is fine. But these people have been hurt by you. Who knows how they will react when they see you?

I had expected something like this. I would not be left free to conduct my own research and talk to the people alone. The presence of an 'official' would surely not allow people to talk freely. I tried to explain to Levent Bey the epistemological problems involved regarding his presence during my interviews. 'Fine,' he said, 'I understand what you are saying, but there is no other way. If you want, I'll wait for you outside the room. Just tell me and it's done. But Ahmet or I have to be around, just in case.'

Unsuspecting of what was waiting for me, we set off for our occupied Kerinia – Girne they called it – a small city on the north shore, for lunch with Levent Bey. As we left Lefkosia, I noted the presence of merchants selling fruit on wooden trolleys. (Were they Turkish Cypriots or illegal immigrants from Turkey?) I saw all kinds of people. (I was trying hard to make out who were Turkish Cypriots and who were illegal Turks.) I saw soldiers of the Turkish occupying forces. (No doubt I would see more of them, since the place was full of them.) I saw villages in the distance that looked empty or abandoned. (Where probably we used to live before we were forced to abandon them.) I felt I was catching glimpses of most of the things I expected to see.

The restaurant was right on the sea outside Kerinia. 'The best fish restaurant around,' according to Levent Bey. The Turkish Cypriot owner welcomed us warmly, expressing joy that he had a Greek Cypriot customer. He too hoped that I would have the courage to report the truth. We sat outside facing the bay. The realization of the trap hit me in the form of an enormous hideous monument composed of a number of lines of thick square concrete – eleven as I learned later – extending from the ground towards the sky. Levent Bey explained that this was a monument to celebrate the 'first landing of the heroic Turkish forces of saviour mother-fatherland Turkey in 1974.'

I had to pretend that all was fine but inside I was fuming. How could he do this to me? Under the cover of hospitality, he had brought me to the bay where the Attila invasion began; where that ugly thing commemorated a hideous crime. It was a sly trick to break my morale, that's what it was; to show me exactly where I was and forcefully impose upon me the fact of the barbaric Turkish invasion, even as I was being treated to a 'welcome lunch'. How foolish of me to relax. I should never trust them again.

THE CRUCIAL QUESTION

After lunch, Levent Bey drove me to the Saray Hotel in the old town, where I was to stay. Just before I came out of the car he grabbed my arm.

> There is something important I must tell you, before you start your research. There is one thing you have to know, if you want to understand what has happened here. I'm talking about the real cause of the problem. You first need to understand how badly we were treated by you, how much we suffered when we lived with you and what you did to us. This is what you have to find out, this is what you have to ask people about.

I gave a diplomatic reply that I would indeed try to find out how people lived before 1974. I doubted whether things were anywhere near as bad as he made them out to be. In fact, I was certain that anything *he* said must surely be propaganda. Plus, I had recently heard so much about how well we had lived from many people who couldn't have all agreed to lie to me. Soon I would get to find out for myself anyway. Next day I could start.

After I had been to my room, I popped across from the hotel to buy cigarettes. I spoke in Turkish, but the owner understood I was not Turkish. When he asked, I said I was Greek Cypriot. 'Oh, but you look just like us, just like a Turk. I would never have guessed,' he said. My looks seemed peculiar to many young people like him just because they were not unusual. They expected Greek Cypriots to look different, and certainly not like them.

CHRISTMAS OF BLOOD

First thing in the morning, Ahmet and I went around the market (*pazari* as we called it, *pazar* for Turkish Cypriots) to meet some of the old inhabitants of Tahtakallas who were working in Lefkosia. I wanted to compare what they had to say about life in Tahtakallas with what I had heard from Greek Cypriots. Ali Bey was the first I met. He was a *kasap* (*hasapis* in Greek), a butcher. He seemed pleased to see me:

> I'll help you as much as I can, Yiannaki. You are young, you don't know anything but I'm sixty now and I lived through it all. I'll tell you all about the war, all about how we became refugees and what happened in 1964 in Tahtakale.

I thought that he had got his dates wrong because he was old. He meant 1974. 'Ali Bey,' I said, 'Thank you for wanting to help me. Yes, we can talk about the 1974 war, what happened then, and how you left Tahtakallas. Let us arrange a meeting.'

We had been talking in Turkish and he thought that I had not understood, so he switched to Greek. He still spoke our Cypriot dialect well. 'Yiannaki, look here, most of the war and the fighting took place from 1964 onwards. It all started in December 1963. That's when we abandoned Tahtakale and became refugees.' He saw that I was lost. 'War' and 'refugees' I immediately associated with 1974. He turned to Ahmet in Turkish. 'Doesn't he know about Bloody Christmas (*Kanli Noel*)?'

Ahmet turned to me with equal amazement. 'Have you heard of Bloody Christmas?' I replied that I had never heard of it before. He looked at me with even greater surprise, mixed with suspicion. People had gathered around us and were talking all at once, some in Turkish, some in Greek, some in English. 'But the war was in 1963, up to 1967... We left our homes in 1963 and 1964... Some left their homes also in 1974, but it was the Peace Operation then...' One of them turned to Ahmet with anger. 'This boy here came to learn about the past and you did not even tell him about the war? About 1963, 1964, 1967?' Ahmet turned back and looked at me. Then he turned to the others. 'How could one read about Cyprus and not know about these things? But he doesn't. Well, he is a Greek Cypriot, what do you expect?' That seemed to have cleared things up. They nodded and looked at me with wonder mixed with pity. A couple of them spoke to me gently. 'It's all right, Yiannaki. You are too young, you wouldn't know about these things. It's not your fault. But don't worry, we'll help you here, we'll tell you what happened from the beginning.'

The beginning always seemed to be the key. We sat down to talk as chairs were offered and others joined us. For the Greek Cypriots, the beginning of the problem always meant 1974. War, disaster, tragedy, refugees, missing people: all these words always spoke of 1974. For Turkish Cypriots things were different. War, disaster, tragedy, refugees, missing people: all this began in 1963. I now remembered having come across such things in certain books but I had discounted them, almost forgotten them, perhaps because I was more interested in how we could live together again, and those negative events did not help. Plus, most of those books were by Turkish Cypriot authors and they were published by their Public Misinformation Office: pseudo-books written by biased 'officials' like my Stepfather.

When people on my side had vaguely spoken about 'incidents' before 1974, they did not seem serious. Or else, they were not serious to them. Perhaps they did not lie to me. They were just not interested in talking about things before 1974. There were many other things they remembered though. When I was in Lefkosia, in Tahtakallas, the elders remembered vividly what had taken place during the EOKA period between 1955 and 1960. How come no one spoke about what had happened in the 1960s? I would have to wait until I went back to Lefkosia and Tahtakallas. Now I was in Lefkosha and I wanted to hear what people here would tell me about Tahtakale.

THE GREEN LINE

A man who had mostly kept quiet approached us. 'When was the Green Line established, Yiannaki?' he asked. 'Green Line' was another name we used for the Dead Zone. I thought I knew that it was established in 1974, when the division took place. But I was beginning to doubt certain things I had taken for granted. Hesitantly, I said 1974. It was the wrong answer, but the one he expected from me. He spoke softly:

> No Yiannaki, the name Green Line was used from 1964, when Lefkosha was divided with barbed wire. That's when the name was first used and the UN first came to Cyprus. That's why you'll find a lot of people here called *Savash* ['War']. They were born during the fighting and that's why they were given this name.

It was still early in the morning but I asked Ahmet to take me back to the hotel. I wanted to be alone. Back in my hotel room, I was feeling depressed and angry. There were ugly sides to our past that I had not known about. The beginning of my research there had been an embarrassing failure in front of the people I was hoping to talk to, and Ahmet. Everyone would soon know. I was so angry with my people... no, with Greek Cypriots, with those who had done those terrible things and never told me anything. I felt betrayed, a sense that would get stronger the more I spoke with Turkish Cypriots.

BARBARISM

Later that afternoon, Ahmet said that after what had happened in the morning we would not meet anyone else until he first showed me something. We drove to an ordinary home, with a horrendous name:

'Museum of Barbarism'. My stomach clenched. This time it would be about other barbarians.

In the first room were black and white pictures of Turkish Cypriots killed by Greek Cypriots. The corpses were sometimes naked, full of bullet holes, half burnt. Then I saw the photos of Turkish Cypriots refugees from 1963, tent after tent in long lines. They had been settled in an area of Lefkosha still called *Gochmenkoy* ('Village of Refugees'). The people were sitting outside, cold, ragged and sad, among puddles of rainwater. Children with their heads shaved were lining up with metal containers waiting for food, looking at me with black, empty, eyes in those familiar pictures. Had I seen them elsewhere, I would have thought they were Greek Cypriot refugees from 1974.

In the next room there were photos of mass graves. One was from a village called Ayvasil, or Agios Vasilios to Greek Cypriots. The text explained that in 1964, twenty-one persons, many of them women and children, had been killed by Greek Cypriots. The next room showed destroyed and looted Turkish Cypriot villages, photos so similar to those of Greek Cypriot villages abandoned in 1974. Ahmet explained that many tourists, officials from other countries, and especially school children were brought to this museum.

I understood what the main exhibit was about when I saw the ordinary pieces of clothing in the glass display: the shoes, socks and trousers. They were children. On the walls of this museum that used to be a family home, were photos of the family, laughing children gathered around their smiling parents. A large photograph told the story: a mother was lying dead in the bath in the blood of her dead children, their bodies piled on top of her.

An old man who had been an eyewitness was summoned by Ahmet to explain. This had been the home of an army officer from Turkey, serving as a doctor in the Cyprus Turkish Army Contingent. The 1960 Constitution of Cyprus allowed for a certain number of soldiers and officers from Turkey and Greece to serve in Cyprus as part of two contingents. The killings took place on 24 December 1963 when the officer was not home. The house was sprayed with bullets and then Greek Cypriots burst in, shooting everyone. The man telling me this was shot but he survived because they thought he was dead. He still could not move his injured arm. He was just visiting with his wife, who was killed. I was given a leaflet that recounted the events, with quotes from British and French journalists who had written about it.

Now I had to see the last room, the bathroom. The paint was peeling from the walls. Signs informed visitors that the stains on the walls were from the actual blood and pieces of brain. I never saw anything as disturbing. Disturbing for what Greek Cypriots had done then and for what Turkish Cypriots were doing now – the hatred this museum would incite.

WHERE IT ALL BEGAN

The next day I was to talk with Hasan Bey, who used to live in Tahtakale. We met at his home and I asked how it all began. I learned that the Dead Zone was born out of events that took place exactly at the place where I had chosen to do my research.

> It all started in Tahtakale, or Tahtakallas as you call it. Back then it was both. No problem, if we used one name or the other. Everything started on 21 December 1963. The first killing was near Hermes Street. Your police shot and killed a woman and a man there, two of ours. From there it spread everywhere. Next day there were more shootings, then real battles, and we began to leave our homes in the darkness. First only some decided to leave, then everyone. If your relatives leave, your children and neighbours, you don't stay behind. Until then we were living OK. There had been some troubles before, in Tahtakallas, during the EOKA period but we thought that they were over with independence. For three years after 1960 all was quiet. Mind you, your people – especially Makarios – never gave up the idea of ENOSIS. Soon after independence, he was still saying that ENOSIS was the final goal. Until finally you staged the coup in 1974 when your EOKA again tried to bring about ENOSIS, but this time Turkey intervened for good.

He paused to compose himself.

> Yes, it was in Tahtakale where the events of Bloody Christmas began. When we got scared we suddenly realized we were surrounded by Greek Cypriots. Until then we never felt surrounded. Until then some of them were our friends, our neighbours. But when things start to go wrong, you can't be sure any more. The real problem was with the younger generation. We had grown up together with the old people. We knew them inside out and they knew us as well. We were close. There was a time when instead of saying *Allah* I would say *Panaia mou* ['Virgin Mary', in Greek]. But with your young ones? Let's not forget what happened during EOKA.

I still remember when I went to buy groceries from Andrikko. We were good friends. Then EOKA began. One day, when I went to buy something, he turned pale. This is what he said. 'Look here Hasani, you know me well so don't misunderstand me. It's better for you if you don't come here any more. You see those boys outside? No, don't turn now. They are keeping watch and if I sell something to a Turk they will report me to EOKA. Anyway, it's not safe any more for you to come here.' I knew that what he was doing hurt him as much as it hurt me. Thank God I had enough money with me to pay my debt there and then. He tried to refuse, just to show that this was a thing that would soon pass, but inside we both knew things would never be the same. So I said goodbye to Andrikko. Your people poisoned the minds of the young. First, they taught you that we are barbarians. In your schools you talk about the Turks like all we do is to kill people and drink their blood. There they taught you all the time about ENOSIS. And you still want that, you'll never change your minds. Look at all the Greek flags on your side. Every day when I read our newspapers they tell us that you still want ENOSIS. Well, we didn't want to become part of Greece, to suffer like our people do in Thrace. And as for your leader, Makarios – that's something I'll never be able to understand.

Hasan Bey continued:

What is this obsession you have with religion? We live almost in the twenty-first century now. What was Makarios, a priest, doing with all the fighters? What was he doing there as the head of our state anyway? I thought that the church was all about religion, not politics, about good things – you know, charity, helping and loving each other. Not about war and killing and guns. We see it all the time on television. Your new archbishop is always there at every military parade, looking so pleased as he watches all those guns. And then as if this is not enough he talks all the time about attacking us. Do our priests, the *hojas*, get involved in politics? Do they stand and watch military parades? Never. They talk about helping other people, about God, about mercy, not politics and guns. We don't go to the mosque any more. So much the better, if you ask me. Only a few old-timers still do and some of those who came from Turkey, but they are poor uneducated peasants, they are behind the world. How can you still obey those characters with the beards and the black hats and robes? People go to your church, children too, and the priests turn them against us. They turn children into proud Greeks and us into evil Turks.

NOT GOING TO THE BEACH

Rain had washed away the city dust, and the sun was shining brightly above Lefkosha. Everything, especially the trees, looked clean and shiny. As I walked alongside Ahmet towards my next meeting, I was surprised that the smell of the wet earth was so familiar. But why not? It was surely a bright spring afternoon in Lefkosia as well, only a few hundred metres away. But I now felt that they were two distant worlds.

I had a long talk with Asim Bey, who had been a grocer – *manav* as Turkish Cypriots would say, *manavis* for Greek Cypriots, once both.

> After the first fighting started in 1963, we moved over to this side of Lefkosha where we lived in tents. May you never have to live in a tent, Yiannaki. You can't imagine what it's like. Later we moved to the back rooms of a relative, where we lived a bit better. As things got quieter after 1964, we gradually started to come out of the enclaves. We even tried to go to the beach a few times in Girne. The children were nagging all the time. 'It's summer, why don't we go to the beach like every summer?' You know how children are. They live in their own world. For them summer meant the beach. So we tried to go to the beach near Girne, where we always went. But this time we were worried. We tried not to speak so that your people could not tell we were Turks. Can you get children to shut up? Impossible. After about an hour, it was not possible to stay any more. We came back, the children complaining all the way. After that we only went to this village in one of the Turkish enclaves with a large reservoir instead of the beach.

COUNTING AGE

Sali worked as a truck driver when he lived in Tahtakale. When he left in 1963, he was able to take his truck with him, but not much else. He moved into the Turkish Cypriot enclave of Lefkosha. As usual, I first asked him his age.

> When we wanted to come to the Greek Cypriot sector we had to go through searches from your police. Not just 'open the door, open the boot.' It was things like 'unscrew your headlights, take

off the cover from the tyres.' You had this done to you every day. You didn't give us gas for the cars and we had to get it from your side. We had to queue and wait and wait to get only two gallons. That was it. You enforced an embargo on many goods. We couldn't get bricks – 'you will build fortifications' – no iron for metal roofs – 'you will build army posts' – no sulphur for our vineyards – 'you will build bombs.' We were refugees and could not even build a roof above our heads.

He paused.

You want to know how we lived then, Yiannaki. We didn't. It wasn't just the humiliation and having to queue and wait at the checkpoints. It wasn't just the fear for myself, whether I would come back alive. Many people who went to your sector those days disappeared, like my wife's brother. You know what she told me when I told her I was going to meet you today? 'Ask him where my brother is.' Every day when I came back my wife was waiting at the door and she brightened when she saw my truck appear. Every morning I had to say goodbye to her and she held me in her arms as if she would not see me again. We had a baby daughter then and before I left, my wife would bring her for me to kiss, like it would be the last time. Can you understand how I felt? It was the fear that if I died I would leave them behind on their own. But I had to work, I needed even the two gallons, I had to do this every day.

Once again he paused.

You asked me my age, Yiannaki. When people ask me my age I subtract four years, those years from 1963 to 1967 when we were in the enclaves. That was not life. *Now* I live. Yes, we may be poor. Once again you have placed an embargo against us and we cannot trade, we can't get tourists, and even travelling with our passports is a problem. I'm not saying life is not difficult. But compared to then, when we were together, now it's like paradise.

Everyone I met there spoke of the difficulties and danger of getting out of the enclaves. A woman described with damp eyes what happened when she tried to go to a wedding. 'To get out of the enclave we had to go through a search at your checkpoint. I was wearing this beautiful white dress. After the search, I cried when I saw it was covered with dirty patches.'

A FAMILY FRIEND

At last I met with Yusuf Bey, the man from Lemesos whom my father had helped in 1974. He lived in *Gazi Magusa*, Famagusta, or Ammohostos as Greek Cypriots called it. He was glad to meet me and immediately asked me out for dinner. His face darkened when I told him what I was doing there, and that I would want to talk about what happened. He sighed but agreed. Even though he was not from Tahtakale, I really wanted to hear his story. After all he was the one person who was a kind of family friend, and I felt I could trust. I had been hearing so many sad things from other people. But Ahmet was with us most of the time, so perhaps people did not talk freely. Not that I thought they were lying, or that they were saying this just because Ahmet was around. But I did hope I might hear different things from him. Perhaps things were different in Lemesos. And his story would be one about my hometown.

I was lucky that evening. Ahmet met a friend and moved to another table some way away. We were enjoying our dinner and I was waiting for Yusuf Bey to move on to the important issue. After we finished and I saw that he wasn't going to start, I decided to ask. His good mood vanished.

'Are you sure you want to talk about these things, Yiannaki?' he said. 'Are you sure you want to talk about what happened then in *Leymosun*?' That was what they called my hometown, which I only knew as *Lemesos*. He lit a cigarette, looking at the ceiling.

> OK, Yiannaki. I don't really want to talk about these things but what you are doing is important and I too want to help. And you are the son of Stathis, so I am even more obliged. But whatever I say, you should know that your father was a fine man. He proved it too. Now where shall I begin? You know I am lucky to even be alive. From 1963 to 1967 we were living closed up in *Leymosun*.

He described how fearful it was to live there and, worse, to go out of the enclave whenever they had to. 'Now, Yiannaki, there is safety. I can go anywhere I want. Can you understand what this means? Now we can *sleep* at night. We lived for years like that.'

He looked me in the eyes. 'Did your father tell you about 1974?' I nodded and he continued:

> OK, he did and you have to know that I'm so grateful. Don't forget to tell him this. For a while after 1968 things were not bad, we felt we had a future here once more, that we could find a way to work

things out, you know, live in peace. But then you had to go on with
ENOSIS. There was the coup and our nightmare started once more.
When will our turn come? Now the Greeks are fighting amongst
themselves but our turn will come when they finish with each
other. And Sampson! He became the new president, that man who
used to kill us in the 1960s, who had said that one day he hoped to
clean Cyprus of the Turks.

Sampson was one of the Greek Cypriot fighters of EOKA during the
1950s. In 1974, he was appointed as president by the EOKA B coupists,
who declared that ENOSIS was to finally take place. But among
Turkish Cypriots he was notorious for having led some of the bloodiest
campaigns against them during the 1960s.

He looked at me, waiting for me to say something, but I did not. So
he continued. 'After the Turkish army landed in 1974, when the… the…
operation took place, they put us in the stadium. They didn't torture us.
I mean there were no killings and such things and some of them knew
me anyway so I was not particularly maltreated. I mean Yiannaki… that
1974…' He paused once more. His eyes shifted onto mine. 'I mean that
1974 when the Turkish army came was real relief for us. Such things we
cannot forget. It's better for us to live separately. It's OK if we visit each
other – I haven't even thanked your father personally. I don't think we
can ever live together again.'

I did not feel like talking much more with Yusuf Bey. I did not like
the things I heard and was feeling bad for pressing him to talk about
things he did not want to. Before leaving he invited me for dinner at
his house on another day, but I never went. I only went back to say
goodbye before I left for good.

LEMESOS

Back alone in the hotel I thought about Lemesos, my home town. How
come I didn't know it had another name? I was only ten in 1974 and was
too young to remember anything from 1963 to 1967. All I remembered
was occasionally driving with my father to the *Tourkomahalla*, the
Turkish neighbourhood, as Greek Cypriots called it. It was roughly
divided from the rest of the city by an empty river bed and it began
from the bridge with the lanterns, the 'Four Lanterns' it was called. I felt
it was like an entrance into a different world, though I did not exactly
understand how. Across the bridge, I would soon see the mosque. It was
big, different, mysterious. We went there during daytime either to buy

watermelons, always from the same man, or to buy yogurt. We also went out a few times for dinner at a well-known restaurant, Arifis. That was all I remembered. I was eleven when the Turkish Cypriots left in 1975, but I had not known any of them. I could not recall having ever met a Turkish Cypriot boy or girl. So when they left, I did not miss them.

But I did remember something of their departure. One day in 1975, we were driving with my father towards Lefkosia. In front of us were long lines of slow-moving UN trucks filled with people. The Turkish Cypriots of Leymosun were moving to the north. The only emotion this stirred was frustration for the long delay due to the traffic moving so slowly and us having to cautiously overtake truck after truck, the line never seeming to end. I did not connect the people in those trucks with anyone I knew. Afterwards I realized that their neighbourhood was empty, but they had never really been there for me anyway. I had been living in Lemesos: they in Leymosun.

PARANOIA

It was around eight in the evening and I was sitting in my hotel room typing up my notes on my portable computer. Just before I crossed I had installed a password system for security. There was a knock at the door. Levent Bey was standing there. 'Hey stepson, I haven't seen you for some time, I missed you and I'm sure you missed your beloved Stepfather too, haven't you? [Smile] Let's go out for dinner.' I meekly objected that I ate out with him or Ahmet almost every night and I needed time in the evenings to type up my notes. 'None of that, my son,' he cut me short:

> I am the Stepfather here, Yiannaki, and I say we go out. So make yourself presentable – you don't want to dishonour your Stepfather, eh? Anyway, you know what I was told when I went high up to ask for you to come over? And I went pretty high up, all the way to the top for your Majesty's sake. The chief told me two things. 'Make sure nothing happens to him and make sure he eats well. We want to show them on the other side that we live well over here, so fatten him up so that people can really tell when he goes back.' Are you refusing our hospitality so that then you'll go back and tell them that we are not hospitable? [Smile]

Great, I thought, not just my mind, my body too was going to be used as an instrument of their propaganda machinery. This was my chance to ask the important question. 'Why was I allowed to come over?' He smiled. 'I'm not sure, Yiannaki, but I think I can guess. The Big Boss was in a particularly good mood that morning and my guess – not a guess really, everyone knows these things here – is that he met a woman the previous evening. Know what I mean, eh?' That was the closest I ever came to an official explanation.

At the usual restaurant with a view the monologue continued:

> Now, you see, because of my job here I deal a lot with your journalists. I read their articles every day and when they come to our side I spend every minute with them. They are so biased. They come here to find out and all they see is what they want to see. Then, they go back and write that the Turkish Cypriots are oppressed, that they are poor and desolate. Yes, there are poor people here, there may even be people who feel oppressed and I don't mind if they write about this but they should write about all the other things too. Not just one-sided articles. If they talk to some-one who spends three hours describing how you made them suffer and in the end sends regards to an old friend on your side, do you know what they do? They cut the rest and only say that the people miss their old Greek friends, they want to see them again and they want to join with you. No one ever wrote one single thing about the mass graves, and they all visited them. Can you believe this?

He drew a deep breath and it was plain that he was about to open a new chapter.

> You won't believe how paranoid they are. They say we are your friends and then they are so afraid when they come here. Take women journalists. When they come, they don't wear any make-up and dress in loose clothes. You know why? They try to look unattractive because they are afraid we will rape them, that their 'Turkish Cypriot brothers' will rape them. The funniest thing is when we sit to eat. In the beginning, everyone says they are on a diet. But I know you well, so I order for everyone. So, everyone sits in front of all this great food we have here and they are all salivating, but no one picks anything up [smile]. I know you well, so I wait a while. Then I plunge some bread in one of the dips and all of them say, 'Oh, well, we'll try a bit of this' and they all take something from the same plate, only after I have put it in my mouth. Gradually you all get thirsty but again you wait for me first – I wait a while to see them suffer. As soon as I drink from a bottle,

everyone drinks from the same one. You are afraid that we will poison you.

Another long breath and a wistful look that meant he was going further back:

> You know what happened to me when I was living in Komotini, my hometown in Greece? When I was serving in the army, a Greek friend invited me to his home. He was the only one to do this in all my time in the army, more than a year. As I enter his house his daughter appears, all joy and smiles to hug her father. 'I brought a friend with me, Marina,' he tells her. 'His name is Levent, he is Turk'. The little girl froze as she was running. The smile disappeared. You should have seen it. She looks at me carefully, as if she is looking at a monster. 'But Daddy,' she says, 'he looks like a human being.' Then she turned to me. She thought her father was joking. 'Where is your knife then, where is your moustache?' That's how life was with you, Yiannaki. Hell every single day.

I shivered when he told me about the little girl, and when I thought what the army must have been like for a Turk in Greece.
  'You say that there are no Turks in Greece, you call us Muslims but you treat us like the monster Turks you believe we are,' he continued.

> Take the way you call the Dead Zone. Sometimes you call it Attila Line and you say it's us who named it like this. You use the name to make us look like barbarians. But we don't use this name, we never did. Once during the Peace Operation of 1974, one of the lines temporarily set up then was called Atilla after a general by that name killed there. You love the name, don't you?

He drew a large breath and grew serious. His fists closed and rested on the table.

> You hate us, Yiannaki. There is no way around it. The hatred is all one-sided, from your side. Throughout history we have been good to you and you have been horrible to us. You were the first ones to revolt against us, you stabbed us in the back, you invaded our motherland in 1920 and then in 1974 you even tried to capture Cyprus and join it with Greece, after you tried to exterminate us here. You say that it is because of your church that you stayed Greeks. Well, who was it that gave all those rights to your church

during the Ottoman period? Throughout history you have been expansionist. You created EOKA and then EOKA B. You still celebrate EOKA, which means you are still trying to unite with Greece. You will never abandon this dream. Don't tell me that EOKA and EOKA B are different. You still want ENOSIS, like you still one day hope to capture Istanbul. I see it in all your school textbooks – you teach the innocent children 'Constantinople will be ours once more.'

For me things are clear, either black or white, there is no grey. That is my philosophy. Your people try to make everything grey, you too Yiannaki, you sometimes do this. I talk to you like a Turk, honest and open and you respond like a Greek, all secrets and not telling me what you think. You don't say much about what you think, do you? But I know your side well. You know the expression you use in Greece, 'He became a Turk.' You use it when someone gets raging angry. But you Greeks here in Cyprus don't use this much, because you use another expression. What is it? Tell me, Yiannaki?

I knew what he meant and I had to tell him. 'Am I a little Turk?' This was a negative expression. 'Now what does that mean?' he asked. He knew the answer but he wanted me to say it. Greek Cypriots used the expression when they were unfairly treated or left out. Say someone gave cigarettes to all his friends but one. The one left out would complain, 'Am I a little Turk?' Greek Cypriots often used the diminutive for Turks when they spoke about Turkish Cypriots: *Tourkouthkia*, 'little Turks'.
Levent Bey went further:

How do you think the Turks of Cyprus felt when they heard this, eh? Tell me now, don't you often say 'Cypriots' when you really mean Greek Cypriots? You do it all the time. You too, Yiannaki. From 'Cypriots' you exclude the Turks of Cyprus, those you now say are your 'brothers', your 'compatriots' whom you pretend to love and care for so much. And you sometimes even call us *Yiouroukkides*.

I tried to explain that Greek Cypriots only used this for Turks from Turkey not Turkish Cypriots and that the hatred was directed against the Turks from Turkey who invaded, not the Turkish Cypriots. He waved my objections aside:

Turkish Cypriots, Turks, what difference does it make? We are all Turks, full stop. Again Yiannaki you try to make things grey. Typical Greek way. But the *Yuruk*, where your *Yiouroukkides* comes from, were a noble tribe. Of course now what you mean is backward barbarians, Turks. That's why I'm so glad to live here. Everyday, when I cut articles from the newspapers, I try to warn the Turks here and the whole world about how you hate us, how you want to exploit us again, how you exclude us, how you claim all Cyprus belongs to you. And all the time you buy more and more guns to use against us.

Not long after, Levent Bey asked to see me one morning. He looked worried.

I need to ask you something, Yiannaki. A Turkish boat has lost its way and ended up on your side, and you are putting the captain on trial. Your side has been persuaded by the UN that someone here should cross to act as an interpreter and make sure the captain is treated well. Our government asked me if I could do it. I know that your people know a lot about me and I know that they don't like me. Do you think I should go?

I replied that it was very unlikely that anyone would harm him, especially if it was the UN who had requested this. 'Would you come with me? I would feel much safer if you came,' he asked. Appearing with him on the Greek Cypriot side, as a friend, a guide, anything, would have meant disaster, disgrace, and treachery. But how could I refuse? My future research depended on whether he would allow me to stay more. I agreed.

'Still, I'm not sure, Yiannaki', he continued:

Many thoughts go through my head. What if your secret police gets a really good-looking woman to just kiss me? Now say she puts a special type of poison in her lipstick and she takes the antidote. Suppose this poison is the type that activates itself after a week, so it gets to me days after I return to our side. Then who could accuse your people of anything?

I half-heartedly tried to persuade him to go. After all, he had never been to our side. He said he would think about it, but the next day, to my relief, I heard that he had decided against it.

BIASES

Latife Hanim (Mrs Latife) worked at the Public Information Office and wanted to meet me:

> I hear you come from a British university. I do hope you'll do objective research. People are saying good things about you and I hope they are right. But there's one thing you must understand: why foreigners are always on your side, the side of Greeks; and why they are so biased against us. I lived in Europe for quite a while and was able to understand a few things. First of all, there are Greeks almost everywhere and most Europeans know some Greeks. You don't find so many Turks around, though these days more live abroad. Then, and this is the most important reason, Europeans adore ancient Greece. They learn about it at school and university. Plus, you sell your case much better than us. The Greeks of Cyprus are much richer than us and you have Greece helping out. Take the Greek lobby in the United States. Everyone knows it's strong and influences American foreign policy. Greeks are better actors, too, you know what I mean? Take the case of the missing persons for instance. Everyone knows that you include in the figures many people whom *you* killed during the coup. Then there are films like *Midnight Express*. Most Europeans only know Turkey through that dreadful film. I am convinced that this film is propaganda made by the Greeks and the Armenians. Why else make such a film?

POST-WAR FASHION

When I visited peoples' homes, I was struck by ammunition shells being used for decoration. They were proudly displayed in the living room, all polished and shiny. These were bronze cannon shell cases, up to a metre tall, that people had found lying around after the 1974 war. Often an ashtray was balanced on top, or plastic flowers were placed inside. I had seen the same things in Lefkosia. I remembered the shell craze that swept the Greek Cypriot side after the war.

Empty bullet cases were precious for us children then. Bullets that had been bent or tarred in action were coveted, but most precious, because so rare, were the bullets that had not been fired, the 'live ammunition'. We collected them, compared them and exchanged them with each other, taking care to do this away from adult eyes when live ammunition was involved, lest it was unfairly confiscated. Those like me who grew up in Lemesos were secretly envious of the boys from Lefkosia. They always had more because they had been closer to the real war.

Boys wore the bullets on black leather bands around their necks. Now I discovered that boys and young men on the Turkish Cypriot side had once prized them too.

WAR FOR PEACE

'Peace Operation' or 'Happy Peace Operation': that was how 1974 was officially designated on the Turkish Cypriot side. But there was a problem with this. It sounded too benign. Where was the sense of heroism, battle and danger?

Photographers in Lefkosha were quick to realize the seriousness of the issue at stake. Turkish soldiers who had taken part in the 1974 war, or others later stationed in Cyprus, often wanted some kind of memento from Cyprus. As I walked around Lefkosha, I saw them in a couple of old photographer's windows: ready-made photos of a drawing of the map of Cyprus with a round hole right in the middle of the island where a photo of the soldier was to be placed. They showed the real thing: war, action and danger. Around the map of divided Cyprus jets were leaving fiery trails, ships in stormy waters were bombarding Lemesos and Larnaka – which, in fact, they didn't – soldiers were standing ready to pounce, a civilian was embracing a soldier. One image wrote in large letters: WAR FOR PEACE. Another wrote: CYPRUS IS TURKISH.

The same shops sold postcards that Turkish soldiers stationed in Cyprus could send back to their loved ones. The message was conveniently printed on the card:

MOUNTAIN COMMANDO

IN OUR BABYLAND,

THE TURKISH REPUBLIC OF NORTHERN CYPRUS

UNDER THE SHADOW OF GUNS

UNDER THE BLUE BERET

LIKE THE HAND OF DEATH

LIKE A LIGHTNING IN THE SKY

LIKE A FLOOD SWEEPING THE EARTH

My best wishes on the occasion of your

....

I send this with my best wishes for days full of happiness and health, with love and respect.

Date: ....

Sender: ....

HOME SWEET HOME

Erkan Bey insisted I should visit him at home. Despite the bitter things he had told me about his life in Tahtakale during a previous meeting, perhaps because of them, he was keen that I spend some time with him and his family. I gladly went along. As we sat in his garden under the tall, shady lemon trees, he explained how he liked to spend time in his garden and tend his trees. The leaves of the old olive tree glistened in the afternoon light as wind rustled them, reflecting the sunrays in their silver underside. As we spoke about his trees, I realized that this used to be a Greek Cypriot home. He confirmed that he had only moved there after 1974, even if he had been a refugee since 1963. The trees were too old to have been planted after 1974.

He was definitely at home. Like others who left in 1963, he spoke of the time when 'we were refugees', using the past tense. Greek Cypriots always used the present tense: 'we are refugees'. He did not feel like a refugee any more. Like many others, he was able to go back to his old home in Tahtakale after things calmed down in the late 1960s but he did not stay:

> My home was looted, even the door frames were missing. Someone had tried to set fire to it. It was all charred and in the middle of the living room was this stinking bucket full of shit. This is the one thing I still remember. The bucket. I never went back again. Before, I had this picture in my mind of how my home used to be. Now it's all ruined. When I think of it now, I can only remember what I saw that day. The bucket.

As in our previous conversation, when he said bad things about Greek Cypriots, he looked at me with a regretful look I had learned to expect by now. 'I'm sorry to tell you this,' his face said, 'I am sorry to tell you how badly you treated us, I know it's not your personal fault, Yiannaki.'

How does one enter and live in another's home? How long does it take for it to become your own? When I met Greek Cypriot refugees who had settled in Turkish Cypriot houses in Tahtakallas, this was easier to understand. The houses were renovated and painted by the Greek Cypriot authorities. There was no trace of the people who used to live there. But what about Turkish Cypriots who moved into Greek Cypriot homes after 1974?

Try to imagine this. You are given a house to move into with your family. When you enter, it still contains many of the belongings, the smells, the stains, the presences of another family who left in deadly haste. You see the marks next to the doorframe charting a child's height, up to the moment when their lives were suddenly divided.

Their photos are still on the wall, their albums in the drawers. You have become the keeper of their most precious memories. You decide to put away the albums without looking – can you actually bear to destroy them? But it's impossible not to look. You have to know who lived there, where you are now starting a new life. A beginning for you: an end for them. You learn every little detail about them as you check the photos. You become an uninvited guest at all the important and intimate moments of their lives: you are there when they first fell in love in those old-fashioned clothes and haircuts, you are present at their wedding, you follow them on their trips, you meet their newborn child, you are there at the baptism, you watch it growing up, then you turn a page – empty.

Then there are the cupboards, the kitchen, the garden. You gradually get to know all the people who used to live there as each day you discover something new about them, the toys the children played with, the type of ties the man preferred, the shoes the woman liked. What do you do with the cot? Do you put your own small child to sleep peacefully in the cot where another was sleeping not long ago? What happened to that child? They are still living there with you. How do you get the spirit of the ones whose home it used to be to leave and claim it as your own?

You, the Turkish Cypriot who moved into the Greek Cypriots' home, know what it means to lose your home. 'Only a refugee can understand a refugee's sorrow,' Turkish Cypriot refugees said, just like Greek Cypriots had also told me. Can you understand the other refugees? Or does it work the other way round? Because you feel that you have been forced to leave your own home, because you lived in fear of Greek Cypriots for many years, because they became the enemy, you feel justified in claiming their homes; you feel that your past suffering justifies theirs. Was there guilt? How could one deal with it? One way was to remember every time it returned how you, Turkish Cypriots, suffered. Is your past suffering used to wash away theirs? Still, how can you be sure that this particular Greek Cypriot, Andreas, whom by now you know by name, is responsible for your suffering? What about his son, Petrakis, and his daughter Elenista who were not born when Greek Cypriots made you suffer, or his wife Mrs Maria who probably did not take part in any of it? Generalize – that's the solution. The absolution. They are all *Rums*. Women and children must be held as responsible as the men; they are all responsible, each and every one of them. Generalization: the drug for peaceful sleep in their, your, house.

What did Turkish Cypriots do? They went away to their new homeland. It had to become theirs, theirs only. Cleansing was the officially designated method to erase any memory of its previous past and inhabitants. All Greek place names in the north – towns, villages and streets – were changed into Turkish. Talk of the previous inhabitants, use of the old place names and especially any talk of Greek Cypriot suffering was deemed treacherous. Only talk of Turkish Cypriot pain, suffering and dislocation was patriotic.

Fire was used to clean houses. When some Turkish Cypriots entered the houses, they burned all the belongings of Greek Cypriots. Others disinfected and repainted. Even so, didn't you unexpectedly discover the boy's toy cars in a secret corner under the hedge? For how long did the owners keep returning? Did their reflections fleetingly appear on the mirrors? If there is some solution, how will you feel when the previous owner comes back, even just to have a look? She may ask you if you kept their previous lives somewhere, those photographs.

Much later when I returned to the north to follow an event, I managed to slip away with a Turkish Cypriot friend who wanted to show me the home of his grandparents. They were glad to see me, but there was something eerie about their home. They had kept the house as they had found it when they moved in. They kept all the photos of the previous family on the walls, adding their own. Next to the Christian religious icons, they placed the Arabic verses from the Koran. In the main sitting room, I saw a high old double bed nicely made with clean sheets. That used to belong, they told me, no, that *belongs* is what they actually said, to the owner. The living room was the only place they had room for it. They chose to live in that house as guests, out of respect for its past inhabitants. They chose to bear the burden instead of erasing it. No, they did not want to go back to their own home in the south. It was too late for that and they would be alone there. Their children grew up here: this was their home. But they could not bear to throw out completely those who used to live there. They showed me the albums of the family, neatly stacked and covered with plastic bags inside a cupboard.

I met other Turkish Cypriots who kept the photos in a bottom cupboard. Some asked me if there was a way to return them. They insisted I take them back. They had not been able to destroy them. The old presences in their new homes, even hidden away in a bottom cupboard, were still a burden.

FRIENDLY WHISPERS, ANGRY VOICES

I had just been served breakfast at the hotel, when suddenly I heard a whisper. 'Welcome, Yiannaki. It's good to have you here. You're the first Greek Cypriot I meet and I'm happy to finally meet a Greek Cypriot.'

I turned around. A young waiter was whispering under his breath, pretending to clean the nearby table. Every morning, he whispered to me, as I chose to sit at an isolated table:

> Good morning, Yiannaki, how are you doing today? I want to get to know you and talk, but these people with you, the police, would never let us. They caused all this disaster here in Cyprus, these fanatics for 'motherland' Turkey, these nationalists and their parties who control things here.

He went on:

> Be careful of what they tell you and of who they take you to see. They don't want to show you the truth. They only want you to think that we want things to stay as they are, us on this side and you on the other. That's not true. Many of us here want to live with you and get rid of all these Turks here.

Next morning:

> We suffer a lot from this situation. Can't even get a job, all are given to the Turks, or to the right-wing fanatics. Or to those who were in TMT. Well, now of course *everyone* claims to have been in TMT. So we have to leave Cyprus and as we leave they bring Turks here, those *karasakals*, and turkify this place. What do we have in

common with those *karasakals*? Nothing. They are uneducated, religious fanatics and nationalists. And they are not Cypriots, they are foreigners. It's with you that we have things in common. We are all Cypriots, aren't we?

Gradually, the whispers also came in other places. Once when I was in the office of the mayor of Lefkosha, waiting for Ahmet to pick me up, a man whispered, 'Hey Yiannaki, tell me what you think of your Companion here? Come on tell us. And do you love your Stepfather?' He understood that I was in a difficult position since I did not know him at all. 'It's OK, Yiannaki, you don't have to say anything. And take my advice, better not to talk too much here.'

I got many other such ironic comments about my 'Stepfather' and my 'Companion'. I really wanted to talk to the whisperers more, but I did not know how. And what if they were planted to ask me things and report to Levent Bey?

The whispers coming from outside were friendly. Gradually, I would be able to guess the parties those who whispered supported. I also began to hear voices. The voices were in Greek and came from inside my head. They were angry, accusatory, and loud, using high-sounding words: *Patriots, Nation, Traitor, Heroes*. They were often phrased as burning questions.

Do you take all this stuff they tell you seriously, Mr Papadakis? These... these lies. This black propaganda. Traitor. You even sympathize with them. If you sympathize with them, how do you feel about those who allegedly made them suffer? So you were moved yesterday listening to their noxious lies. What about us, the real victims? The only victims? And why don't you ever argue back? Why nod as if you agree with all they tell you? Don't you see that this makes them more certain of their distorted views? What is this stuff about northern Cyprus instead of occupied areas? This Lefkosha instead of Lefkosia? Why aren't you using quotation marks now for their so-called state? How about invasion? Why have you stopped using that word? Wait until you come back over. Let's see then, if you'll dare do this.

'SCHIZOPHRENIC GREEK CYPRIOTS'

I read this headline in a right-wing pro-government Turkish Cypriot newspaper. I took it personally, even if it was not meant to be about the voices I had been hearing. How much more biased can you get! I read further in the small print. To my shame, it was I who was biased. I had misinterpreted the title. The clip was entirely objective and taken from Greek Cypriot sources. 'According to the newest research on the Greek Cypriot side, the level of schizophrenia among Greek Cypriots now lies at about 1 per cent of the population,' the newspaper reported. Now why was this news?

This article was taken from the paper's daily page devoted to 'News from the South'. Anything negative about the Greek Cypriot side was good news over here. They adored Greek Cypriot extremists. Any statement they found in the Greek Cypriot press about Turkish Cypriots by extremists, made it to this section. If someone said 'A good Turk is a dead Turk' not only did it become news, it was presented as a general Greek Cypriot outlook. (In my mind, I could hear my Stepfather's scissors joyfully working, '*clip, clip*'.) The Archbishop was another hot favourite, always a good source of inflammatory statements. Never mind that they were a cause of great embarrassment among Greek Cypriot politicians.

But did I have a right to criticize them? Did I have a right to criticize them from the outside? It was always easy to do this. Get the job and then we'll see what you can do, and how easy it will be to change things, my father used to say. My Stepfather would soon offer me the job – his job. Hand me the scissors. I could be in charge of selecting and cutting out bits from Greek Cypriot newspapers to be translated. Of course, a certain *quid pro quo* would be involved.

RIGHT AND LEFT

I wanted to talk to some Turkish Cypriot political leaders and asked Levent Bey to arrange it. He was pleased when I asked for Hakki Bey and Dervish Bey, both belonging to the National Unity Party (UBP), the right-wing party in power. Displeased, when I mentioned the two left-wing opposition leaders: Ozker Bey, of the largest left-wing party, the Republican Turkish Party (CTP) and Mustafa Bey, mayor of Lefkosha and leader of a smaller left-wing party, the Communal Liberation Party (TKP).

Levent Bey accompanied me to each meeting. But he did not stay with us every time. When I met the two UBP leaders, with whom he appeared comfortable, he sat with us. But in Ozker Bey's office we entered together, spoke for a few moments about this and that and then Ozker Bey nodded towards Levent Bey. It was a signal to leave and he did. He did not even try to come into the office of the other left-wing leader.

I posed exactly the same questions to each leader but received different replies to many questions. The two left-wing leaders were in agreement, but they disagreed with the two right-wing politicians. I met with the two right-wing leaders first, then the others.

'What have been the main political mistakes made by Greek Cypriots since the 1950s?' I asked this first in the certainty that it would be appreciated in order to ease the ground. All four were more or less in agreement, but some went much further than others.

ENOSIS was the biggest mistake. 'The Church instigated all this ENOSIS business and created hatred and chauvinism among Greek Cypriots, as it still does,' Dervish Bey replied. 'As if there were no Turks living here. The same mistake was made by the chauvinist nationalists of Greece, first for supporting the Greek Cypriot demand for ENOSIS and then for trying to enforce this in 1974.' Hakki Bey spoke in a similar manner. But he said more about the 1960s. 'In 1960, we saw that the Greek Cypriots did not want the status of independence that Cyprus had received. They had higher aspirations: to take control of the whole island and enforce ENOSIS. That's what the Akritas Plan was all about. You know about this, don't you?' I had heard about the Akritas Plan countless times, but only on this side. It was a Greek Cypriot document discovered in the 1960s after the inter-ethnic fighting had begun, outlining how to bring about ENOSIS, including a swift, full-scale attack against the Turkish Cypriots if they tried to react. It was signed by 'The Chief Akritas'. On the Greek Cypriot side, no one spoke about it, as if it had never existed.

The two left-wing leaders also spoke about ENOSIS as the root of the problem. But they had things to add. Ozker Bey started with ENOSIS and then continued:

> Now the violent means through which they tried to bring it about were totally wrong. We had to defend ourselves. We set up our own organization called TMT and TAKSIM, partition, became our goal. Now that too was wrong, but unfortunately after what the Greek Cypriots did no one here could possibly disagree with TAKSIM. The correct path would have been the cooperation of both against the colonial power. And then, of course, ENOSIS gave the British the opportunity to use their well-known Divide and Rule tactics. But they did not start the division themselves, they exploited what was already there. Our policy of TAKSIM, though understandable, was equally wrong. It stirred up ugly Turkish nationalist passions

among our people. But if anyone tried to disagree, then they were traitors. Some of those who tried were shot by TMT.

Mustafa Bey's reply was almost identical. In fact, both had answered my second question before I had posed it, so I did not ask them.

'Now, what were the major political mistakes that Turkish Cypriots made since the 1950s?' The two left-wing leaders had already pointed these out, feeling that Turkish Cypriots too had made serious mistakes. Unlike the other two. Dervish Bey: 'If we committed any mistakes, I would have the courage and honesty to admit so. But I cannot see any. It was only natural that we had to act in self-defence and that is all we did.' Hakki Bey spoke in similar terms: 'We, the Turks here, were just reacting, initially to stay alive and then only in self-defence.'

The next question I posed was about ENOSIS again. 'Do you think that Greek Cypriots still want ENOSIS, or have they abandoned the idea?' The replies of the two left-wing leaders were once more in agreement, as were the other two. Mustafa Bey:

No, I am convinced that Greek Cypriots don't want ENOSIS any more. It's finished. But many people here, on our side, don't want to admit this. Two years ago I said here that Greek Cypriots don't want ENOSIS, and I was attacked for this. Most people here believe that Greek Cypriots still want ENOSIS and our government propagates this view all the time.

Ozker Bey said:

ENOSIS is no longer a Greek Cypriot aim. How could it be? After all the destruction it brought about in 1974, the Greek Cypriot people would be crazy if they still wanted this. Plus, things have changed a lot since then. Now there is the possibility of Cyprus joining the European Union. Now our government here speaks all the time about uniting with Turkey.

The others disagreed. Hakki Bey: 'To be frank the Greek Cypriots want a sort of solution to the Cyprus Problem that cannot block the way to something like ENOSIS in the future, so yes they still want it.' And Dervish Bey said:

Through their actions they show that they still want ENOSIS. Makarios, for example, outwardly defended an independent Cyprus. But up to 1974 even, he still speaks about ENOSIS as the ideal solution. He was only saying that the time was not yet right and that people should wait patiently. Then, the Akritas Plan openly speaks of ENOSIS. The difference between Makarios and Sampson, you see, was that even though both wanted ENOSIS, Makarios was trying to get it step by step whereas Sampson wanted it all at once.

Sampson was the person the coupists appointed as president. I was tempted to press on with Dervish Bey since he had only spoken about the past, the period before 1974, not the present as I had asked, but I did not. His manner of speaking already gave me the answer. He was employing the present tense for a bygone era in order to suggest that ENOSIS was still pursued. 'Makarios... up to 1974... *speaks* about ENOSIS... The Akritas Plan openly *speaks* of...'

My next enquiry was:

There are two fundamental tenets of Greek Cypriot political thought: a) that there is no real democracy on the Turkish Cypriot side, which is totally controlled by Turkey; and b) the idea of Turkish expansionism, i.e., that Turkey always wanted and still aims to capture the whole of Cyprus. What are your comments on these?

To the first question, the replies given by the left-wing opposition politicians once more differed from those given by the two politicians in power. As far as the second went, they all agreed. The two right-wing politicians replied that they lived in a strongly democratic state with freedom of the press and free elections. The others disagreed. Ozker Bey replied:

We are very dependent on Turkey here and this is a fact. There is no point in hiding that during the last parliamentary elections here, Turkey intervened in favour of the right, and so they were not truly democratic. There was even intervention during the latest presidential elections. There are also serious doubts whether the government here truly represents the will of the people. You know, our people are often afraid to talk here.

Mustafa Bey's view was that:

We have a serious problem with democracy here. One half of our budget relies on Ankara, our security relies on Ankara, investment relies on Ankara. Ministry budgets have to go to the Turkish embassy for approval. No, we don't even have a freely elected government. During the last elections there were many interventions by the Turkish government, even by the Turkish state television, all in favour of UBP and in support of Denktash. Even the Generals in Ankara made their choice known and wielded their influence.

As for Turkish expansionism, they all agreed that this idea was totally unfounded. The UBP leaders argued that there was a serious problem with expansionism coming from the other side. Ozker Bey told me:

I know that Greek Cypriots are totally obsessed about Turkish expansionism, but they are wrong. There is no such thing and Ataturk set the legitimate borders of Turkey in order to counter any expansionist policies. Yes, there are some extremists in Turkey in favour of Turkish expansionism but the national policy is guided by Ataturk's principles. Turkey is not interested in grabbing Cyprus. You know that as a party we strongly criticize Turkey for many things. But this, no.

Mustafa Bey said, 'No one in Ankara wants expansionism and I don't agree with this notion that Greek Cypriots always repeat. In 1974, there was a good reason for Turkey to intervene and if a solution is found over here, then Turkey will go.' Dervish Bey, however, said:

This is wrong. Turkey did not want to capture Cyprus or else it would have taken the whole of the island. Turkey came here using her guarantor rights, even asking Britain to join her in this, which Britain refused to do. You know that in the 1960 constitution of Cyprus there is a clause prohibiting the union with another state, or its division, and that Greece, Turkey and Britain were placed as guarantor powers of the island's integrity and independence. After the 1974 coup for ENOSIS, it was clearly legitimate and within Turkey's rights to act.

Hakki Bey was the one who went furthest forward, and back:

Has Turkey ever expanded during the last 200 years? The maps show Turkey shrinking during the last 200 years. In 1821, for example, it was Greece that expanded on Turkish land. And Greece has since been expanding against Turkey all the time. How about the campaign of the 1920s for *Megali Idea*? That's what they tried to do in Cyprus too, with ENOSIS in the 1950s with EOKA, then ENOSIS again in the 1960s, and finally with the coup for ENOSIS in 1974.

The issue of Turkish settlers was next in line. 'How do you personally, and Turkish Cypriots in general, feel about the people from Turkey who come to work or live here?' The two right-wing politicians were concise. According to Dervish Bey:

> They are people like us, Turks like us belonging to the same nation, so why shouldn't they come? And after all our motherland did for us in 1974 with the Peace Operation, it would be utmost ingratitude to refuse entry to our Turkish co-nationals. But on your side they use this all the time for political propaganda and always exaggerate the numbers.

The two left-wing leaders were very uncomfortable with the rising numbers of Turkish settlers. In Mustafa Bey's view:

> One of the problems is that we have no verifiable numbers. Even though our government conducted a census, they never disclosed the results. I as a Cypriot want to know how many came here and am unhappy if this intrusion continues. Then our young people leave our country, or others come to the Greek Cypriot side to work. Did you know that around 500 Turkish Cypriots come to your side every day for work?

Ozker Bey said:

> This is a big problem, I would say a methodical campaign of colonization. They are exploited here both as voters and as cheap labour. The more this inflow continues, the more of a long-term problem this becomes. And as people from Turkey move in, our people are leaving. You know what Denktash said when he was challenged on this? 'A Turk leaves, a Turk comes, what's the difference?' Now for me as a Turkish Cypriot leader this is unacceptable. But in any solution they too must be treated humanely and some of them who married and have established roots here should stay.

The next question was easy again. 'When you hear Greek Cypriot politicians talk what are the things that seem dangerous or harmful in terms of reaching a solution?' Hakki Bey replied:

The basic problem with your political rhetoric is that your politicians find the present completely unacceptable. They insist that everything should be turned upside down. All the refugees must return, they say, but how about our people who don't want to return to your side? Where will they live? I know of no one here who says he wants to return.

Dervish Bey said:

This thing that all your politicians say, that all refugees have to return, is impossible. We don't want to move back. Another thing that is repeated is that Denktash and Turkey oppress the Turks here with the force of arms. This is completely wrong. The problem you know started in 1963. If Greek Cypriots had given up ENOSIS by then, we would have been on good terms.

According to Ozker Bey:

One of the biggest problems is that people tend to forget what the others suffered and remember only their own sufferings. We went through difficult times after 1963 but Greek Cypriots never mention these. They prefer to forget them. But Greek Cypriots too went through difficult times in 1974. Greek Cypriots try to present the problem as one of invasion and occupation alone, and say that if Turkey leaves everything will be OK. They claim that the problem is simply one of foreign invasion by another state and ignore all the internal dimensions, especially the violent conflict before 1974. But the Cyprus Problem did not start in 1974. First we have to remember that Turkey intervened because of the coup. Then that from the 1950s on there were serious problems between Turkish Cypriots and Greek Cypriots. But our leadership too says many wrong things about the Greek Cypriots. That Greek Cypriots have never given up ENOSIS, that Greek Cypriots want to grab the north, that Greek Cypriots want to rule the Turks and the like.

Mustafa Bey told me:

There are big problems with what politicians say on both sides. The Greek Cypriot position is that all refugees have to go back. On our side, the party in power, UBP, says no one can return. It's either black or white. We go for the compromise, for something in between. We must have a Turkish Cypriot majority on our side, but many Greek Cypriot refugees could return. There is a need for compromise, not just black and white. Then there is the issue of the withdrawal of Turkish troops. On our side they say all have to stay, on yours that all have to leave. We stand in the middle. There is a nasty saying on this side: *Domuz'dan post, gavur'dan dost, olmaz*. 'You can't make a hide from a pig, you can't be a friend of an infidel Greek Cypriot.' All the philosophy of the authorities on this side is based on this, that Greek Cypriots are our enemies and that we should never trust you. On your side – and I am pleased to say this – things have changed, especially with the new government. Now with Vasiliou, Turkish Cypriots are no longer the enemies.

Naturally the next question was about the negative aspects of what Turkish Cypriot politicians say. The two left-wing leaders had already answered this while the others saw nothing wrong.

The next was about propaganda. 'Do you see Greek Cypriots pursuing a propaganda campaign?' Hakki Bey said:

This is a very important question. Greek Cypriot propaganda is very effective, it is merciless. They do it because they are recognized internationally and they use this to their advantage by doing everything possible to stop the Turks of Cyprus from participating in international sports meetings, in academic conferences, everywhere. So we are completely denied a voice in international forums. Then you try to create a false image about what is happening on our side. You try to give the impression that the opposition parties are in the majority and that they want a solution, just like the Greek Cypriots. But this is wrong. All the people here want the same thing.

In Dervish Bey's view:

Greek Cypriots have been active in propaganda for a long time. They say there is only 'one people' in Cyprus and no separate Turkish people, that there is only one legitimate government, the Republic of Cyprus, that there are no Turkish people in Cyprus who also want their own self-determination.

According to Ozker Bey:

We have to realize that the Cyprus Problem has two important dimensions, the internal one and the international one, and that both are as important. Greek Cypriots only want to talk about the international aspect and Turkish Cypriots only about the internal one. None of them wants to see the whole picture. Another issue is the issue of rapprochement, one so important on the Greek Cypriot side. By repeating that 'we used to live like brothers in the past', even if this is true for certain periods, they deny the inter-ethnic problem, the fighting and our suffering during the 1960s. My party too supports rapprochement but our views are not identical with those of Greek Cypriots.

Mustafa Bey said:

> The biggest problem is this thing we have with mothers, the motherlands, and this applies to both sides. Our government and right-wing parties talk about the motherland all the time and so do the right-wing parties on your side. I dislike this motherland-baby relationship and criticize it. We both need to grow up without the protection of mothers. But they, the mothers, don't really want the baby to grow up because for many years Cyprus has been their main staple for internal political consumption. In Greece and Turkey, the opposition, whoever they are, always criticizes the government for selling out on the Cyprus issue. We, the opposition here, are accused of being traitors when we talk of the need for us to become independent, to grow up. Because our government has been a total failure on economic and social issues, all they can do is use this motherland talk. Your side is not very convincing either. They spend one million dollars a day on arms and then say it is defensive, but there is no such thing as purely defensive arms. This has to stop and what we need is a mutual reduction. We also need practical measures. As the Turkish Cypriot mayor of Lefkosha, I have managed to work closely with my Greek Cypriot counterpart to create a Master Plan for the future development of Lefkosha. In the Master Plan, we also comment on other things such as the need to revise the educational curricula on both sides in order to converge as far as possible towards a shared view on history.

'Are Turkish Cypriots also pursuing a propaganda campaign?' I only needed to pose this to two of them, first Hakki Bey: 'We only say that we are a different people with our own religion and language, that we were never the same people and that we are distinct. We just try to survive. I don't think there is any distortion in this.' Dervish Bey: 'Our propaganda is based on facts. The basic fact is that there are two peoples in Cyprus.'

The final question was on the topic of federation. During the political negotiations, the two sides had agreed on a federal, bi-zonal, bi-communal state. Despite protests on both sides, it was felt that this was the only way to a solution. UN Resolutions strongly urged the two leaders to work towards federation. Hakki Bey: 'Both sides talk of federation but they mean different things. Greek Cypriots treat our notion of federation as confederation. For us it is bi-zonal and bi-communal, while Greek Cypriots want everyone to return, which would not be possible if we are to have a majority in our zone.' Dervish Bey told me:

> Yes, we want federation but not as Greek Cypriots describe this. We want a true federation between two peoples, where each will be a majority on their side. Your leaders don't really want this. They want something like the unified 1960 Republic of Cyprus. This can't happen. We all know the dreadful results of that and we should never go back.

Ozker Bey thought:

> First thing is that it will not be possible in a bi-zonal federation for all the Greek Cypriot refugees to return. Our people don't want to go back anyway. But when Denktash speaks about federation he means something more like confederation, almost two independent states, whereas when your leader Vasiliou speaks about federation he means something more like a unitary state.

Mustafa Bey's view was:

> Our government one day speaks about federation, the next about confederation. Even though they agreed to this, they, the officials, often say that federation is the graveyard of Turkish Cypriots. We don't accept this. We feel that a federation will bring an end to this nasty situation here but our government does not truly strive for this. Denktash is more interested in two separate states and in unification with the 'motherland'.

As I was about to leave Ozker Bey, he took my arm. At first, he was deadly serious: 'Yianni, our generation destroyed this place. Not my own generation but surely the generation of Denktash, Makarios and Grivas. Now your generation must clear up the mess.' Then a twinkle appeared in his eyes: 'Now tell me, are you getting along with your Stepfather? It would be much better if you were allowed to work on your own, but they won't let you.'

DANGEROUS CYPRIOTS

One evening I was invited to watch a film by a woman who said she would also introduce me to her friends. I was tempted and concerned. I had heard of Emine and her other left-wing friends even before I had crossed over, and they were the people I wanted to meet most. But, if I showed too much enthusiasm to meet with them, perhaps the authorities would think I sympathized with their views and not allow me to stay longer. Then again I really wanted to meet them. I called up my Stepfather:

> Hi, I am calling to see if I can go and see a film tonight… Well, with some friends… With Emine and her friends…Yes, *that* Emine… Oh, come on, it's just a film. And please stop calling me 'Yiannaki', I'm not a child. Listen, I promise to only go there, nowhere else and be back here by ten. At ten I'll call you from the hotel… OK, done, thanks, bye, I'll call you.

Talk about a strict Stepfather! I hadn't spoken to anyone like this for years, having to beg just to go and see a film, and promise to return by ten. But my Stepfather was the old-fashioned type. He wanted to protect his innocent son from bad influences.

I went to the movie theatre where I met Emine, her son and some friends of hers running a small bookstall in a room outside the projection hall. We didn't have a chance to say much, because the film was starting. In the movie theatre it was just myself, Emine's son and someone else. The others had seen it. After the film, I only spoke with them for a few minutes before it was ten and I had to head back to the hotel. I called up my Stepfather. He wanted a full account. He asked for details: who was there, who I spoke to, and I told him. 'Good, I see you are telling me the truth,' he said, sounding pleased as he hung up. At the movie theatre, I had asked Emine if one evening she and her friends would like to come to the hotel since I could not go out. This I did not tell my Stepfather.

I had heard that Emine and her friends belonged to a radical group of intellectuals, one that the authorities regarded as highly subversive: 'the Cypriots'. That was what they called themselves. Others called them various more unpleasant names. They had been very active in creating links with the Greek Cypriots, and in organizing bi-communal meetings to promote dialogue and understanding between people of the two sides.

They came to see me a couple of days later. Mayhem broke out in the hotel. They called me from downstairs saying that the receptionist had been given firm instructions that no one could see me without prior permission from my Stepfather and was now calling to check. Then I received a call from reception saying that we could all go upstairs to the bar. I went upstairs and saw my friends there, but the barman said that he had instructions from reception that we should sit separately until further notice. We did as we were told and began to talk from adjoining tables. We were interrupted by the barman, who said that the instructions were that we could sit there but not talk until official approval was received from Levent Bey. Finally, my Stepfather called. It was mixed news. We could sit close by if we wanted but we were not allowed to talk. I could see him smiling. So they left. I was angry and vowed to get revenge. The day would soon come. In the meantime, I became a disobedient stepson. In the morning, before Ahmet arrived at the hotel, I sneaked out, saying I was going to buy cigarettes, to a nearby café run by Emine and her friends just to talk for a few minutes.

When we next met, Emine explained what had happened at the movie. Her friends were shocked because a well-known secret policeman had gone there and was looking at the books, waiting for the film to start. They were surprised because this was a kind of artsy movie and he did not seem like the type. A few minutes later, when Emine arrived with me, they understood. He watched the whole movie with her son and me. These were the people who were not allowed to talk to me, the left-wing voices I had been hearing in whispers.

THE BLACK BEARDED

I now came down for breakfast very early, taking my time and asking for refills of coffee from the waiter. 'You see all those *karasakals* here walking around Lefkosha? Now we can't leave our doors open as we used to,' he whispered. 'Not safe any more. I can pick them out from the way they dress, their baggy trousers. You see them in mosques too all the time. In fact, only they go there, we don't. So now, as if we didn't have enough problems, we also have those religious fanatics from Turkey all around us.'

I got to hear more about the *karasakals*, the people from Turkey who had come to live or work in the Turkish Cypriot side, mostly in whispers. *Karasakal* meant 'black bearded'. It was the equivalent of *kalamaras* for Greek Cypriots. But the meaning was different: religious fanatic, backward peasant, and more.

Early one morning as we were driving in Lefkosha with Levent Bey,

I saw them sitting in groups near the injured statue of Ataturk. He pointed at the statue. 'It was you who did this to our greatest hero,' he explained.

> You, Greek Cypriots, don't only attack people who are alive, you even attack statues. You even attack dead people. Look in any old map of Lefkosha. What happened to those places marked as Turkish cemeteries? Take the one in your sector next to the Omeriye Mosque. It's become a parking lot. What about the names of streets on your side of Lefkosha where Turkish Cypriots lived in the past? After we left in 1963, you erased the Turkish street names. Now you like to accuse us of desecrating your cemeteries, your churches, and changing your street names, eh, Yiannaki?

As I was duly informed, the statue of Ataturk was shot by Greek Cypriots the night when the fighting began in 1963. It was not repaired to act as a reminder.

I tried to change the topic, successfully for once, asking who the people sitting around so early in the morning were. 'Oh, them' Levent Bey responded. 'They are just *karasak*... I mean people from Turkey. They are Turks like me and everyone else who lives here.' I then saw a truck stop to take some of them on board, presumably for work. Since I had seen this, Levent Bey had little choice: 'They are workers and they wait here for people to pick them up for work on farms.'

They sat there desolate every morning waiting for Turkish Cypriots to load them into trucks or cars and take them to work for the day. *You feel sorry for these backward Turks who took our homes?* They sat at Inonu Square, the end of Istanbul Avenue near the statue of Ataturk. I was reminded of Lemesos, where I saw the same sad sight with foreign workers from Syria and Egypt. They waited for Greek Cypriots to load them onto trucks at the place where three streets met: Freedom Street, Peace Street and Greece Street.

TURKS, CYPRIOT TURKS, TURKISH CYPRIOTS AND CYPRIOTS

This was the official ranking of possible identities for Turkish Cypriots, in descending order of preference. The official view was that they there were first and foremost Turks, always had been, and always would be. 'Cypriot Turks' was tolerable, since it was still clear they were Turks. 'Turkish Cypriot' sounded suspicious, perhaps in need of occasional precautionary police surveillance. 'Cypriots' should certainly be locked away under accusation of national treachery. Not only was the 'Turk' bit entirely missing, the name implied unity with Greek Cypriots. According to more liberal views, such 'Cypriots' were merely deranged, lost or paranoid – that they were watched by the police.

Right-wing parties in the north, which had monopolized power since 1974, were in full agreement with this ranking. Other parties, especially left-wing ones, disagreed. Their ranking of preferred Turkish Cypriot identities was exactly the inverse. They considered themselves as Cypriots first, a category that could include Greek Cypriots too. Why so? For many reasons. Like left-wing Greek Cypriots, they had found themselves in the past excluded from the dominant political definitions of identity as these had been formed in the mother-fatherlands and later in the babyland. In both mother-fatherlands communists had been treated as unpatriotic traitors. Because of this, they had been violently persecuted in Cyprus by right-wing groups. In Cyprus, there had been a lot of cooperation within the institutions of the left, especially trade unions, and as things started to get rough such people attempted to provide bridges, even work towards cooperation. Some were then killed as 'treacherous collaborators with the enemy'. They knew well that violence was not the prerogative of the other community for they had experienced it from their own. After 1974, they had added reasons for dissent. Power was controlled by right-wing parties and the economy was still in ruins. The few precious government jobs went to people of the right who came to enjoy the monopoly of economic resources. In patron-client societies like ours, political and economic power were inseparable. They hoped that a solution might reduce the control of power from the right and give everyone new opportunities.

Then there was the problem of the Turkish workers. In the evenings, I sometimes took a break by leisurely walking – only one occasion did I walk fast, for reasons of revenge – around the Old Town, which was full of cheap hotels where Turkish migrants rented rooms with as many as ten people in a room. They worked for lower wages than Turkish Cypriots were prepared to accept. So, they represented unwelcome competition to Turkish Cypriot workers, but a welcome pool of cheap labour for employers. This made it difficult for local workers to organize and demand higher wages.

Eventually, I had the opportunity to meet some of the Turks from Turkey with my Stepfather. The ones I met were successful, established businessmen who had settled in Cyprus, and some had married here.

They never used the word *karasakal* for themselves, of course. They used another name: Cypriot. They proudly called themselves Cypriot, even in the presence of my strict Stepfather. They were the only ones who could use it with impunity. They did this in order to make it clear that they belonged there and that they should be treated as locals, as official policy decreed. But if someone from Cyprus tried to call herself 'Cypriot' then all hell broke out, because they were supposed to be Turks and nothing but Turks. On the Greek Cypriot side, members of the smaller minorities such as the Latins and the Armenians could also call themselves Cypriot with impunity. But, if any Greek Cypriot did so, he ran the risk of being accused as a traitor to the Hellenic nation.

FANATIC CHRISTIANS

'Religion is your problem,' Fikret, an old man from Tahtakale stated angrily. This was a topic that enraged people. 'Your Church has always been the strongest force of chauvinism and nationalism.'

He was only partly right. The Church always was a misunderstood institution. He was judging from his own perspective. In Turkey, Ataturk's reforms had tried to sideline religion and Turkish Cypriots were much more secular than Greek Cypriots, and than Turks. He was right that the leaders of the Church often made fiery proclamations that never failed to make it onto Turkish Cypriot news, thanks to my Stepfather. Some Turkish Cypriots had heard rumours that each knot on a priest's knotted string corresponded to a child the priest had killed. (During the 1974 war, Greek Cypriots heard rumours about Turkish soldiers having worry beads made with women's nipples.) But Turkish Cypriots were wrong in believing that the Church wielded such a powerful influence. Because they saw Archbishop Makarios as the archetypal Greek Cypriot leader, they felt that the Church was still a dominating force. It was still a force, no doubt about it, but not with regard to morality – in fact, quite the opposite.

Greek Cypriots, in perfect agreement with Turkish Cypriots, held the view that the Church was historically the leading force of Greek nationalism. But things were never so simple. Adamantios Korais for example, one of the intellectual fathers of Greek nationalism, referred to priests as 'monkish barbarians'. He advocated the liberation of Greeks from the double tyranny of the Ottomans and the Orthodox Church. Patriarch Anthimos of Jerusalem had argued at the end of the eighteenth century that the Ottoman Empire was a creation of divine will, and urged the Orthodox to remain loyal to their Ottoman masters. Later when the secret organization called *Philiki Etairia* called for an uprising against the Ottomans, they were condemned and anathematized by the Holy Synod. Some of its leaders were Freemasons. In Cyprus, the local archbishop denounced them in even stronger terms at the start of the nineteenth century. But by the end of the century they were able to re-emerge as strong proponents of Greek nationalism in Cyprus, working through their Masonic lodges.

The Church no longer represented moral force but an economic one. Its own TV station, The Word, showed all kinds of American films laced with the standard sex and violence, with sporadic religious programmes on the side. The Church invested heavily in hotels and business. It came into conflict with environmental groups trying to protect natural reserves that the Church wanted 'developed' into tourism complexes. Bishops only travelled in Mercedes cars. Archbishop Chrysostomos' name, 'the Golden Mouthed', was said to match his deeds. Foreign visitors and dignitaries found him more eager to talk about money and real estate investments than about the Cyprus Problem. Greek Cypriots called him 'Tommy' to indicate that he behaved like an American businessman. My own favourite church symbol would be the two-headed eagle of the Byzantine Empire with two crossing golf clubs underneath, the emblem of a church-owned golf club. As the promotional leaflet explained: 'Historically, it [the golf-club] has been part of the monastery of "Stavros tis Minthis", which gives an air of timelessness and romance. A monk may often be seen in the garden from the 7th tee.'

TAHTAKALE

'Tahtakale was a good neighbourhood, the water there was sweet, and the air was cooler than other places,' Asim Bey explained. 'The people were good, rowdy yes, but warm-hearted. So it hurt even more when we had to abandon our homes there.' I explained that refugees lived there now. 'So now refugees live there,' responded Asim Bey.

Lucky them. Well, not so lucky perhaps. They must have done a lot of rebuilding because after we left everything was ruined. Ironic, isn't it? We are forced to leave, and your people are put inside houses that had to be repaired because your people destroyed them. It just goes to show how crazy this place Cyprus is. You even say that you want your people to return, all of them. This means that you are asking us to become refugees again and go back to Tahtakale, and the refugees who after twenty years have made a life there, will become refugees again. Now you show our mosques every day on your Turkish programmes on TV and call us to come back. Back then you threw us out, destroyed our homes and changed the street names. And how about your own people? Where will they return to? Every day before the news, you show photos of a village with that 'I Don't Forget'. But the photos you show are all of the village before 1974. Nothing is the same any more but you still show them photos of the place as it used to be, never as it is.

He paused and looked at me seriously:

Yiannaki, I know who stole all my carpentry machines from my shop. Later, I saw them in his shop. This is the problem you see, we know who took our things, we know who killed our people, and we know them all by name. Can I walk out of my house in Tahtakale, pass outside his shop and say good-morning to him, while he is using my own machine?

He mentioned the name of a man – the Greek Cypriot who told me smoking was not allowed in his shop because he did not want to see me any more when he learnt I would cross to meet the Turkish Cypriots of Tahtakallas. 'He was one of those Olympiakos people, you know,' he said, as if that explained it. Olympiakos was the Greek Cypriot right-wing coffee shop in Tahtakale. Asim Bey's face clouded and his voice became hoarse as he said the name. Others had a similar reaction:

Olympiakos… Olympiakos. Those people were the cause of all our problems. I mean for all of us, Yiannaki, first our problems, then yours. All the time ENOSIS this and ENOSIS that and glorious mother Greece and we will one day make you pay for what you made us suffer when we Greeks in 1821 revolted against you the Turks. As if it was me, or my neighbour Kemal, who had done it to them personally. In 1963, when the troubles started they had the machine gun up in the house of their president from where they shot us. I know them all by name. We all do. So it's still there? Full of Greek flags I am sure as it was then.

THE VILLAGE OF WOMEN

When I asked Levent Bey why the enormous flags had been painted on the slopes of the Girne mountain range, he reacted as if I had reminded him of something. 'I will take you there, Yiannaki, and you will understand.' These were two enormous flags, of Turkey and the TRNC, each the size of many soccer pitches, that Turkish Cypriots had whitewashed on the side of the mountain range, making them visible from far away on both sides. A quote from Ataturk was written under the Turkish flag: 'How Happy is the One who Says I am a Turk.' It looked like the mountain was officially stamped, to show who the land belonged to. This was the contribution of Cyprus to the Guinness Book of Records: the largest flags in the world. (Later, the largest chicken kebab too.)

We drove to the village below the flags. 'This is Tashkent. You may know it as Tohni. People here lived in Tashkent or Tohni on your side until 1974 and then they all moved here.' It was a warm day and the villagers were sitting outside their homes – all were women dressed in black. They seemed to know Levent Bey well. He only had to nod towards their house and they understood he was asking to enter. In every living room, photos of men were hanging on the wall. We entered and left in silence. Levent Bey explained. 'All the men of the village were rounded up and murdered in August 1974 in their village in the Greek sector. This is why you only see women.'

We passed a monument with 'DO NOT FORGET' engraved on it. Levent Bey found the man he was looking for at the coffee shop. He was the only one to survive. He explained what had happened, with many details and names of the perpetrators. He pointed to numerous Turkish Cypriot news reports describing the killings. 'Now you see, Yiannaki, why we placed the flags here.'

There was a strange kind of pleasure in the way the man had told me his story. It was present in Levent Bey's eyes too, as he smiled suggestively throughout the man's gruesome description. It was a pleasure I had also encountered on the Greek Cypriot side, a feeling I had once experienced too: the pleasure of absolute self-righteousness, felt whenever such self-evident and unshakeable proof of others' atrocities was presented. Unshakeable proof that a Dead Zone divided the world into devils and angels.

ENOSIS WALL-DECOR

Once, way back in the 1950s and 1960s, ENOSIS posters were the favourite decor in Greek Cypriot coffee shops and schools. Now I was in a place where ENOSIS posters were once again appreciated: the National Archives Centre in Girne, the Turkish Cypriot historical research centre. Levent Bey took me there to teach me some history lessons, in his usual style.

Most of the posters I had never seen before. One showed a young maiden in chains standing on Cyprus, beckoning towards Greece, shown as an Athena lookalike. The maiden was waiting for the chains to be cut in order to reach the embrace of the mother-fatherland. The previous day I had seen its counter-poster in a coffee shop. A hand was moving towards Cyprus from the side of Greece; another hand with a Turkish flag was bloodily severing it with a knife, and Ataturk was watching from behind. Some of the posters were made in Greece during the previous century at the time of the *Megali Idea*. It was unnerving to encounter these remnants of a long dead past. Greek Cypriots and Greeks no longer believed in them, but Turkish Cypriot researchers did. As was explained, the posters were there to motivate the researchers. The imminent threat gave meaning and purpose to their hard labour, their existence even, and that of the Centre.

I was introduced to the deputy director. I described my research, and said that I wanted to talk to Turkish Cypriots who had lived in the same... He cut me short, shouting. 'This is nonsense. There is no point in what you are doing. The problem is clear to all with eyes to see. The problem is ENOSIS. You started it all with ENOSIS, you continued with this after independence and you still do.' I tried to explain that things had changed after the late 1960s; that after 1974 ENOSIS died, that the coup was not a mass movement but the opposite, a terrorist movement by a despised few and that Turkish Cypriots wrongly saw the coup as a popular movement. He cut me off with the usual arguments. 'Don't you use the Greek flag all the time? Don't you still commemorate the terrorist EOKA struggle on 1 April when it began? Aren't the two educational systems closely linked? How about the army? Not to mention the European Community, where Greece belongs and where you want to become a member, which is another way of uniting with Greece.' Again I tried to explain that, yes, Greek Cypriots leaned on Greece for protection; that fear of Turkey was one of the main reasons why. That there were cultural links, but that did not mean ENOSIS. That the Greek flag had become a symbol of the right. That the commemorations of EOKA were now presented as commemorations of independence, not ENOSIS. Instead he continued. 'You say you are doing research in Tahtakale. The proof is right there. You threw us out and then filled the place with prostitutes to say "You see this is where Turks lived" like you did in Rhodes and all over.'

I did not like his arguments, nor the tone and volume of his voice, which reminded me of the other voices in Greek I had been hearing. I wanted to tell him that 'ENOSIS and only ENOSIS' was indeed still a problem. The problem was that Turkish Cypriots now vehemently believed in ENOSIS, when Greek Cypriots no longer did.

THE MUSEUM OF NATIONAL STRUGGLE

The next day, Levent Bey arranged for me to visit the Museum of National Struggle, a new building on the walls of Lefkosha, next to an army camp. The curator was expecting me. She greeted me warmly, gave me the explanatory leaflet and offered to accompany me. The layout was like a long corridor. It was, after all, a museum of history and the story it told progressed linearly from the beginning to the end. I read the first sentences in the leaflet: 'The Museum was built for the purpose of immortalizing, displaying and teaching the generations ahead the conditions under which the Turkish Cypriot people gave their struggle from 1955 till the present.'

The beginning of the museum was a large room. The first person I saw upon entering was – who else? – Ataturk, and 'How Happy is the One who Says I am a Turk'. The TMT fighters' anthem was on display:

A spark is burning inside the fighter.

It is the flame of Turkishness.

There is nothing like it

on the face of the earth.

Cyprus can't be Greek.

The Turkish fighters will not stop.

Either Turkish Cyprus will exist

or the fighter won't live.

If the Greeks come and stand in line,

and even if the whole world comes with them,

until the fighters die,

this earth won't be given to them.

The painting on the wall showed Ottoman soldiers heroically scaling the walls of a city. The legend explained that it depicted the conquest of Cyprus in 1571. This was the start of the museum's story, the beginning of history: 1571, the heroic conquest of Cyprus by the Ottomans.

The corridor beckoned, dark and crooked, hiding the end from view. In just a few steps I made a huge historical leap, from 1571 to 1958: the start of TMT, the Turkish Cypriot fighters' organization. The three large letters were placed high on the wall. I found myself staring into dozens of pairs of eyes looking down on me. The letters had been written using photos of the dead heroes of TMT. Perhaps it was guilt that made me feel they were looking accusingly at me, guilt that we... no, not we, they, the Greek Cypriots – certain Greek Cypriots – had killed them. Many of them were young. A painting of the first TMT hero killed – *you call those terrorists of TMT heroes?* – showed a young man, high-school age, with tidy parted hair, and a gentle face – *you feel sorry for him*? The loud voices in Greek began again.

I was about to enter the corridor, each step lined with new facts. *Facts? You call their propaganda facts?* Facts I had never known, dates that had never meant anything until I crossed the Dead Zone. This corridor explained what happened between 1963 and 1974. Only eleven years, but the largest part of this museum beginning from 1571 was devoted to them. That was why their monuments all had eleven lines. From 1958 I walked into 1963. Nothing in between. No 1960. The year of independence that Greek Cypriots gloriously commemorated did not matter here.

I stepped into the dark corridor, which felt narrow and oppressive. First, I encountered two paintings. A man standing with arched back and outstretched arms, eyes closed and head tilted to the heavens, in front of a dead body. And a woman in bridal clothes weeping in front of the corpse of a young man draped with a Turkish flag. Next were photos of the missing persons between 1963 and 1974. I saw refugees fleeing for their lives. Further on were photographs of the mass graves at Murataga (Maratha), Sandallar (Santallaris) and Atlilar (Aloa), where men, women and children had been killed and buried by Greek

Cypriots. I had been there with my Stepfather to see the monuments bearing the names and ages of those killed. But his presence there and his insistence on telling me the same things over and over had left me feeling cold. One photo showed an old man on his knees on the ground pulling his hair as others around him dug out a corpse. A painting showed soldiers with Greek flags on their sleeves and EOKA on their berets shooting a group of old men, women – one was naked – and children.

Then there was a collection of strange guns. They looked like toys put together by children, made of water pipes, locks and other pieces of metal. Next to them was a display of real, modern, factory-produced guns. The curator explained: 'We used those hand-made guns when we were forced to move into the enclaves. We could not acquire real guns to protect ourselves, nor could we buy the materials we needed to make our own. The real guns are the ones you were using.' One painting summed up the history of Turkish Cypriots. It showed a peasant loaded with a heavy bag and a blonde gentleman (the British) demanding money (taxes); Turkish Cypriots living in tents, Turkish Cypriots killed by Greek Cypriots, frightened Greek Cypriots fleeing in the wake of Turkish soldiers, Turkish Cypriots bathed in light rejoicing next to Turkish soldiers, a stern figure of Ataturk watching them from behind as a dove flew over, and in the background modern factories (the road to progress and prosperity).

A small entrance beckoned me out of the solemn corridor towards the light. I walked into a large, round room bathed in light from high windows. It was the last room, the end of the story. The room was devoted to the '1974 Happy Peace Operation'. The leaflet explained:

> As a result of the set up, the visitor entering the museum will initially experience the painful days of the struggle given by the Turkish Cypriot people in order to keep the enemy off its precious soil. Upon leaving the museum, the visitor will feel the air of freedom and peace breathed by the Turkish Cypriot people who did not lose their hope despite the migrations, mass murders and economic and political pressure imposed on them by the Greeks during the eleven years from 1963 to 1974; a hope which materialized with the 1974 Peace Operation, a result of the protection and support given by motherland Turkey. '

The first painting in the room showed people rejoicing, their arms high in the air. The display on my left showed helmets, insignia and flags captured from Greek Cypriot soldiers. Another display showed a phoenix rising from the ashes, the mythical bird that was reborn out of its own ashes, with the outline of a soldier in front of it, over the date when the Colonels of the Greek junta seized power: 21 April 1967. It symbolized the rebirth of Greece, which the Colonels said was being reawakened to past glory under their firm guidance. I knew this well because it used to be on all our school books. The display right at the end presented the 'Foundation of the Turkish Republic of Northern Cyprus' in 1983. This was the standard happy end in stories of national struggle: the foundation of an independent state.

The final display showed Greek Cypriots demonstrating on the Green Line. I had seen many photos of such demonstrations in the Greek Cypriot news, taken from the Greek Cypriot side; these were from the Turkish Cypriot side. The crowds now looked threatening, eyes wide open, clenched fists in the air, faces twisted in frozen screams of hatred, Orthodox priests and Greek flags menacingly visible in front. 'Peaceful demonstrations of refugees claiming their right to return' was the usual comment when the images were shown on the Greek Cypriot side.

This last room was the room of liberation, triumph, and elation, devoted to 1974. 'The Happy Peace Operation'. I understood how Turkish Cypriots felt then. But I could not share their joy, it made me feel sadder.

WE WON'T FORGET

After talking to many Turkish Cypriots about the recent past, I noticed that some things were mentioned as I was about to leave, usually after I had switched off the tape recorder, like afterthoughts. The tape recorder signalled that we were talking about serious things, about History. As I was getting ready to leave they sometimes stopped me to add something. 'Look for Kostaki, he was my neighbour, a good man. We built his house together when he got married.' It was as if a door had been pushed open a little and light came through the crack. At those moments, their stories resembled the things – the good things – I had heard in Tahtakallas. But these descriptions were not as vivid as those of Greek Cypriots, who spoke as if it had happened only yesterday. The stories did not flow as smoothly, as if their narrators hadn't thought about them for a while. The colours were faded. Even good friends' names were sometimes accompanied by a question mark. Sometimes the icy touch of death crept in. Had the Zone of the Dead already claimed their friend? 'Please say hello to Yiango… if he is still alive. Is he, Yiannaki?' These comments led to other dark thoughts. 'What's going to happen to us all, Yiannaki? How can people ever come together? Only us old ones knew each other. And we are passing away.'

'Those who forget their past don't know where to head in the future.' I had heard this so many times in Greek, and now just as frequently in Turkish. 'I Don't Forget' for Greek Cypriots; 'We Won't Forget (*Unutmayacagiz*)' for Turkish Cypriots. 'I Don't Forget' was all about the homes and villages in the north. This symbol sometimes showed Cyprus painted as a blue-white Greek flag, with dripping blood – the red of the Turkish flag – covering the northern part. Now, I considered how this must look to Turkish Cypriot eyes – Cyprus as a Greek island, Turkish barbarism. 'We Won't Forget' meant something different: we won't forget the martyrs who died, what Greek Cypriots did to us, the sacrifices of those who shed their blood for us, our past sufferings, the pain. It also meant 'I never want to live with Greek Cypriots again, I never want to go back.' One was about land, homes, and the good life. The other was about people, those who died, the horrible aspects of the past. Some Turkish Cypriots were surprised when I told them of the same slogan on the Greek Cypriot side, but many knew of it. Greek Cypriots were even more surprised when I told them.

One day, I stumbled upon the two confronting each other in capitals across the Dead Zone. 'I DON'T FORGET' in Greek was inside Lefkosia, while in Lefkosha the reply in Turkish went 'WE WON'T FORGET THE SLAUGHTER EITHER'. They were meant to be read by those on the other side, but since each was written in a language which the other side no longer understood, the effect was largely lost. Two desperate screams that remained unheard. A wall reflected them back.

BIRTHDAY OF A SPY?

A couple of times, I was given permission to cross to the Greek Cypriot side for the day. I was missing my girlfriend – a Dead Zone now lay between us. I also wanted to see my parents and friends. More than anything I wanted to escape. Spending the day hearing Turkish Cypriots recount their sad lives with Greek Cypriots and then having to write their stories up night after night was too much. It was during a dinner that Levent Bey first asked me to spy for them, I think.

The day I asked to cross happened to be the birthday of Greece: 25 March, the anniversary of the independence of Greece, commemorating the 1821 uprising against the Ottomans. Even though this date belonged to the history of another state, Greek Cypriots also celebrated it. Levent Bey put it gently. 'Would it be possible to take a couple of photos of the parade for me? Just a couple. The parade is all over your newspapers anyway and all over your TV news. But if you don't feel like it, don't worry, you don't have to do it.'

I had to think quickly. Naturally, before I had crossed I had discussed the issue of spying with a couple of trusted friends. One had said that the way to turn someone into a spy was to first start by asking for small favours – it would not be top military secrets straight away. But the month was running out and Levent Bey would soon tell me whether I could stay longer, which I desperately wanted to do. I was also curious. And he was right about the papers and TV. It was not even a military parade, just school children marching. What possible harm could there be? So I took some photos of school children and just to show diligence I took a photo of the officials' stand, but from far away so that faces would be difficult to tell apart. After he saw them, Levent Bey called to say that they were good and that I was doing really well. I felt that my chances of staying had improved significantly. Then I made my biggest mistake.

APRIL THE FIRST

The date when the EOKA struggle began, 1 April 1955, was an important commemoration on the Greek Cypriot side. Sadly, in Cyprus, and elsewhere, it had another meaning: April Fool's Day. This was the reason I chose 1 April 1991 to get my revenge on Levent Bey. This coincidence now made me wonder. How come April Fool's Day was chosen for the start of EOKA? In fact, it was all a historical accident. The original plan was that the EOKA insurrection for Union with Greece was to start on 25 March to coincide with the 'Greek' insurrection against the 'Turks'. Due to unforeseen problems, it had to be postponed for a few days. Exactly when the insurrection had begun in Greece was still an issue of debate, but eventually 25 March was settled upon. This date had a big advantage because it was an important religious date: the conception of Christ by the Virgin Mary. As the new-eternal God began to be 'created', so was the new-eternal Christian Greek nation. If God could not be created anew – for he is eternal – so the eternal nation was not created anew but awakened.

I knew that important decisions were being made as to whether I would be allowed to stay on. And I still did it. I just couldn't help myself. I was so angry with Levent Bey. He made my work difficult because his unending insistence on Turkish Cypriot victimization made me all the more hesitant to accept what I was hearing from others. Plus, I was angry with him for having become my Stepfather without my permission, for strictly controlling my movements and, of course, for pointing out all the Mercedes cars. And, for not letting me talk freely to my compatriots, the Cypriots. It was that incident, I think, that did it, creating a maze of convoluted historical symbolisms.

The day before I asked him if he knew the meaning of the day. Of course, it was the anniversary of EOKA, he replied with pride. I asked if he knew the other meaning. Of course, it was April Fool's. I regarded that as more than fair warning. His words echoed in my ears: 'If anything happens to you all these buildings will fall on my head.' First thing in the morning, I went over to the receptionist. 'Will you help me play a small joke on Levent Bey? Just an April Fool's joke. All you have to do is call him and say that I popped out to buy cigarettes and a car hit me. Then I'll immediately grab the phone and explain that it was a joke.' He would do it! Was he a crypto-Cypriot? I wondered. It all went wrong. By the time I was handed the phone, the line was dead. We tried to reach him again and thankfully we did through his secretary. She caught him in his car. I tried to be funny about it, explaining that the original idea was to tell him immediately, but he didn't see the humour. He wanted to see me. Now.

His secretary received me first. She was furious. 'What did you do, Yiannaki? I never saw a man go white and perspire all over at once. He picked up the phone, turned white and his shirt stuck to him. What a horrible joke!' When Levent Bey appeared in his fresh shirt, he was more composed. 'Yiannaki, that was a bad idea. I told you what would happen if anything happened to you. And after all I did for you.' I was ashamed and apologized. I was to stay put at the hotel.

A couple of days later I was informed that it had not been possible to arrange for an extension. Levent Bey said that he had tried hard but that his request was refused higher up. Perhaps he just said that. Perhaps he was angry and did not even try. Or, perhaps, just perhaps, there was another reason, as I came to suspect.

BACK TO THE ZONE OF THE DEAD
Before leaving I needed to read their historians and collect their books. Would they confirm what I had been hearing? Back to the Zone of

the Dead then, only I was not returning to a place I had been before. Previously, on the Greek Cypriot side, I thought that I had been reading about the history of Cyprus. But I had only visited the Greek Cypriot Zone of the Dead. The Dead Zone had divided the Zones of the Dead too. The dead I had been meeting on the Greek Cypriot side were not those I met on the Turkish Cypriot side. The cemeteries that found themselves on the wrong side of the Dead Zone had been buried, turned into parking lots or destroyed. The other side's dead were killed again and cleansed away. Not even they could rest in peace. The Dead Zone extended all the way into the afterlife: our glorious heroes in paradise, their terrorist-killers in hell.

The first things historians and officials in Lefkosha's Public Information Office were keen to show me were about our side: ENOSIS. Oaths were their big favourite, especially those given before 1960 that 'we will fight for ENOSIS until it is realized and *never* give it up.' 'Never' had been underlined in case the reader failed to notice. Still, it was disturbing to encounter all the pronouncements in favour of ENOSIS that Makarios and others had been making after 1960 and into the 1970s. I had thought that ENOSIS died after 1960. In fact, almost nothing was said in Greek Cypriot textbooks about the period between 1960 and 1974. I did not know that as late as 1967 the Greek Cypriot parliament had passed a resolution in favour of ENOSIS that was supported by all Greek Cypriot parties. Greek Cypriots did not like to remember that period, nor their demands for ENOSIS then; Turkish Cypriots showed no interest in documenting how it was abandoned after 1974. I had often wondered why many Turkish Cypriots believed that Greek Cypriots still wanted ENOSIS. Now I understood why ENOSIS was so important to them. It stood for the ever-present threat that allowed them to righteously insist on the division and continue to claim what they had gained in 1974. The coup was the second grand absolution. On this side it was presented as a mass movement by Greek Cypriots, not an act of a despised few extremists, to justify the widespread Greek Cypriot suffering that ensued.

The most important period of the history of Cyprus for Turkish Cypriot historians were the years between 1963 and 1974 as if the whole of the history of Cyprus was encapsulated in those eleven years. I read the standard school textbook of the history of Cyprus written by a man high in UBP. The largest part of the book was an account of how many *Turks* the *Rums* had killed, how, where and when. He mentioned the famous Akritas Plan, which had escaped the attention of Greek Cypriot historians. The book gave details about the mass graves and how bulldozers were used to bury people.

There I found out that in January 1958, the British killed seven Turkish Cypriots during pro-TAKSIM demonstrations. That date had become a yearly commemoration. I had never heard of this before. The Greek Cypriot view was that Turkish Cypriots had always been in close cooperation with the British. But things were not so simple. After the rise of Kemalism in Turkey and the creation of Turkish national identity, the British supported the religious anti-Kemalist factions among Turkish Cypriots in order to prevent the rise of a Turkish identity in Cyprus. A similar strategy had been followed in Greece with regards to the Turks of Thrace. The Greek authorities had supported the religious leaders who declared themselves faithful to the Supreme-Father, not the new usurper.

The beginning of the history schoolbook was highly important; beginnings always were. It began with geography. 'The closest neighbour of Cyprus is motherland Turkey.' The Girne mountain range in Cyprus was 'a continuation of the Toros mountain range of Turkey'. Population statistics ensued, showing how, during the eighteenth century, the population of Turks in Cyprus was larger than that of the Rums. Another fact followed: the first inhabitants of Cyprus originally came from Anatolia. Then another fact – an all time favourite – that 'Cyprus was once a part of Anatolia until later it became separated.' He then commented that 'for Greece, Cyprus carries neither any historical nor any strategic significance.' Just in case students still missed the point: 'The Rums found in Cyprus nowadays are not Greeks. This is confirmed by various foreign historians, since Cyprus was conquered by many foreign nations.'

Real history begun with the Ottoman conquest of Cyprus, and one of the largest sections was devoted to the Ottoman period. The section was titled 'Turkish Hegemony' even though at the time the Turks were still to be born. The Ottoman Period was presented – not surprisingly – as one of benevolent rule that left a rich legacy of monuments behind, giving Cyprus its current Turkish character. The book contained lists of fountains, mosques, tombs of saints, aqueducts, *hans*, which used to function like hotels, and *hamams*. They were scattered all over Cyprus, though I had never noticed. Driving outside Larnaka, I regularly passed in front of an imposing aqueduct but I had no idea it that was Ottoman. This was never mentioned in our books. All we knew about the Ottomans was that they were barbarians who never built anything. And what had happened to all the *hans* and *hamams* on the Greek Cypriot side? In Lefkosha, I saw two well preserved *hans* and a beautiful *hamam*, but I had never seen those said to have existed in Lefkosia. Either they had been destroyed or they too had somehow become invisible.

In Turkish Cypriot history books, Turks 'killed' only when they had to, either in self-defence or to capture a land such as Cyprus because it was vital for their strategic *defence* interests (which would then lead to the capture of another place necessary for the defence of Cyprus and so on). Expansionist Greeks and the Rums always 'slaughtered'.

Statements by Rum extremists were once again hot favourites, presented as the general Greek Cypriot outlook: 'One day we must exterminate the Turks in Cyprus. Slaughter those Turkish dogs. We want to drink Turkish blood.' (Naturally, statements from Turkish Cypriot extremists were absent.) I remembered us shouting slogans like 'We want to drink Turkish blood' when I was in the army. But the slogans were meant for the Turks from Turkey, not Turkish Cypriots – not that this made them palatable.

Some books included fascinating cartoons of Makarios, as I had never seen or thought of him before, taken from international newspapers like the *New York Times* reporting on the 1960s violence. This Makarios was not the gentle, white-bearded grandfather I had known as a child. The one I saw in the cartoons had thick tense eyebrows, dark menacing robes, and an unruly beard as he sat contentedly among piles of Turkish Cypriot corpses.

Many books published his address to the UN Security Council on 19 July 1974, four days after the coup, and one day before the impending but unbeknown to him Turkish invasion. On the Greek Cypriot side, I had never come across this speech, where he warned the world of imminent danger. As I read it, I could hear his voice: 'The coup [caused by the Greek military regime] has cost much bloodshed and many lives… But this was an invasion which violated the independence and sovereignty of the Republic of Cyprus…The Turkish Cypriots are also affected. The coup of the Greek junta is an invasion and from its consequences all the people of Cyprus both Greeks and Turks will suffer.'

If Makarios now looked evil on this side, Denktash looked no less than saintly. When I first saw Denktash's photo, I was surprised. I could not help admire how good he looked. He looked good in more ways than one: good looking but also a decent chap. Greek Cypriot politicians now appeared bad and ugly. The trick was simple. Each side used photographs of its own politicians taken in professional studios with special lighting that sometimes created a real saintly halo around their head. For the other side's politicians bad photographs were chosen with as much care. Such photos only reinforced what people already knew. 'Our politicians are good inside and out. Theirs are nasty and ugly. Their looks confirm their inner natures.'

On this side, I had also met the children called War. Many were born around the time I was. How come I was only called 'Yiannis'? What was happening in Lemesos/Leymosun those days? I should find out. Now I saw history from the other side of the Dead Zone. This history, like its reflection on the other side, was built on the basis of truths and facts made to lie. 'The best lies are made with truths,' as Erkin, my friend in Turkey, had said. Even if everything asserted was true, a great deal went missing. The dead of the other side did not matter, their pain did not count, their experiences were silenced, their fears declared unfounded.

APHRODITE

She looked different from this side. I remembered the Turkish Cypriot poster at the Izmir International Fair Trade, 'Cyprus, the Island of Venus', turning her into a Roman instead of a Greek. But the Turkish Cypriot authorities did not hesitate to advertise ancient Greek ruins in the north. When it came to tourist money, northern Cyprus happily emerged in tourist leaflets with abundant ancient Greek heritage. Unlike history schoolbooks, where nothing mattered before the Ottomans and no Greek monuments were presented. 'Cyprus has never been a Greek island.'

On the Greek Cypriot side, everyone knew the place where Aphrodite was born: the Rock of Aphrodite. It had two other names, both with Byzantine associations. The Rock of Digenis, after *Digenis Akritas*, the most famous of the Akrites, a legendary defender of 'the Byzantine borders against infidel attacks'. Or the Rock of the Romios, after the Orthodox Christian inhabitants of the Byzantine Empire. The three names together suggested an ancient Greek and a Byzantine heritage: the Hellenic-Christian ideals, myths and legends all condensed in the names of this place. In Lefkosha, I learned of another name for the rock, in Turkish: Rock of the Infidel (*gavur tashi*), meaning the rock of Greek Cypriots. The accusation of unbelief – or should it be infidelity, since Aphrodite was implicated? – was reversed.

The Rock of Aphrodite had many sides to it and so did Aphrodite. Once I knew Aphrodite as the Greek Goddess of Beauty and Love. But the Goddess of Beauty had married Hephaestus, the ugliest God, and the Goddess of Love had taken Ares, the War God, as her lover. Her own beginning was caused by an act of violence: the castration of Uranus by his son Cronus. Now, I vaguely remembered some things I had read about the Goddess of Love in the Greek Cypriot side that seemed unimportant at the time, something about her as a 'warrior' Goddess. I should read them again.

ADVICE

'Be careful, Yiannaki.' I heard this all the time as I was saying goodbye and thanking those who had helped me. 'Be careful, Yiannaki. When you go to your side people will not like what you have to say. But try to be objective, to write about what you saw with your own eyes here.' Others were more concerned about the British. 'Will the English who are on your side ever allow you to write this?' Whispers: 'Try to come back and work on your own to hear all the truth.' Loud voices: 'Well, goodbye Mr Papadakis. Make them understand it's all your fault with ENOSIS.' Further whispers: 'Try to go somewhere where you can meet Turkish Cypriots freely, where they can talk to you without officials around.' Someone even involved the ancient Greeks: 'Watch out, your people won't like what you have to say. Wasn't it the ancient Greeks who spoke about killing the messenger with the bad news?'

GOODBYE FROM MY STEPFATHER

Levent Bey insisted on driving me to the Ledra Palace checkpoint. 'After all, I am your Stepfather, Yiannaki, who else should deliver you to your father, who will no doubt be waiting there, so happy you are still alive? [Smile]' I was disappointed that I only stayed for a month and blamed myself. Even so, the previous night I extracted the final piece of revenge by walking furiously – running almost – for two hours during the evening around Lefkosha, just to make that nasty, fat policeman at the lobby – the one who had told on my Cypriot friends when they came – follow me. It was because of the stupid joke that I was now leaving. Or, perhaps, he had decided it was time to see how far I was prepared to go. I had come this far. Filled in an entry form. Crossed a Dead Zone. Taken photos for them. Would I go all the way to the other side? It was time to see exactly where I stood.

We stood a step away from the Dead Zone. Levent Bey spoke gently: 'I'm sad to see you go, Yiannaki. I really got to like you here. Who am

I going to tease now? [Smile] And I really started to believe in you. You are beginning to understand what happened and let go of all the Greek Cypriot propaganda. You are not the same as when you came.' I replied that I too was very sad to go before I finished my research, and I apologized once more for the joke. His eyes sparkled. Something was coming.

'You know, Yiannaki, there may just be a way,' he said as I stood one step from the Dead Zone, having lost all hope:

> You are clever and know a lot about the two sides. You see how overworked I am. I have been looking for years for someone to help me. For someone who speaks good Greek and who can help me with the newspapers. [Here it comes!] All I need is someone to read the Greek Cypriot press and cut out what should be translated. You'll just spend a couple of hours in an office each morning and then you are free to do your research alone as you please. Complete freedom. No one will ever know about this either on this or the other side. It's nothing serious, and we do it anyway. If you don't, someone else will.

I was lost for words. How should I react? I was angry, but I did not want to show it. I was still under his authority, a step away from the Dead Zone. There might still be a chance. But this? 'Thank you for the offer, but it is impossible for me to do this. If you want to let me stay, because you feel that I truly came to hear what Turkish Cypriots have to say, then do it.' I waited with faint hope. 'Then it's goodbye, Yiannaki. I don't hold this against you. It's OK. Try to come again and I'll help. But in the end it's not up to me. Take care when you get across, be careful with what you say. Regards to your family.' I took a step into the Dead Zone.

ACROSS THE DEAD ZONE

I was now walking the other way round: from Lefkosha (which once also used to be Lefkosia), towards Lefkosia (which once also used to be Lefkosha). I was feeling heavy, not just because of the extra body weight. Not even with the extra weight of books and pamphlets from the Public Information Office in my bag. I felt upset for not having been able to stay longer, but pleased that now I would be able to see my girlfriend, family and friends freely; sad for all the misery I was carrying inside me and in my notes; angry for all the things Greek Cypriots had never told me; those that even my own father had not explained properly; and for those that my Stepfather did not allow me to hear on the Turkish Cypriot side. Still, whenever I got angry with my Stepfather, I couldn't help thinking of the incident with the little girl and his life in Greece. Had I turned into a traitor then, by taking photos and in other ways? I felt betrayed by the things Greek Cypriots had never told me. Perhaps, that was how traitors were created: they first had to be betrayed. At that point, I did not even know that in a few days I would hear myself talk just like my Stepfather. More than anything I was ashamed. But what had I done? What was I responsible for?

I had often felt ashamed of being a Greek Cypriot. Now I was feeling ashamed of Turkish Cypriots. Even if I was sad for what they went through, I was angry with them. I was ashamed of the way they insisted only on their misery and refused to see that of the Greek Cypriots. For doing exactly what they accused the other side of: obliterating their pain, reducing it to mere propaganda.

I passed by the Turkish flag and the posters presenting information about Cyprus… no, presenting propaganda… this was not right either. I passed by the posters presenting their views… still not good enough, presenting the official Turkish Cypriot view – that was the best I could do. I passed by, this time without glancing at them. They were so familiar by now. There was an additional reason why I no longer wanted to look at such things. It had to do with what Turkish Cypriots had done at the Museum of Barbarism.

As I kept walking, the voices in Turkish were fading away while those in Greek were becoming threatening and loud. I was heading towards Lefkosia. But I would never be able to go back to that place called Lefkosia. It could never be just Lefkosia again.

CHAPTER FOUR
LEFKOSHA/LEFKOSIA
APRIL 1991–JANUARY 1992

ACROSS THE DEAD ZONE

I walked once more past the bullet holes of the wounded Ledra Palace Hotel until I saw the Greek flag ahead of me. Its presence there now seemed such an affront to Turkish Cypriots. Yet how my Stepfather must have loved it! I walked past the Greek Cypriot posters presenting our... no, presenting the Greek Cypriot official view. I did not look at them. I walked towards the Greek Cypriot police checkpoint. I had never noticed anything interesting about it. But from now on, after having been to the Turkish Cypriot side, I had something to compare with. I noted how small it was, a shabby temporary structure, compared to the large, concrete checkpoint on the other side. One side saw the Dead Zone as temporary, the other as permanent. On the Greek Cypriot side, the Dead Zone was marked by barbed wire that could easily be removed, whereas on the other walls had been built in the middle of the road.

ARRIVAL ON THE GREEK CYPRIOT SIDE

At the checkpoint I explained that my stay on the other side was over. I was told to wait. I protested that I felt tired and wanted to go home.

'You'll see, we have orders,' was the short ask-no-more-and-do-as-you-are-told reply of the officer in charge. I had not anticipated what was awaiting me, my welcoming reception as a potential spy, though in retrospect I was surprised by my lack of foresight. Especially given the offer that had been made to me only a few minutes ago.

The welcoming committee caught me by surprise when they arrived in what I thought then was an ordinary civilian car. It was only when the Dead Zone became my real home that I would learn to recognize the cars and faces instantly. But that would come years later when I would live in the place where, like me, everyone was a potential spy or traitor. 'You are coming with us to the police station,' I was informed by a man in civilian clothes. At the police station I was shown a chair to sit on, as three men stood around me and started to fire questions. I had to turn my head each time to be able to face the person asking, leaving me exposed to the eyes of the others, unable to see what they were doing, or their expressions.

'So what is your name? OK, yes we know it is Yiannis Papadakis. Well, Yiannaki, tell us now, did you see Turkish soldiers standing with guns over Turkish Cypriots?' 'N...no,' I stuttered, 'that I did not see.' 'Is the place full of Turkish army then?' 'There are quite a lot of soldiers around, more than one would notice here, b...but because here we are more...' 'How are they oppressing the Turkish Cypriots?' 'I did not see them actually oppressing them... but I felt that many did not like them, well maybe they want the army for protect...' 'Did they mistreat you?' 'No, I was staying in a hotel, Saray Hotel in Lefkosh... in Lefkosia... in occupied Lefkosia.' 'Did they force you to sign anything, anything at all?' To that I replied with confidence. 'No.' 'Not even the entry form?' 'NO.' 'Who did you meet?' 'I tried to meet with people who used to live in Tahtaka... kallas.' 'What did they tell you?' 'A lot of them described how they left in 1963, their lives in the enclaves and...' 'Did you believe their propaganda?' 'Well... actually... I think...' 'Did you or didn't you? Just tell us. Didn't you tell them the truth?' 'Yes of course,' I said with more confidence now, 'I tried to explain what 1974 meant for us...' 'Who was in charge of you and accompanied you there? They didn't allow you to speak to them freely on your own, did they?' 'No,' I said beaming with pride because now I had a chance to re-establish my slipping patriotic credentials. 'There was a man called Levent Bey in charge of me who...' 'Levent, that sneaky fox, eh? What can you tell us about Levent, their top spy? You know he works with MIT, the Turkish secret services. That he is a fanatic Pan-Turkist, not a true Cypriot, not even a Turk, but a

Muslim from Thrace, don't you?' I was in trouble here. Should I betray my Stepfather? What if he could somehow learn that I had said things about him to our secret services? It was their job to know things like that and to have informers inside the other side's secret services. 'Well, I kind of guessed this because he speaks *kalamaristika*, but I don't have any proof of where he comes from.' 'Any more things you can tell us about him?' 'No, I can't think of anything now.' 'OK, Yiannaki, you may go now. Give us your address and we'll call you a taxi. One last thing, what are you carrying in your bag?'

I froze, afraid that they would ask to see my notes from the interviews, where I had also included a lot of personal thoughts about both sides. Even worse, I was carrying publications from the Turkish Cypriot Public Information Office, photos of the mass graves and the Museum of Barbarism that now felt like incriminating evidence. To top it all, I had a book with me personally signed by Levent Bey with a dedication: 'To my Stepson Yiannaki, with Best Wishes for a Successful Research in the Quest for the Truth about Cyprus.' And he had written this in Greek.

I refused to let them see what I had. 'Yiannaki, do you mind leaving them here with us, just for a couple of days? We promise we won't lose anything and we will return them to you soon. Matters of national interest you see. You may have overlooked to tell us something which will be of use for the country and the nation.' 'I am afraid that is absolutely out of the question. These are my own things, *academic* things that belong to me. Even on the other side they did not ask this.' (That should do the trick.) 'Are you sure? OK, suit yourself, Mr Papadakis. We are not like them on the other side who work by force.' (Worked!) I was free to go at last. I found the whole encounter daunting. Why did I feel so guilty? How was it that they would always make me feel guilty? My only consolation came a few moments later as, in the back of the taxi, I jotted down all the things I had been asked. I had the distinct feeling that someone in the police station was probably writing up his own notes too.

FURTHER QUESTIONING

'Do they have a life there? Do they have food? Cinemas? Are they oppressed by the Turkish army? Did they treat you well? You seem to have put on weight. What did they tell you about us? Did they tell you how well we used to live together? Do they all want to return?'

Everybody in Tahtakallas had questions when I returned. But it was so hard to reply. Even when it came to things I thought I understood, it was still difficult because of the fear of how people would react. My replies felt cumbersome, complicated and defensive.

'They have food and cinemas but they are not as rich as we are.' Now I had to use 'we'. Neither 'you', nor 'Greek Cypriots' would do. 'But they often compare this with how they lived before 1974, especially from 1963 to 1967 when they were in the enclaves, and they are grateful for what they have now.' Some became suspicious. 'Yiannaki, don't tell me you got carried away by their propaganda? That you believed what they told you? It was the presence of the policemen with you that made them say these things. That proves that they are not free.' For everything I said, actually for everything Turkish Cypriots had told me that I now repeated, a refutation was readily available.

I began to hear whispers again. 'So they did tell you about these things. Of course they would, why not? After what they went through. After what we, no not us, they, our fanatics did to them. We don't like to talk much about these things over here. But we will have to face up to them eventually.' These were in Greek, the others had been in Turkish, but they spoke the same language. I could feel lines drawn around me. Some left me out, others embraced me; some placed me on one side of the Dead Zone, some on the other; and a few neither here nor there.

If I tried to press my – their – point harder, it could be disastrous. 'They went through real suffering, you know. They too have refugees, they had refugees in 1963 like the people who left Tahtakallas in 1963, they too have missing persons, dead and...' I stopped myself short. What I was saying sounded familiar. I was beginning to talk like Levent Bey. People pointed this out at once. 'Yiannaki, be careful, you are beginning to talk like Denktash.' It was the strangest feeling. The more someone rejected what I said, insisting that she knew everything that was happening on the other side, the more I talked like their official propagandists. Then I felt that I was forcibly catapulted across the Dead Zone, made to argue as if I was standing on the other side. But there was no way around it. I would have to tell people what I thought, what I had heard, what they had told me. Or else, I would feel ashamed for having betrayed the Turkish Cypriots, even some Greek Cypriots. I tried to be straightforward, and in return I felt that people became more honest with me, whether they liked me or not.

Some became angry and shouted. 'After all we went through, they complain? The people who took our homes?' But there were also whispers. 'We did bad things to them when we were in control. I can't forget that man boasting how he shot a Turkish Cypriot boy. "He would have grown up to be a snake that would one day bite us, to become a Turk," he said. I wanted to say something but I didn't. But don't write this.' Others insisted the opposite:

> You must write these things. Just don't write my name. About people boasting about what they were doing to the 'dirty dogs', the Turks. I tried to say something, and the answer was like 'What, you are with them?' and the gun would turn and point at me. So we had to bite our tongues. Shame on them who did these things, and on us who kept silent and did not do more to stop them.

From that time on the accusation of treachery, though rarely expressed to my face, followed me like a shadow. I heard that the young man, the proud Hellene, who was angry with me before I crossed, now called me 'Yiannis the Turk'.

INFECTIONS

I noticed that something had happened to my hearing and eyesight. Many Greek Cypriots, myself too, were worried that I might have been contaminated by my visit. Not just by poisoned food, but poisoned words: propaganda.

Things now looked different. 'Kofinou – Central Slaughterhouse': I had often driven past this sign to the village of Kofinou and the slaughterhouse. It had meant nothing to me. But that was before I went to Lefkosha. For Turkish Cypriots the place name seeped memories of their dead. A clash had taken place there during the 1960s in which many Turkish Cypriots died. It took a society very confident in its collective amnesia to put a sign like this on the island's busiest road. But the whole of Cyprus was such a place; almost any site carried within itself the memory of an atrocity, a mass grave, a rape. And what applied to space, applied to time. Any date could be special, a birthday, a death-day, an anniversary. People on each side only remembered theirs, the rest were just days.

Things also sounded different. Say someone said: 'We used to live well with the Turkish Cypriots. I had this boy working for me...' Before crossing, what I heard was: 'We used to *live well* with the Turkish Cypriots, I had this boy working for me...' Now, I heard this: 'We used to live well with the Turkish Cypriots, I had this boy *working for me...*'

My ears hurt when I heard certain things. Sometimes they hurt from the sheer volume of things said to drown out the voices I had carried over. Usually, it was small things said in passing, but they hurt as much. Like when grandfather Kyriakos was telling a fairy tale to his granddaughter: 'And so the handsome prince asked for beautiful women to come to the palace so he could choose the one he would marry. He could marry any princess from any place, except a Turk.' Mrs Elisavet described a fight many years ago with her Greek Cypriot neighbour: 'I went out of my mind with anger. I called her a thief, and I called her a whore and I even called her a Turk.' Mr Constantinos remembered how naughty the man, now passing in front of us, was thirty years ago as a boy. 'Now you see him serious, established and well dressed. But he was such a nasty thing when he was a boy that people called him "the Turk".' Mrs Hara spoke well of Katiris, the Turkish Cypriot old man living among them. 'He only shops from me. Such a faithful customer. He is a good man, Yiannaki, even if he is a crazy Turk.' I knew how much my Stepfather would have appreciated these. As I wrote them down, I now heard inside my head the sinister 'clip, clip' of my Stepfather's scissors. I wondered whether he had been successful in his proposal after all.

Mr Yiorgos remembered how he had been captured and tortured by the Turks back in the 1821 Greek Revolution. He was an old man – not that old of course – and a supporter of left-wing AKEL (Uprising Party of the Working People):

> I was standing like that saying 'Come and get me you infidel Turks if you dare, I am not afraid of you.' And then when they got me, I said the poem:
>
> See what time death has chosen
>
> to come and take me.
>
> Now that the branches are blossoming
>
> and grass is growing on the earth.
>
> That is how the school play ended, you see. In those days, it was school plays all the time. We had to do them on every national day. But even then, well before the days of the EOKA troubles and with the Turks, I did not like those plays. You see where my house is, next door to the Turks of Tahtakallas. Then most of my friends were Turks. So I didn't like the things we were learning at school. What

did those things have to do with my friends Ersen and Ibrahim – may God rest their souls, they are dead now I heard. I wish I could have gone to their funeral. Anyway, why were they making us hate them? My family was poor and both my parents worked together with Turks all the time.

How did people change the way they saw their friends? How did chasms appear that denied any common humanity? Mr Yiorgos pointed to the two educational systems in Cyprus:

We can't always blame outsiders. 'The British and their Divide and Rule.' We were creating hatred in our own schools. Same in both communities. We both created divisions. Yes, what the British did *sparked* the violence. Everyone says that. They lit the spark and built on the divisions we had already created. But we had already spread the gunpowder on the ground ourselves.

I heard similar thoughts often when I sat at Orfeas, the local left-wing coffee shop. 'The two educational systems infected the young ones with their propaganda and hatred.'

WEATHER FORECASTS, DWARF ELEPHANTS AND THE CYPRUS PROBLEM

Weather forecasts in Cyprus did not just tell the weather, I now noted. They expressed positions on the Cyprus Problem. 'The Flag', the Turkish Cypriot TV channel, broadcast a daily news bulletin in Greek for the enlightenment of Greek Cypriots. During the weather forecast, they gave temperatures only in towns in the north, where no Greek Cypriots lived. The towns were called by their Turkish names. On the Greek Cypriot side, RIK, the state TV station, used a map of Cyprus without a dividing line, but only mentioned the temperatures in the south. Other Greek Cypriot channels, right-wing private ones, regarded this as unpatriotic. They also showed temperatures in the north to make the point that those areas too belonged to Greek Cypriots.

Maps in Cyprus, as elsewhere, were a political instrument. I remembered the map of Greece – not of Cyprus – at school. In order for Cyprus to appear in the map of Greece, it was cut and placed in a box next to Crete. I only became aware of this when I first saw Turkish Cypriot maps. Geography, politically speaking, sided with the Turkish Cypriots. No need to cut and paste to include Cyprus in the map of

Turkey. Greek Cypriot maps showing Cyprus in the world at large always extended westwards, positioning Cyprus in a European context. They never showed Cyprus in the Middle East or Africa. The problem with the 'Cyprus in Europe' maps was that bits of Africa, the Middle East, and – sadly – Turkey were visible. One such map by the Greek Cypriot Public Information Office presented such undesirable bits as blank. The biggest challenge was to make a map of Cyprus that included Greece but not Turkey. The map shown as background during the news on The Word, the Church channel, managed best, with Turkey obscured by mist, as if the weather conditions had rendered it invisible. There were, however, special cases when Cyprus was shown in an exclusively eastern context. A shop in Lefkosia, for example, sensationally advertised itself as 'The Largest Darts Shop in the Middle East'.

Turkish Cypriot political parties employed different maps of Cyprus during election campaigns. The left-wing CTP, which favoured reunification, used a map of the whole of Cyprus with no line dividing it in green – neither blue nor red. The right-wing pro-division UBP showed only the northern part of Cyprus – in red of course – with the south having completely vanished. The standard official practice on both sides was to show Cyprus whole in outline but with the other side blank.

Despite the political advantages that the map offered to Turkish Cypriots, they still tried to improve their lot. A map in their history schoolbook showed lines extending from Cyprus to indicate distances. The line joining it to the south coast of Turkey, the nearest possible point, was just a few kilometres. The line joining it to Greece went hundreds of kilometres, to Athens, not to the nearest Greek island.

If maps were on the side of Turkish Cypriots, earthquakes were politically on the side of Greek Cypriots, unlike dwarf elephants. A Turkish Cypriot book dealing with the last thirty years explained how Cyprus had thousands of years ago been a physical extension of Anatolia, later separated by an earthquake. (I remembered my friend Erkin in Turkey telling me that when he was a child he thought that it was Greek Cypriots who really cut Cyprus off from Turkey.) The mountain range of Girne was geologically speaking still an extension of the Toros mountains in Turkey. The book further stated that the millennia-old skeletons of dwarf elephants had been found both in Cyprus and in Anatolia. Greek Cypriots, of course, did not take this sitting down. A Greek Cypriot newspaper carried an almost triumphant article explaining how the fates of Cyprus and Greece were joined by a common seismic fault line.

TAHTAKALLAS OR TAKTAKALAS?

I looked at the large sign recently installed by the Greek Cypriot authorities: 'Taktakalas Settlement'. It was the first time I had seen the name spelled that way. Changing 'h' into 'k' and using only one 'l' made it sound less vulgar to Greek Cypriot ears, that is, less Turkish or Arabic. Perhaps the official hope was that people would more easily to move into Taktakalas than Tahtakallas.

After 1974, when Greek Cypriot refugees were asked to move into the houses Turkish Cypriots had abandoned in 1963, they were not pleased. Mrs Eftihia remembered vividly the first day they brought them to see the house they were to be allocated as refugees:

> I was so upset when I heard where they were going to put us. *Tahtakallas*. What kind of a name is that? It sounded horrible. When I came to see it for the first time, it was even worse. Not like now that they fixed the houses, and people moved in all around. It was in ruins then. Then I saw the mosque, it was in ruins too, like a stable, and we were going to live right next to it. And the houses were Turkish Cypriot. OK, they were big – you see what good houses we had the Turks living in before? – but we didn't like it here. Who would be crazy enough to come and live here next to the Dead Zone? All there is apart from us is a bunch of abandoned old people. We protested a lot. We tried to change the name but the government refused. Our case went high up in the Ministry of the Interior but they told us that we couldn't change place names because that's what the Turks were doing in our occupied areas.

But locals were proud of the name Tahtakallas. Many elderly ones shared a story about the area's name:

> The name means 'Wooden Tower'. In the old times, when we were ruled by the oppressive Turks, our brave young men stood guard during the nights. They stacked their wooden clubs one on top the other, making them look like a small wooden wall. This is how the area got its name. In those days, the Turks could simply come in the middle of the night and kill people. Or come after young girls. In those times, when a Christian wanted to marry, the woman was forced to sleep with the Turkish lord first.

I heard the same story from many different mouths. It seemed like a common memory from the distant past, each version confirming the others. When I asked how they knew the story, however, a different picture emerged: 'Oh, we heard it from Mrs Marianna, she knows everything about the area's history.' I asked Mrs Marianna:

> Yes, I told them the story and that's how everyone knows it. I personally heard it from the mouth of the most important folklorist of Cyprus. He was the man who created the discipline of Cypriot folklore studies. In fact, he was a teacher from Greece who came here to teach students about the glory of Greece and our Greek identity. He also collected a lot of material on folklore, including many stories, like this, on how the Turks used to oppress us in the past.

I wondered if Turkish Cypriots had ever heard the story, and what they would have made of it.

AKRITIC PARISHES

The day of the annual fair of Tahtakallas came. It was called 'The Fair of the Akritic Parishes'. This was an effort to gather funds for local charities. It was the only fair I had come across in Cyprus, on the Greek Cypriot side rather, that was not named after a local saint. The present day *Akrites* were demanding from others recognition of their debt to them. If it weren't for them, they said, the Turks would have taken over the area, and, given their insatiable expansionism, the rest of Lefkosia. So others had a duty to support them.

I had previously assumed that the area must have taken this name after 1974 because I had assumed that the Dead Zone was born in 1974. 'It was in 1968 that we started this fair with this name,' said Mrs Maria. 'In fact, we have been *Akrites* since 1963 because the dividing line cut across this area. In those times, we had to defend ourselves from the mania of the Turks of Cyprus, now from the Turks of Turkey.' So, then they were 'Turks' too, neither 'Turkish Cypriots' nor 'brothers'.

When I began my research, everyone told me that they had consciously chosen to stay in the Akritic Parishes for 'national reasons', to protect and save Lefkosia. That was what they still told journalists. But as time went by, I noted a gradual shift in what they told me. Doubts were first expressed about other people. 'Don't believe them, Yiannaki, when they say they stayed for patriotic reasons. They just live here because they have nowhere else to go.' And later: 'Look, Yiannaki, I don't really have anywhere else to go. With my pension it would be impossible to rent anything. I'm stuck here all alone in this damp old house.'

Still, I often felt that they would not have liked to live elsewhere. In Tahtakallas, the presence of so many old people meant that they shared the same problem: loneliness. The solution was close at hand. They kept each other company, and because they had grown up with many of those living around, they had many things in common to talk and reminisce about. They sat together in the sidewalks of narrow roads that now led nowhere. They had turned them into narrow gardens, full of pots that sometimes made it onto the blue-and-white army checkpoints. Better to be there, I thought, than isolated in a block of flats somewhere.

Loneliness was also one reason for the presence of so many cats. 'She's my baby,' Mrs Eva said, pointing to a ginger cat, 'and every night when I go to bed she comes and looks me in the eyes. It's like we talk to each other. I do talk to her and I'm sure she understands.' When it came to some of the oldest and more disabled people, the cats had taken over the house. The people became guests, not the other way around. In Katiris' poor home, the cats ruled and would frequently eat his sparse food.

Sometimes I envied those cats because they could cross any time. I knew that there were other lonely old people, just across the street, so far away on the other side. Some of them were old neighbours. I suspected that some cats had two homes and two feeding places.

Loneliness must also have been one of the reasons people wanted my company. The more we spoke together, the more I understood how memories came from the past like faraway voices, indistinct whispers that people formed into thoughts through their own firm voices. As I compared stories from the two sides, I came to see how the faint voices from the past were transformed into echoes of their current thoughts and desires.

The old Tahtakallites lived in the company of ghosts: those who had left but were not completely gone. Numerous other marginal beings also lived there in the area. Many destitute people, Greek Cypriots, migrant workers from Syria, Egypt and Pakistan could only afford to live there. The prostitutes had been born into multiple margins of poverty, abuse, gender and migration. And there were some Turkish Cypriots around. Of all those living on the edges, these were the ones who most concerned the Greek Cypriot authorities, who wanted to remove them from the area.

TAKTAKALAS REFUGEE SETTLEMENT

'We are all foreigners here,' Mrs Eftihia, an elderly woman from the Taktakalas Refugee Settlement, explained. 'We don't know each other. We come from different villages. What do we have in common to talk about? Nothing. No one here knows about my village and its people.' The houses of the refugee settlement had been recently renovated but the paint was peeling off and no one seemed to care enough to repaint them. The houses were not theirs. The government did not give them ownership, fearing that the Turkish Cypriot authorities could then argue that there was nothing wrong when they gave away titles of Greek Cypriot houses. The Greek Cypriot refugees' real homes were in the north. Until they reclaimed them, they were not allowed to have homes. For the time being, they were permitted to live nowhere, neither here nor there.

Even if locals and refugees shared a common loneliness they did not mingle much. 'I really tried to sit and talk with them when we first came,' Mrs Eftihia pondered:

> But what could we talk about? They spoke about their own things, about all the people they knew, about what had happened in their lives, about people who used to live here, people who died. What could I say? Nothing. We had no common memories. Sitting with them made me feel worse. It made me feel twice a refugee, all alone, away from home and with no one to talk to. I wish I could explain to them why it's difficult to join them, but only a refugee can understand a refugee.

So what about the other refugees? They were no good either, because they came from different villages. The only thing that joined them was belonging somewhere else, but this was a different place for each one. Couldn't they have made the Settlement their home by now, twenty years later? Officially, no. It would amount to treason. Their true homes were in the north. They were commanded not to forget and condemned to a lonely life in exile. The photographs of their old villages shown on Greek Cypriot TV showed them as they used to be, never in their present state. Even the children of Greek Cypriot refugees were asked at school to talk to parents and grandparents about their 'real' home, which they had never seen, and then write essays about it.

Right next to the Taktakalas Refugee Settlement, I met an elderly couple living in a crumbling rented house. 'We were twice refugees,' they bitterly pointed out:

We left our homes before 1960 when there was violence here, and again in 1964 when the place we had moved to became a Turkish Cypriot enclave. But our government never gave us any help, as if we were not refugees. Only the 1974 refugees get brand new houses. We don't count as refugees. Make sure you write about these injustices.

So who were the refugees of Cyprus? Opinions were divided. For Greek Cypriot officials 'the refugees' were the Greek Cypriots who left their homes in 1974. Greek Cypriots did not regard the Turkish Cypriots who had left their homes in the 1960s as refugees but as people who willingly conspired to destroy the Republic of Cyprus by creating enclaves. They were 'mutineers' and the 1960s conflict was called 'the Turkish mutiny'. Not even 'the Turkish Cypriot mutiny'. A more refined version of the argument was that the Turks did not really want to leave, since the people had always peacefully coexisted, but were brutally forced to by their own leadership. Even in this version they could not count as refugees, because Greek Cypriots did not want to admit there were problems before 1974.

The Greek Cypriots who left their homes due to the inter-ethnic violence during the 1960s, some even in the late 1950s, were not refugees but were officially designated as *Tourkoplihtoi* ('those struck by the Turks'), a word that implied a natural calamity, as in 'struck by an earthquake'. If the problem began in 1974, there could be no refugees before then.

The Turkish Cypriot authorities took a different view. Their refugees had been the Turkish Cypriots displaced during the 1960s. Then there were those who left after 1974. But neither group could be called refugees now, since they now lived in their true and only homeland. Except in one case. When Greek Cypriots demanded a solution that would allow all Greek Cypriots to return, Turkish Cypriot officials replied aghast: 'You can't possibly expect us to make our people refugees a third time?'

Officially, Turkish Cypriots had to forget their old homes in the south. Talk of a past life in the south with Greek Cypriots could only include the bad times. Now they lived in their homeland. To become a homeland, it had to be rapidly provided with their memories. Their own ghosts came to populate the land as those of others were exorcized. The land was baptized anew as the others' presences were cleansed away. New memorials and statues were erected, heroes inhabited street-names, and Turkish place names were used everywhere.

Both sides had a sad record, when it came to the political management of ghosts. Turkish Cypriots who moved to the north were housed as communities. People from one village in the south were settled together in the north. Thus the authorities placed their people, and their accompanying joint stock of ghosts, together in one community, at the same time as prohibiting them from talking of the place that linked them, except in negative terms. Greek Cypriot refugees had spiritually to stay put in their homes in the north, but in reality were placed with people from different villages. These policies denied what both governments claimed to defend as a fundamental human right: the right to choose one's home in the present and to choose how to think about one's home in the past.

THE CIA

'TURKISH CYPRIOT STABBED CO-RACER AND DISAPPEARED' was the headline of a front-page article in a Greek Cypriot newspaper. The article was about two Turkish Cypriots who chose to make the Greek Cypriot side their home. This was a moderate newspaper. I checked to see how a right-wing paper reported this: 'MURDER ATTEMPT OF TURKISH CYPRIOT BY ANOTHER TURKISH CYPRIOT IN LEMESOS ... He has repeatedly troubled the police in incidents of fighting, drunken behaviour and for causing trouble... The other had previously been arrested for spying...'

I wanted to find out more. Who could know? Katiris perhaps. I found him alone as usual, sitting in his favourite spot with cats rubbing against his feet. The dirt covering the floor had formed a small pile, like hard-set mud, which he used to rest his feet on. He was short and ordinary chairs did not allow his feet to reach the ground. He welcomed me warmly as usual and we lit cigarettes together. I asked him about the events in Lemesos. He knew the family well and said that he had heard it on the news. He had the radio tuned to a Greek Cypriot channel that morning. Other times, he listened to sad Turkish songs on a Turkish Cypriot channel.

As we were talking, three men entered without knocking. His posture became one of submissive politeness even before a word was spoken. I looked at them, they looked at me, in mutual surprise and suspicion. It took me a few seconds to understand who they were, as I had not yet learned to recognize them. They belonged to the Cyprus Intelligence Agency.

They were in their early thirties. They did not bother to introduce themselves but asked who I was, what my business there was, and about my relationship with Katiris. They were surprised and interested when I told them. One of them took my phone number and said he would call me later. He spoke Turkish to Katiris. It was the first time I had come across someone his age on the Greek Cypriot side who spoke Turkish. Later when I enquired, I found out that the only people now who learned Turkish were from this special branch of the secret police. He asked Katiris if he knew anything about the stabbing, if he had seen anyone around, or if they had come through his place. Katiris politely replied that he did not. 'Yes Sir, if anyone comes around I'll let you know, Sir'. Stupidly, I too said something in Turkish. On their way out they muttered and looked at me suspiciously.

'They come and see me every now and then and I give them information,' Katiris explained:

> Many people come to stay with me, sometimes it's 'crazy Turks' like me, other times poor foreign workers who don't have a place to stay. If this man who did the stabbing came here, I would tell the CIA because I don't want any more killings. If I know something I tell them, but they never say they got their information from me. I have to do it, otherwise they say they'll kick me out of here.

I began to take note of newspaper articles about Turkish Cypriots living on the Greek Cypriot side. The right-wing press was especially fond of this topic. For example, 'The authorities believe that it may be Turkish Cypriot renegades, acting as instigators under instructions of the Turkish Cypriot pseudo-state, who tried to burn the mosque in the free areas in order to create tension.' Turkish Cypriots living on the Greek Cypriot side mostly appeared as troublemakers, spies or saboteurs.

In my own way, I understood how that must have felt. On another visit to Katiris, I encountered the three policemen who had interrogated me when I crossed back to the Greek Cypriot side. Their usual work was to check on the few Turkish Cypriots who had crossed to the Greek Cypriot side.

INVISIBLE PEOPLE

After Katiris and the CIA, I checked if other Turkish Cypriots lived in the area. Most people said there weren't any. Others were vague: 'I think there is a man living there in that house but I am not sure.' Very few people knew about them – and this in a neighbourhood where everyone knew everyone. By then I had been doing research there for almost a year and had never heard about them. Unlike Katiris, who everyone knew, the rest preferred to live unobserved.

Ziyat Bey was in his early sixties and I had previously seen him sitting outside his house. I had said 'Good morning' in Greek and he had replied in Greek. When I discovered that he was a Turkish Cypriot, I went over to talk to him. Initially he was reluctant. 'I can't. I have serious blood pressure problems, and sugar problems, diabetes, so please leave me alone.' But another day, when we exchanged greetings he invited me for coffee and we started talking.

> The sugar… the blood pressure… Mr Yiannaki, if you knew what I went through. I used to live here and when everyone left in 1964 I decided to stay. The children, your children, threw bricks at my house. They called me names: 'crazy Turk', 'dog-Turk', and more. It was hell. That's when I began to get ill. So I went to the other side and there I was a traitor again because I had stayed on this side. They did not leave me alone either. I tell you, and I know because I've lived on both sides, it is the exact same shit here and the same shit there. Finally, I decided to come back here after 1974. Wrong decision too. All the time I'm in the wrong place. The story of my life. Well, here it's not that bad. I get some pension money and get by quietly. But listen to what your people did to me one day. I was sitting over there at the kebab place, Orfeas, near the Dead Zone, where I would go just to find someone to talk to, and two young guys came up to me in front of everyone: 'What are you doing here?' I replied that I was just eating my kebab. 'But you are a Turk. You cannot come here so close to the Dead Zone. Opposite you are our soldiers and you can see them. We don't want to see you here ever again.' You understand, Mr Yiannaki? They were from your secret police. They accused me of spying, in front of everyone. I was so ashamed. Even some of your people looked away when this happened and I could tell they felt bad. After that I was in the hospital for a week. And I never went to sit there again. All I do is sit here alone on my front-step. I tell you that it is exactly the same shit on this side like on the other side.

Later I found out that many Turkish Cypriots on the Greek Cypriot side had rented places in Old Nicosia because it was cheap and there were other Turkish Cypriots around. The issue of spying had then been raised at the highest levels and the government had offered them extra money for rent as long as they moved away from the border.

Hristoulla lived in a single dark room behind a shop. It was difficult to tell her age. Late forties, perhaps. Her name came from Hristos, 'Christ'. Her room had a single window high in the ceiling and when I went to see her the light entered through the window like a golden beam in the dark room, illuminating her as she sat on the bed. All around, staring from the shadows were crude brown wax replicas of babies hanging from the walls with beans, 'black-eyed beans', for eyes. They were Christian Orthodox votive offerings placed in the church by people who had asked the help of God. The place had an eerie voodoo-like feeling. The Greek Cypriot grocer opposite had told me that a Turkish Cypriot woman lived there. 'She is a kind of a crazy witch. She reads your fortune in the coffee cup. You can't imagine how many of our young women come and pay her for this. But it's all lies, isn't it?'

Hristoulla told me that she was baptized Christian and had chosen the name herself. 'I believe in your Christ and pray to him. That's why I put all these votive offerings on the walls.' She spoke of a child she had had with a Danish man, but she had not seen her son for years. She showed me the photo of a smiling blond boy. The father took him away to Denmark and did not contact her again. 'Every now and then I have to go to the psychiatric hospital for my injection,' she said. 'Sometimes they keep me inside for a while but then they let me out again. There they don't use my name. They call me "the Turkish woman" [*i Tourtzissa*].'

The next time, Hristoulla told me a story about love. I sat on the chair as the light-beam falling from the window above moved over her face, changing colours with the setting sun, until the room got dark. It was about a young Turkish Cypriot woman she met at the psychiatric hospital. A young Greek Cypriot man had been in love with her since long before she entered the hospital. She loved him too:

> He loved her so much, Yiannaki. He saw her withering away and disappearing, leaving this world day by day in the hospital. He loved her so much that he took her out one day, secretly, and brought her right to the Dead Zone. He showed her the way, they kissed, and he told her to cross and never come back. That is how much he loved her.

Becoming inconspicuous like Ziyat was one way Turkish Cypriots chose to become invisible. Changing names like Hristoulla was another.

Gradually, I met more Turkish Cypriots living on the Greek Cypriot side. Some were young, fairly established with good jobs. They chose names to render their children invisible, names like Jan (Soul) or Deniz (Sea) that sounded like the English John and Denis. A young woman I met later first told me her name was July. As she got to know me, it became Guly and finally, only after she trusted me enough, she told me she was Gul, the Turkish word for Rose.

It was not easy for Turkish Cypriots to live among Greek Cypriots. In theory all was fine. But when it came to real persons now living among Greek Cypriots, the ever-present accusation of spying forced them to live as inconspicuously as possible. They had to become invisible, like real spies. In the end, they turned into what the newspapers made them: people living unseen among the Greek Cypriots.

ARMY MEMORIES

Panikkos who lived in Tahtakallas told me about the time he had served in the army when he was eighteen. He was stationed at a military outpost on the Dead Zone:

> We were here and they were there, and we could see each other all the time. I liked it, it was quiet and only a few steps from home. I could sneak out any time to eat at home. And I had a girlfriend who I was crazy in love with in the neighbourhood. Then one day we heard they were going to transfer us to another place far away, near Paphos. How would I see her? Just to get home would take three or four hours and who knows how rarely we would be home again. So, Nikos and I, who also lived around the corner decided to do something about it. We had found a couple of hand grenades lying around. They were not listed in the army book, no one knew about them, they were just spare it seemed. One day, I waited for the Turkish guard to go inside his concrete watch-post – I didn't want to hurt him you see, we knew each other well, we sometimes spoke – and then I threw the hand grenade right in the middle of the Dead Zone. BOOM, it went and then TAKA TAKA TAKA TAKA TAKA I started to spray around their watch-post with my gun. Their guy who was inside must have gone crazy but he was not hurt. I was aiming for the ground. There was mayhem. All our generals immediately rushed down on us with their stars on their shoulders. It became like the Milky Way here! They were going crazy. They wanted to know if war was breaking out. I told them

everything myself: 'The Turks threw the hand grenade just like that, without provocation. It exploded there in the middle of the Dead Zone. So we had to defend ourselves and started shooting. That scared them and kept them quiet.' So, we received an honorary citation for our brave defensive action, were given leave and as a reward they did not transfer us.

PARADE PROBLEMS

Military parades were the highlights of army life. They were presented on both sides as the ultimate show of unity and strength. All men marched in the same uniforms, to the same rhythm, in perfect coordination, in the same direction. The nation was shown as strong, united, equal, single-purposed and male. Men and machines blended into each other; their colours were similar; the guns became part of the body; the men half-protruding from the tanks appeared as an extension of the machine; the men, walking like robots, had become the perfect fighting machines. I had participated in one when I was in the army. I remembered how many weeks beforehand we had to practise and practise under the scorching sun. Then just before the event everything – boots, cars, guns, teeth – had to shine. The parades were presented as emblematic of military alertness and capability, in commentaries by politicians and TV announcers on both sides. 'Once more our soldiers have shown their high level of training and readiness to defend the country.' But dissenting voices were sometimes heard. Archbishop Golden-Mouth, present in the officials' stand next to the politicians never failed to embarrass them: 'Why do we only talk about defence? It is my personal hope that one day we will also talk of offence.'

That was not the real problem with parades. They were meant to be a show of strength, order and discipline as if soldiers were asked one day, out of the blue, to march and show off their skills; as if they had not been practising for weeks beforehand; as if the parade was not the opposite of real army life: disorder, favouritism, inefficiency, dissent and negligence. But parades were a show, a show of strength to raise morale and scare the other side.

This led to problems, especially when it came to the other side's parades. They had to be shown on TV in order to prove once more, as everyone knew, how aggressive, war-thirsty and provocative the enemy was. They had to be shown in order to warn the people against slumbering into warm self-assured rest, while the other side was amassing deadly armaments. The question was how do this without creating a scare?

The two sides found similar solutions. Only a few seconds were shown of the other side's parade. The Greek Cypriot solution was to show some quick shots of the other side's officials, tanks and guns followed by lengthy clips of the last section of the parade: grown-up men in funny red robes with tall silly hats, holding sticks with fake horse-tails, all bearing identical, large, masculine, plastic moustaches. The glorious Ottomans looked like a carnival show. The Turkish Cypriots' solution was similar as far as the quick first shots – officials, tanks and guns – went. They too focused on the small unit that ended the parade. Those were not ordinary soldiers, nor the elite units but the reserve civilians who were ordered to wear their uniforms and march each year, despite their frantic efforts to avoid it. They were not a pretty sight either, though they must have been to Turkish Cypriot eyes. Their military caps bounced somewhere among their fully grown hair, many of them had beards and moustaches of various styles, their marching was not coordinated, their lines were those a child would draw, and some grinned sweetly at the camera when it focused on their tired sweaty faces.

OLYMPIAKOS

Olympiakos was so keen on patriotic symbols that they overflowed onto the street. Olympiakos was the local right-wing coffee shop, aligned to DISY (Democratic Rally), the largest right-wing Greek Cypriot party, which controlled around a third of the votes. The walls of Olympiakos were full of Greek flags that reached out onto the balcony, and continued on lines to the wall across the street. Only Greek flags, not a single flag of Cyprus. Its walls were full of slogans in capitals: 'LONG LIVE THE NATION', 'LONG LIVE EOKA', 'LONG LIVE THE 25 MARCH 1821'. All around were large photographs of dead heroes of EOKA and images of Greek heroes from the 1821 uprising. A large photograph of Grivas, a leader of EOKA and later of EOKA B – the organization that had staged the 1974 coup – was hanging on the wall of a more private room. Displaying a photo of Grivas, whom many Greek Cypriots considered as the prime culprit for the 1974 tragedy, was a gesture of defiance against those who blamed Grivas and his Olympiakos supporters.

On the balcony, two large flags waved on wooden poles. Next to the blue-white Greek flag hung the green-black flag of Olympiakos.

Black symbolized mourning for living under a colonial yoke, and green stood for the hope of redemption and Union with Greece. The club had been founded as a cultural-athletic-educational club during the British colonial period. Its aim was to support ENOSIS in every possible way. According to the club's constitution, the colours of the flag were to change to blue and white, echoing those of the Greek flag, once ENOSIS was achieved. This brought to mind other stories of 'unfulfilled national aspirations' that Greek Cypriot school children knew well. The fish were frying when Constantinople fell, so they jumped half-cooked into the pond and will return to cook on the other side when the City becomes Greek once more; the king turned into a statue but will that day come back to life, and so on. The *nom de guerre* of Grivas, *Digenis*, also brimmed with historic associations. Digenis Akritas was the bravest of the *Akrites*.

'We were the front-bastion of Hellenism and resistance in Tahtakallas,' Mr Marios, an old member of Olympiakos proudly explained:

> We were the leaders of the anti-colonial struggle in the area, and some of our members died for EOKA. Not like the communists. I will say it openly, out of the teeth: the communists were traitors. They were against EOKA. First, our club was stoned by the communists in the forties, and later it was burnt by the Turks in the fifties. That was in 1958 and the British just stood there and watched the Turks jumping outside like rabid dogs rejoicing at the flames. Olympiakos is the *akritas* of Tahtakallas, the local bastion of resistance and Hellenism, here in *akritic* Cyprus, our island lying at the edge of Hellenism. In the 1960s we were the ones defending the area against the Turks during the Turkish mutiny. Yes, we defended the area in 1963, we fought against the Turks of Tahtakallas with machine-guns. I don't understand all this new talk about 'our Turkish Cypriot brothers'. When we fought them then, everyone was with us, everyone treated us like heroes. Now we are made to feel ashamed of those times.

Another day, after we had drunk a bit, he whispered: 'We fought for ENOSIS and we did not stop. That is why we did the Revolution. You see Makarios had betrayed ENOSIS and was behaving like an autocrat...' 'Revolution' was a word suggesting a noble cause that people of Olympiakos, especially the supporters of EOKA B, sometimes used among themselves for the coup. Others accused EOKA B, DISY

– the self-declared party of Hellenism where many of the coupists now belonged – and Olympiakos of being responsible for 1974.

But not everyone there agreed with Mr Marios. Mr Iakovos was sad when he spoke about EOKA, in which he had participated. 'That was a truly noble struggle. We were all so young then, so idealistic. We really were the cream of the youth. But later it all went so wrong when they used the name again. There was nothing noble in what the EOKA B coupists did in the name of EOKA.'

Hellenism was such a grand word the way Olympiakos supporters used it. It meant the unbroken continuity and existence of Greeks, from the ancient times through Byzantium to the present; the unity of Greek people living in Greece and outside; the historic fight against the barbaric expansionist Turk, who had belittled Hellenism from its rightful Byzantine Empire to its current small state. It was also used for something more specific: an absolution. Mr Constantinos made this clear. He was standing next to me as I explained what the Turkish Cypriots had told me. He became upset when he saw that some were nodding with sympathy. 'So this is what they told you then? But look at what the Turks did to us in Constantinople, in Smirni, every place that was historically ours where they slaughtered us and sent us away. Right here in Cyprus too.' As an afterthought he added:

> The Turk brutalized us here in 1974 and now we can't even say we
> are Greeks and we say they are our brothers. After all the history
> of killings by the Turk, we are now accused of having harmed a
> few Turks here. Our people now even blame us for the coup, which
> they say 'brought Turkey to Cyprus'. But the Turk always wanted
> to capture Cyprus. The Turk is expansionist and history proves
> this. They would have captured Cyprus anyway. The coup was just
> an excuse. A pretext.

Hellenism was a word he employed to suggest that the 'Turks of Cyprus' were part of the larger whole of 'the Turk', the historic aggressor, and deserved what they got. As for the coup, historic Turkish expansionism rendered it insignificant.

Some Olympiakos supporters did not want to talk to me after my return, in contrast to people who frequented another coffee shop a few metres away, who were now keener. Some of those who did not want to talk to me were people that Turkish Cypriots had mentioned by name. When the leader of DISY came to talk to Olympiakos, carnations decorated the podium. Their colour matched his name: Glafkos, meaning pale blue. But that was not the reason why they specially ordered blue carnations. Carnations were normally found in red and white. Red would have been doubly offensive. It was the colour of communists and the Turks. Blue was the colour of the Greek flag.

ORFEAS

As in many other neighbourhoods, Orfeas, the communists' coffee shop, was very close. In villages, the two politically opposed coffee shops were often opposite each other. One day the leader of AKEL, the largest left-wing Greek Cypriot party, one that like DISY controlled about a third of the votes, came to talk to his supporters in Orfeas. He never mentioned the word Hellenism. When *he* spoke of brothers, it was about Turkish Cypriots not Greeks. He spoke about his party's traditional cooperation and good relations with 'our Turkish Cypriot brothers and compatriots.' He referred to the history of cooperation between Turkish and Greek Cypriots, to the common workers' strikes and membership in the same unions when AKEL offered the major platform of cooperation. In the past, the party had been accused by the right of cooperation with 'the Turk', of treachery. But after 1974, when Greek Cypriots began to think of the past as one of peaceful coexistence and the idea of rapprochement emerged, AKEL was able to argue that it had always been in the forefront of such efforts.

When I spoke with members of Orfeas, they confirmed their leader's view about a peaceful past. Only in one part though, the one that was not whispered. 'We tried to get along well with Turkish Cypriots who lived here,' Mr Ilias said. 'We made them welcome in Orfeas, not like those of Olympiakos.' He lowered his voice. 'You know, they were the ones who were shooting the Turkish Cypriots in 1963 from the machine gun up on that house. I'm sure they told you all that on the other side.' Then he continued:

And in 1974 Olympiakos was the nest of the coupists, the followers of Grivas and the Greek junta. An EOKA B hotspot. Whereas AKEL supporters resisted, took arms against the coup and died during the resistance against the coupists. Members of EOKA B who were directly involved in the coup, and those who supported them like the people of Olympiakos, now try to forget about the coup. They don't like to talk about it. But they have not repented, they never asked for forgiveness. Some of them are now in top government jobs. Some have even become MPs. But you the young ones don't know who they were. Only those who lived through those times now remember the supporters of the junta by name and their dirty deeds.

AKEL supporters in Orfeas had a great deal to say about the coup: how the Olympiakos people were jubilant, how they roamed the streets brandishing guns and how afraid *they* were. 'You can't imagine, Yiannaki, what it meant to be an AKEL supporter during the coup,' Mr Kostas said:

> Even before, my son was in the army and suffered in the hands of the fascist *kalamarades*. In the coup we all thought our time had come. They went around dragging people out of their houses. They don't tell you this at school. Write it all down and write down what they did to the Turkish Cypriots even if they call us traitors. Even if they call you one day.

It was interesting to hear where some of them sought protection from EOKA B during the dangerous days of the coup:

> We sent our families elsewhere and then went to stay for a couple of nights with Turkish Cypriot friends in the Turkish sector of Nicosia. It seemed the safest place for a communist. But our Turkish Cypriot friends were really worried then that if the coupists prevailed, their turn would come.

The period of EOKA was as dangerous, if not more so, than that of EOKA B. All of them spoke with dread of what it meant to be a communist from the time of EOKA in the 1950s, through the period of the Greek junta, then EOKA B in the early 1970s up to 1974. When they spoke of EOKA, one story was always repeated, as well as one fact regarding Grivas:

> Everyone knows the story of the man who was stoned to death by the masked killers of EOKA. They tied him to a tree and stoned him to death because he was a communist, with no proof that he had done anything wrong. Maybe not everyone knows it now. You are young. But we AKEL people all do. EOKA killed so many communists they accused of treachery. Did you know that EOKA killed more Greek Cypriots than English? But what can you expect with Grivas as a leader? Everyone knew how he hated communists

even more than the Turks. During the German occupation of. Greece, he cooperated with the Germans by hunting down and handing in communists who fought in the Greek resistance against the German fascists.

Two coffee shops next to each other, the two largest Greek Cypriot political parties and two so different views of geography, history and identity. For DISY, Greek Cypriots were *Greek* Cypriots, for AKEL Greek *Cypriots*. Hellenes, Cypriot Hellenism, Greeks of Cyprus, Greek Cypriots, Cypriots: the DISY rank in order of preference. The reverse order applied for AKEL. Similar outlooks were echoed by the right and left among Turkish Cypriots. Right-wing parties on either side were joined by their identification with the mother-fatherland, by mutual hatred and by hatred of communism. Leftists on both sides were joined by their identification with Cyprus as Cypriots first, a past of cooperation, and the common experience of having been victimized by right-wing nationalists of both sides. I was beginning to sense another chasm in Cyprus, as serious perhaps as the Dead Zone, this time between left and right.

Leftists were also united by their manner of talking. They whispered. I often felt as though they whispered even when they spoke normally. The right had in common the use of high-sounding words. The walls of Olympiakos shouted with slogans, those of Orfeas were mute, devoid of symbols and pronouncements. Such large words of glory emerged from the material that history schoolbooks were made of: wars, fighting, deaths, heroes and enemies. These, it seemed, were the only possible ingredients of glory. It was not possible to use large words for 'small' everyday acts of goodwill, 'insignificant' workers' struggles, 'invisible' acts involving cooperation that cut across ethnic boundaries.

THE RISE OF YELLOW

In the beginning, all symbols were blue and white on the Greek Cypriot side – until yellow appeared. Before 1974, Greek Cypriot organizations like the Cyprus Broadcasting Corporation and Cyprus Airways used blue and white, the colours of the Greek flag, which was the only flag used at the time. Yellow was the main colour in the 1960 Republic of Cyprus flag, but this was despised as a symbol of defeat, the defeat of ENOSIS. After 1974 things changed, as the island was divided and ENOSIS was abandoned for good. Enthusiasm for ENOSIS had already begun to fade away with the rise of the Greek junta in 1967.

Independence emerged as the new aim, now meaning the reunification of Cyprus as a unitary sovereign state. The once scorned flag of the Republic of Cyprus re-emerged as the symbol of this state.

The anniversary of the 1960 independence was re-remembered by Greek Cypriots and officially instituted by government decree in 1979. Prior to that, it was not publicly commemorated. This explained why I was taken by surprise by the celebrations when I returned from my studies abroad. The date of the anniversary was moved from 16 August to 1 October, when the fact that schools were open would enhance its impact. Until then, the largest military parade had taken place on 28 October, a Greek national commemoration. Now this too was moved to 1 October, a Cypriot 'historical date' and a Cypriot commemoration. A Greek Cypriot commemoration, to be more precise.

Now the colour yellow crept into state symbols. After 1974, the flag of the Republic was added next to that of Greece on the Greek Cypriot side. This flag showed an orange-yellow map of Cyprus on a white background, over two crossing green olive branches. No one now remembered that it was a Turkish Cypriot who drew the flag Greek Cypriots would come to love, and Turkish Cypriots to detest. The 1960 Republic flag already spoke of conflict and the hope of reconciliation in a peaceful future. All its components, all its hopes were to be refuted by history. White stood for purity and honesty. The map of Cyprus was the map of a united island. The two crossing olive branches symbolized the two communities coexisting peacefully, intertwined in the management of the new state. This was a flag with no cultural allusion from either community, drawing its symbolism from nature instead: yellow for copper, the shape of Cyprus, olive branches. Given the climate of intolerance and animosity prevalent during the late 1950s, it was impossible to use cultural or religious symbols, or the colours of the mother-fatherlands. The hope for a peaceful future was also embedded in the emblem of the Republic: a dove carrying an olive branch. Yet, as Greek Cypriot President Glafkos Clerides later remarked, 'Ours could be the best flag in the world because no one is prepared to die for it.'

What about the other distinguishing symbol of any state, the national anthem? When the Republic of Cyprus was created in 1960, it acquired a flag but no national anthem. When the President of the new state, Archbishop Makarios, prepared for his first official visit abroad to Egypt, he was asked to send them the national anthem. A piece of classical music was hastily chosen. The story went that as Makarios emerged from the plane in Egypt, the 'anthem' was performed and he proudly began to walk along the red carpet. An aide rushed up and told him to stand still. He had to stand to attention when the national anthem was played, but the President had forgotten this was meant to be his state's national anthem. Now, when I asked, no one knew what it was. The first and only national anthem of Cyprus was lost in oblivion.

If the Greek Cypriot state now used two flags, placing equal weight on the two sides of Greek-Cypriot, political parties made clear choices. AKEL used only the flag of the Republic of Cyprus, DISY only that of Greece. 'Cyprus belongs to its people' was the cry of AKEL supporters. 'People' included Turkish Cypriots. 'Cyprus is Greek' was the counter-cry of DISY supporters. 'Shame on the treacherous coup and the Turkish invasion,' wrote the banners of AKEL during commemorations. 'Shame on the coup and the barbaric Turkish invasion,' wrote those of DISY during commemorations.

PARTIAL MEMORIES

Of course, the two parties commemorated different dates. DISY preferred dates from the history of Hellenism like 25 March 1821. Its youth section commemorated events from the 'history of Hellenism' that were not even commemorated in Greece: the 'Fall of Constantinople to the Turks', and the 'Destruction of Smirni by the Turks'. Only two dates from the history of Cyprus were commemorated: 1 April, 'the start of the glorious EOKA movement for ENOSIS', and 20 July, 'The Barbaric Turkish Invasion'. Taken together these pointed to a 500-year-long conflict between 'Greeks' and 'Turks'.

AKEL chose dates from the history of Cyprus and events of cooperation with Turkish Cypriots. Its largest commemoration was held on 1 October, for the 1960 independence, that DISY ignored. AKEL also held a week-long series of commemorative events in support of rapprochement. Turkish Cypriot groups and artists were always invited to participate. This week began on the date that two AKEL members, Kavazoglu and Mishaoulis, both in favour of cooperation, one Turkish Cypriot, the other Greek Cypriot, were killed together by right-wing Turkish Cypriots in 1965 as a threat to all those who cooperated with the enemy. Of the two significant dates for 1974, 15 July for the coup and 20 July for the Turkish offensive, AKEL preferred the first. Only the Republic of Cyprus flags waved during the commemorations as people chanted, 'The people don't forget the fascists and the tanks.'

DISY never held a commemoration on the date of the coup because it advocated forgetting, not remembrance. Given the number of ex-coupists under its wings, this was not surprising. Its position regarding the coup was stated again and again: 'It is time to forget past divisions. It is best not to dwell on the coup, a source of division among us in Cyprus, and between us and Greece. We have to remember who the common enemy, the common threat, is: Turkey.' Openly advocating forgetting in a society where people were constantly asked not to forget was not easy. A special word was employed for this purpose, an archaic word rarely used in modern Greek. DISY officials could not say 'we need to forget' which would necessitate using the verb *xehno* ('forget'). What they said was that 'we advocate a policy of forgetting' (*lithi*). The use of the archaic *lithi*, gave rise to new problems related to etymology. Problems that those who revered etymology and the ancients, were unaware of. In ancient Greek '*a-lithia*', the opposite of '*lithi*', meant truth.

AKEL too now wanted to forget certain things, especially the periods when it had supported ENOSIS. In 1990, the party only critiqued its own stance in support of ENOSIS during 1964–1967, despite continuing sporadic allusions to ENOSIS. During the 1965 funeral of Mishaoulis and Kavazoglu, the left-wing leaders who spoke over their coffins presented them as fighters for 'self-determination' and 'for the fulfilment of the people's national aspirations'. At the time, both statements were implicit allusions to ENOSIS. Turkish Cypriot Kavazoglu was inadvertently turned into a fighter for ENOSIS.

How did Turkish Cypriots stand on the issue of commemorations and flags? I had not been able to examine this on the other side. It would take time, but eventually I would find out, when I lived among the people without a flag.

HOPE

Mihalis, a DISY supporter, was in his mid thirties with a fine moustache and a fine sense of humour to match. We had become friends and every now and then would go for an outing together. That was before crossing.

His father was one of the first Greek Cypriots to die in the area during the inter-ethnic fighting of the late 1950s. His brother went missing in 1974. I thought that his support of DISY fitted well with his background and personal tragedies. He was denied a father by Turkish Cypriots and a brother by Turks. But other things did not fit that well. He had told me the story of how his father died, as if he had witnessed it, even though he was a baby when it took place. He had often heard it from his mother. He had told me the story before I crossed to the other side. Now he was asking me what I had heard. I had dreaded this moment. When I was in Lefkosha, I imagined myself talking with Mihalis, worried how he might react to what I would say. Now he let me talk for a long time without interruption and gave me time to explain myself. All the time I spoke, his eyes focused on mine.

'What is done is done, Yiannaki,' he replied softly, with what seemed like sadness and resignation:

> I can't bring my father back and I doubt my brother will ever return. My mother still hopes, but I tell her nothing. Why should I take away her hope? I only hope we can live a better life ourselves. Especially now that I have become a father. I know it's my own father that they killed and that many will say I should not talk like this, especially me, but that's how things were in those days. They killed us and we killed them. And when we found the chance later in the 1960s, we attacked them with a vengeance. OK, people over here don't speak about this, but it's not as if they don't know. Anyway, the Turkish Cypriots told you everything when you went over. In the end we both lost and if we continue we will lose again. We both paid so dearly. And what did we win? In the end no one won. We ended up with the disaster of 1974. They had a horrible time living with us, but then is 1974 a victory for them? Living in a country that is not recognized, in poverty. Not being able to have a passport, travel and trade. And with the Turkish army all around them. No one should live that way. You said that they feel the army offers them protection. That maybe they want it there. I can understand that, and it's our fault if we made them feel that way. But who wants to live anywhere where the army is so powerful? So, should we continue as we did before? Then how will it ever end? No, we have to put an end to it. We, the younger ones, have to start. No one else can do it for us.

DIVIDED LEFKOSIA, UNITARY LEFKOSHA

Maps, like memories, only came in parts. The other side was always erased so it was difficult to find a map of the whole of Lefkosia/Lefkosha, except one which was of no use anyway. Officially, Greek Cypriots lived in a divided city, in divided Lefkosia. Officially, Turkish Cypriots lived in a whole city, Lefkosha. What lay next to them was of no interest, it was the capital of another country.

This was a city – *a* city? – with two municipalities, each with its own logo. At first sight, both logos showed the city united. Both showed the circular medieval walls. The city walls were built by the Venetians to prevent the Ottomans from capturing Nicosia, and in the process caused the deaths of many Ottoman soldiers. The Venetians also destroyed many houses and churches of the local Christians to build them. Nonetheless, the Venetian walls were presented with pride in both logos – they were after all western. Both sides felt equally proud of this western heritage, as proof that they truly belonged to the West. Both regarded western monuments as theirs – no problem – but never those of the people on the other side. For Greek Cypriots, Ottoman or Turkish monuments stood as reminders of the barbaric Ottomans, sad Muslim remains. For Turkish Cypriots, Greek or Byzantine monuments were those of the evil Greek Cypriots. On Greek Cypriot maps, the walls appeared with the Venetian bastion names; on Turkish Cypriot maps, with the later Ottoman names.

The logo of Lefkosia employed, as one would expect, three colours – blue, white and yellow – and a dove. The walls were in yellow, matching the colours of the walls, and of the flag of the Republic, with a dove flying inside representing the peaceful past and the hope for reunification in a peaceful future. This logo spoke of peace, the other of conflict. The logo of Lefkosha showed a Muslim religious monument inside the outline of the walls, a site of worship for the Whirling Dervishes. A date appeared underneath, one that did not say much to Greek Cypriots but spoke plenty to Turkish Cypriots: 1958, a year of serious inter-communal clashes in what was then both Lefkosia and Lefkosha. It would soon cease to be both as the clashes led to the first physical separation of the city, when people were for the first time forced to choose sides. The British called the division the 'Mason-Dixon Line', after another line between north and south during the American Civil War. In 1958, Turkish Cypriots unilaterally declared their own municipality, and included the date in their logo. The issue of municipalities remained unresolved in the 1960 constitution.

Maps also revealed the sad story of Nicosia, how from Lefkosha and Lefkosia it turned into either Lefkosha or Lefkosia. When Turkish Cypriots moved after the Bloody Christmas of 1963, the Turkish street names were changed – an indication that they were neither expected, nor wanted, back. This did not happen in the areas Turkish Cypriots left behind in 1974. Now they were expected back, so that Greek Cypriots could return to the north. But Turkish Cypriots erased all Greek Cypriot place names.

On the Greek Cypriot side a sign revealed the extent of the problem. The same sign announced *Elliniko Loutro* (Greek Bath) in Greek and, underneath, 'Turkish Bath' in English. The same circular road that ran inside the walls was Athena Avenue on one side, and became Istanbul Road on the other.

SHIT MANAGEMENT

There was only one whole and mutually accepted map of Lefkosia/ Lefkosha: the map of the city's underground sewerage system. The Sewerage System of Nicosia was the best example of inter-ethnic cooperation in Cyprus. It was the largest, longest-running – and clearly it was running well – and most successful bi-communal project. Cleansing activities this time brought the two sides together, though admittedly different from the ones they usually engaged in.

It was the two mayors who accomplished this. How did they pull it off? The answer to this was one of the Greek Cypriot mayor's favourite stories. 'I realized that unless we did something about sewerage, something drastic and quick, soon we would be up to our socks in it,' he said with a mischievous smile:

> I had to persuade people from both sides that it had to be done and this was no easy job so soon after 1974, when the traumas were so raw and the passions running high. I managed to invite the leaders of the two sides together at my house for dinner. I made sure that we had a really large, sumptuous dinner and after we finished I asked them if they wanted to use the toilet. Both, of course, said yes. After they finished, I brought the issue up. 'Your Excellencies had to use the toilet and this was a vital need. Imagine how much this city needs the same.' Both saw my point and agreed. We worked quietly, underground so to speak, and when we were ready we first connected vital buildings like hospitals on the two sides and foreign embassies to the sewerage system. That way no one could try to take it apart. Even then, there were some fanatics on both sides who shouted things like 'What, are they going to send us their shit now too?'

After the project had been established, a cartoon was published in the

Greek Cypriot press. It showed the two smiling mayors with their pants down, sitting on toilets opposite each other, jointly pulling the single overhanging flushing chain. Another was published in the Turkish Cypriot press showing a mighty wall above ground as two metal pipes shook hands beneath. Divided on the ground, Lefkosha/Lefkosia was unified underground.

THE STORY OF THE DEAD ZONE

A line ran through walled Nicosia in medieval maps; another through contemporary ones. The two lines were almost identical, dividing the city along an east-west axis. The line crossing the medieval city was a river. Later through human effort it became a long bridge; later still, through more human toil, it was to turn into a chasm, a dangerous no man's land. It still remained a site of division and one of contact: the paradox of borders.

The river was called by various names: proper and improper, official ones appearing on maps and unofficial ones that people used, clean and dirty, Turkish Cypriot and Greek Cypriot. The proper name Greek Cypriots used was *Pedieos* (from *pediada*, meaning plane) but it was colloquially called *Pithkias*. Most Greek Cypriots knew it that way, and some Turkish Cypriots too. Among Turkish Cypriots it was also called *Kanli Dere*, meaning 'Bloody Torrent'. They also called it *Chirkefli Dere* (Foul Torrent), while Greek Cypriots used an even stronger name, *Kotsirkas* (Turdy). As time went by, it lived up to all the associations of its names.

The river flowed through the city walls until 1567, when the Venetians diverted its course for strategic reasons. In the subsequent Ottoman period, the old riverbed through the walled city was left open. The Ottoman administrative centre lay north of the now empty riverbed, with the Orthodox one on the south. Powerful Muslim and Christian families congregated around the two administrative centres, on either side of the riverbed. The river acquired a new name in Turkish, *Kanli Dere* (Bloody Torrent), due to the red hue of its water on the occasions when it still flowed. Later, it took the two other names associating it with dirt, one in Turkish and the other in Greek, due to the refuse it carried along. By that time, it only flowed through Nicosia as an occasional torrent, when rains were heavy and the water followed its old course. Later when the British took over in 1878, the old riverbed inside the city was gradually covered up for hygiene reasons. As the riverbed was covered, a road emerged over the ground, a road that was in effect a long bridge over the riverbed.

This road was called Hermes Street. The various personas of Hermes would, in due course, also emerge on this river-bridge. It became the major commercial axis of the city, bringing people of different groups together for the purpose of trade. Hermes was the ancient Greek god of traders. He was also associated with Hades, the Kingdom of the Dead, the ancient Greeks' own Zone of the Dead. He was known as *Psychopompos* (the bearer of souls to Hades), for he could cross the most difficult boundaries, like the one between the living and the dead. After 1963, the Green Line emerged along Hermes Street as the Dead Zone was born, first drawn by a British officer in green. The darker associations of Hermes with Hades too came to be fulfilled. As Hermes Street became a savagely fought-over boundary, as it was drenched in blood, the older associations of the river's name with blood were also fulfilled.

It was not long before the Dead Zone of Hermes Street acquired its own Cerberus. Cerberus was the fierce, three-headed dog guarding the gates of Hades, to prevent the souls from escaping. This time Cerberus guarded a different kind of memory: that of its previous name. *Cerberus Street* lay at the edge of Tahtakallas. Before the area's Turkish Cypriot inhabitants abandoned Tahtakale in 1964, the street had a Turkish name, *Chinar Sokak*, Plane Tree Street. It was changed by Greek Cypriots.

Later still, a few years after 1974, this river-bridge regained its older function associating it with excrement. The old underground riverbed became the main artery of the jointly administered sewerage system. It became the city's main carrier of dirt and a site of underground cooperation. On the ground a site of bloodshed and danger: underground a project of mutual benefit and a bridge between the two sides.

Even on the ground, the Dead Zone later became a site of underground cooperation, a unique kind of bridge. Just outside the old city walls, next to the riverbed, was the only point of contact and communication: the Leda Palace Hotel. During the early 1990s, as I was starting my research in Cyprus, the UN-managed Ledra Palace was the only site where people from the two sides could meet. Initially, the meetings took place quietly – almost underground – because those who participated were branded as traitors on both sides. Gradually, the meetings became more common, as the UN, various embassies, and other organizations actively encouraged them.

Was it just a series of coincidences that the various names of the river-bridge and of the Dead Zone came to be fulfilled one by one? Or could it be a kind of destiny? I wondered too about my own preoccupation with the Dead Zone. Was that just coincidence?

BIRTH AND THE DEAD ZONE

I was walking inside the empty riverbed, the Greek Cypriot side of the city on one side, the Turkish Cypriot on the other, a machine-gun post right in front of me. Behind the abandoned machine-gun post I saw the Turkish Cypriot houses, decaying, crammed together and bullet-hole torn. I was in my birthplace.

I was in Limassol, which I had known only as Lemesos, where I was born in 1964. I had come to see the other side, the abandoned side that Turkish Cypriots called Leymosun. Lemesos had recently become sister city with other cities in Greece: Thessaloniki, Zakinthos, Rhodos. Was Lemesos ever a sister city with Leymosun?

After 1964, Leymosun became an enclave, but I remembered going there later, when things quietened, with my father to buy watermelons and yogurt. That was all I remembered of Leymosun, and that I never actually knew anyone there. By the time I was ten, in 1974, the Turkish Cypriots would soon be leaving. When I went to the other side, I decided that I should visit Leymosun. The houses were tiny and poorly built. When it was an enclave, Greek Cypriots did not allow them to obtain building materials for fear they would be used as fortifications. Greek Cypriot refugees now lived crammed in some of those sad houses.

I crossed the riverbed into Leymosun towards the place I wanted to visit, that strange place that I used to see on my right when I was driven to Leymosun as a child. It was a conglomeration of three buildings with a large square in front. One was probably a club or administrative centre, another was a hospital, and the third was a mosque. It was the mosque that used to fascinate me. As I walked towards it, I stopped to examine the base of a departed statue. It had *Turk, Ogun, Chalish, Guven* ('Turk, Be Proud, Work, Trust') written on the base, followed by *K. Ataturk*. Ataturk must have stood above it. Did Greek Cypriots destroy him? Or did Turkish Cypriots take their father along when they left? They had sometimes carried their statues with them when they left after 1974. I did not know for sure. The mosque seemed in good condition and its door was locked. I walked into the adjoining cemetery. It was in ruins with weeds growing all over and ornate tombstones carved with Arabic calligraphy lying around broken.

Then I saw them. Lying there mute, one next to the other, with a detail in common: fourteen Turkish Cypriot graves with the same date, 13-2-1964, all killed together during the fighting. That was a few days before I was born, on 18 February 1964.

I went straight to see my parents. I asked them if they remembered what was happening at the time of my birth. 'Well,' my mother replied, 'something was definitely happening back then. Yes, there were some troubles back then. That was why you were born a bit premature. It all had to do with the political situation. I got scared.' They could not remember any more than this.

Everything became clear to me. My premature birth was caused by the fighting. I was born at the same time as the Dead Zone, under the same circumstances, for the same reasons. Perhaps, then, I was marked from the beginning. The Dead Zone was my own kin; my own kind of calling. And where was the Dead Zone born? It had all started right in Tahtakallas with the killing of the Turkish Cypriot woman, setting off Bloody Christmas and all that followed. It was born in the place I had chosen to do my research, unaware of its role in my own birth. Perhaps that was why I had chosen it, why I was so obsessed with the Dead Zone, why it kept on pulling me. I did not know even then that it would pull me until I went there to live, and would never let go.

Even my trusted parents never told me any of this. I had to find out for myself. They did not remember much, since they were living in Lemesos. Had they been living in Leymosun, they would have remembered. They gave an ordinary name to a child born in ordinary circumstances, when other children were receiving names like War. My father was present at my birth. As other children were born, their fathers did not know if they would ever meet them. As I was born, others were dying. Their deaths caused my premature birth. Even my own parents hid things from me; even they betrayed me. What did those who were betrayed become?

THE PEOPLE OF THE DEAD ZONE

Marios and I were walking inside the Dead Zone. It was his first time there. Many had told him not to go. He had been told that people who went there were traitors. We were going to one of the bi-communal meetings that had started taking place at the Ledra Palace Hotel.

These meetings were becoming more frequent and new groups were constantly created: groups of teachers, lawyers, women, artists and others. Many of the people who went to the meetings belonged to the two largest left-wing parties on each side. The two parties, AKEL and CTP, along with the smaller left-of-centre Turkish Cypriot TKP, often organized their own meetings and activities. But people from many other parties – some DISY supporters were actually in the forefront – also joined the 'bi-communal meetings' as they came to be known. 'Conflict Resolution Seminars' were also organized by academics or professionals who had experience in places like Israel and Ireland.

The aim was to meet people from the other side, talk to each other and hear what they had to say: their experiences, memories, views, fears and hopes. The hope was that these meetings would lead to mutual understanding and conciliation, that some common ground could be created in an island divided by a Dead Zone. People there first tried to listen to what the others had to say. That in itself was a revolutionary act in Cyprus. So much so that participants were accused of treachery.

Despite the opposed official positions – Greek Cypriots insisting on rapprochement and Turkish Cypriots on separation – the people of the Dead Zone often found themselves condemned on both sides. On the Greek Cypriot side, the accusation usually came from the right:

> Why do they go there to talk to each other? We never had any problems between us, we lived well in the past. It is all Turkey's fault. These meetings clearly imply that we had problems in the past, as Turkish propaganda insists. Plus, they provide international recognition to their illegal state.

But, given the official Greek Cypriot policy of rapprochement (*epanaprosegisi*, 'coming together again'), the meetings were generally grudgingly allowed and even at times encouraged by the Greek Cypriot authorities. On one condition: that they 'did not bestow recognition to the other side as a legitimate state'. When it came to the two political leaders meeting during talks, or party leaders meeting in Ledra Palace too, the issue was never raised.

Things were complicated on the Turkish Cypriot side too. Given the official position that the problem was between the two communities in Cyprus, if there was a real official will for a solution, such meetings should have been encouraged. Instead, the accusations were sharper, and the meetings were often prohibited. In this case too, it was the right that sounded the alarm. 'What are those people doing there conspiring with the savage Greek Cypriots, and talking with those who slaughtered us? Only traitors would talk with people whose hands are dripping with our blood.'

THE LANGUAGE OF THE DEAD ZONE

The accusation of treachery was not the only thing we had in common. We also shared a speech impediment. We stuttered.

Being inside the Dead Zone was a kind of internal exile. People found themselves in a place that belonged to neither, estranged from their own people, outsiders treated with suspicion. When it came to the language of the Dead Zone, the exile was triple.

First, we were exiled from both our native tongues, Greek and Turkish, neither of which could provide a common medium of communication there. Even within the 'native tongue' we were already in exile. Our native tongue was neither the standard Greek nor the standard Turkish that we had learned at school, but our own dialects. When one tried to talk, the 'standard' language did not seem so standard after all. The standard languages were created by Turkey and Greece by expunging 'foreign' words, as 'foreign people' were exiled in the bosoms of the mother-fatherlands. Speaking the 'standard language' in Cyprus was arduous. Unlike the dialects that flowed easily, talking in the standard languages required effort, and led to stuttering. Many people in Cyprus had been bilingual, or rather bi-dialectal. As animosity grew and people were separated, as people were learning to talk like true Turks and Greeks, as the other dialect was becoming that of the enemy and fines were imposed for using it, we were left with no language in common. Except that provided by our common colonial past and desire to be western: English. That was the second exile. We discussed the Cyprus Problem in English.

Talking about the Cyprus Problem was also separated by the Dead Zone. Our heroes, their murderers; our rights, their wrongs; our history, their mythology; our Happy Peace Operation, their barbaric Turkish invasion; our state, their so-called state. It was so easy to talk in the official idiom. Words, thoughts and arguments flowed because they were already out there, ready-made, used all the time. One had to invent from scratch a language to talk about Cyprus as a whole, one that both could use: a language of understanding, empathy, and forgiveness. It was one that had to be invented as people hesitantly tried to talk to each other inside the Dead Zone. This was a language of uncertainty and questioning, not one composed of readily found, capitalized, sacred truths. When people tried to talk there, they often stuttered.

This difficulty emerged even when trying to talk of a basic human experience like pain. The language of pain had been hijacked by the two officialdoms' politics. The language of politics in Cyprus had been turned into a language of pain and suffering by both sides, but in a way that never allowed consideration of the other's pain. Both sides were screaming with pain, with true pain, even the same kinds of pain. They were locked in an perverse screaming match to make one's pain heard over the other's. Peace activists inside the Dead Zone even had trouble talking about peace. The word 'peace' had been torn apart. The language of peace had been hijacked with talk of the 'Happy Peace Operation' and 'peaceful coexistence'; talk of peace used to deny others' pain and hide one's own violence.

The language of pain was the only one allowed in Cyprus to talk about Cyprus. Actually, only the language of the pain of Cyprus was taken seriously. Other problems elsewhere received scant attention. The same took place within. Only the Cyprus Problem counted as a real problem worth talking about. Everything else was minor; it could wait. Problems of discrimination against migrants, religious minorities or women, were waved away. If anyone dared breach the silence, one was accused of – what else? – treachery. 'How dare you accuse us of violating human rights when we accuse the other side of this?' The Cyprus Problem became the perfect alibi for abuses within. And talk about the Cyprus Problem always had to be in tears. Smirking, let alone laughing at us, was a highly improper manner of conduct.

Another reason why the people of the Dead Zone stuttered was the constant fear of moving a bit too close to the other side; the fear of saying something that someone would report back to their own side, where they would be publicly condemned as traitors. To speak there was a dangerous tightrope: a scary experience for which none of us had practised. It could only be learnt on the spot during the performance, inside the Dead Zone.

THE FEELING OF THE DEAD ZONE

The people meeting there were said to share another dangerous vice: a shameful feeling.

Shame. This was the emotional equivalent of the Dead Zone in space, a peculiar feeling of closeness and distance, identification and disavowal. It was the opposite of pride, the predominant feeling on both sides, expressed in parades, flags, heroes, and grand political statements. Pride employed a strong, loud language. Shame was like a confession timidly whispered. As people tried to talk in the Dead Zone, as they spoke of their personal suffering in their own voice, with details that said so much, about their son's eyes, the roses they had planted in their garden and how they still woke up with their smell, about the last time they spoke to their husband, not knowing it was the last time, about how at the last instant they decided not to put their baby daughter in that car that never reached its destination, as they tried to say all this, keeping their voices steady to maintain their dignity, the others heard as if for the first time. For those from the other side, it was often indeed the first time. For those of their own side too, who had heard nothing but this for decades, the words were movingly new. Heard afresh, in a different voice, separated from the years of official use, they became human once more. As this space for empathy opened up, the one for shame opened up alongside it. Shame for the pain inflicted upon those of the other side; for still not admitting this and not acknowledging any responsibility.

There were different kinds of shame. There was shame for doing things one later came to regret, but more common was shame for not having acted at all. Shame for not speaking out when other people were harmed, even those once-upon-a-time neighbours and friends. Shame for having allowed extremists to determine the course of history. For allowing them to set the rules of the game among themselves. People who once felt ashamed decided they could no longer remain inactive. They had tasted the bitter harvest of not daring to act humanely, the consequences of keeping silent. This was the shame older people often expressed.

How about younger people like me? I too had often felt ashamed. First as a Greek Cypriot, later for Turkish Cypriots. Ashamed for how little shame people expressed on either side. But why should I feel ashamed? No one could blame me for anything. I tried to rid myself of this feeling. I felt it was unfairly imposed on me like a second skin. It just so happened I was born on one side of a city called Lemesos. I did not choose my birth. Clearly I was not to blame for anything. Was I?

MUSEUM OF NATIONAL STRUGGLE

The young men behind the hangman's noose looked at me accusingly. They were hanged by the British during the 1955–1959 EOKA anti-colonial insurrection. Their photos were later placed on the wall, behind a replica of the gallows in the Museum of National Struggle of Lefkosia. Something about those photos, in that room with the two thick wax candles, reminded me of church icons. In the modern secular era, these museums became the sacred places for our new religion. Except, this church was empty.

In the next room, others looked at me from across the Zone of the Dead, from their photos that spelled the letters EOKA. Many were high-school boys, boys who joined the struggle with their heart and soul. Boys or not, the British treated them as terrorists posing a challenge to the glory of Her Majesty's Empire. Turkish Cypriots also regarded them as terrorists. Other rooms showed photographs of bodies scarred by torture, presumably inflicted on the 'savage terrorists' by English gentlemen. The clothes of those who no longer had any need for them were displayed in glass cases. There were notebooks where these young men had written thoughts and high-school poetry about love and glory.

Once more I found myself under the stern gaze of young men looking down on me. Once more their gaze weighed on me like an unspoken accusation. This time it was not like in the other Museum of National Struggle. It was not a charge of responsibility, atrocities or blame. It was an accusation of treachery, disrespect, desecration even, for having also felt sorry for the deaths of those whose photos spelled TMT.

The Museum of National Struggle in Lefkosia was situated inside the Walls, as was the Museum of National Struggle in Lefkosha. The two were so different, and yet so similar. They passionately disagreed by speaking the same language and in the same tone of voice. In Lefkosha a single Turkish flag flew outside, a single Greek flag in Lefkosia. Only those two flags appeared, in spite of the two museums being about independence.

This was a museum of history, but this time the story was not clear, with a beginning and an end. The museum of Lefkosha was built in a line, while this was just composed of various rooms. The Turkish Cypriot museum was built in the 1980s, the Greek Cypriot one back in 1964. A placard set in a glass case told the history of Cyprus:

> The island became Greek during the fourteenth century BC, when the Mycenaeans settled here. Since then the monuments, language, customs and traditions of the Cypriot people have all been Greek. No foreign rulers managed to change the national character of the Cypriot people. The Turkish occupation was succeeded by the British one... The struggle broke out on 1 April 1955 and all the people took part, even the children. After four years of unimaginable heroism and sacrifice the struggle ended with the

unjust London-Zurich agreement. The museum exhibits illustrate
the ethos and spirit of this struggle.

This was a sad story. The aim of the struggle was not achieved despite
the deaths. It spoke of the 'Cypriot people', meaning Greek Cypriots. If
the fourteenth century BC was the beginning of history, if Cyprus had
been Greek ever since, then Turks living in Cyprus did not belong here.
They were mere remains of foreign oppressors. The Turkish Cypriot
museum chose a different beginning as it told a different story. History
began with the Ottoman conquest of Cyprus in 1571. Until the British
took over in 1878, Cyprus was Ottoman. Historically, then, Cyprus was
Turkish. That Greeks lived there, as a majority even, was the outcome
of an unjust turn of events.

Strange things, the beginnings. They lacked what everything else was
supposed to have: a beginning. In the historical path, beginnings were
made to stand out large and clear. They had to be large to hide things
behind their backs. And, because they were born pregnant with the
end. They concealed other possible beginnings behind them. One could
always take a step back and ask what caused a beginning. Beginnings,
then, didn't just happen; they were chosen much later. It was the
political goals of the two sides, the desired future, which determined
the beginnings of their stories – one claiming that ENOSIS and only
ENOSIS was the command of history, the other positing TAKSIM as
the only just historical outcome. The end caused the beginning, not the
other way round.

Both museums had clear beginnings, but the Greek Cypriot one
lacked an end. A happy end, to be precise, one to be rejoiced in, like
the happy ending of the Turkish Cypriot museum. As the historical
text explained, the Greek Cypriot struggle ended with the 'unjust
London-Zurich agreement'. The aim of ENOSIS was not achieved, as
independence was the sad outcome. When the decision to create the
Greek Cypriot museum was taken in 1964, many Greek Cypriots were
opposed to it. The struggle for ENOSIS had not ended, so how could a
museum be built? In order to urge future generations to continue the
struggle for ENOSIS, was the reply. Another room, the proper ending,
was to be added.

The Greek Cypriot museum created in 1964 spoke only of Greeks
and Turks, not Greek Cypriots and Turkish Cypriots. Nothing here
suggested Greek rejoicing for 1960. Instead, the enemy celebrated: a
display showed the Turks of Cyprus rejoicing at the achievement of

independence. The major enemy here was the British. The Turks of Cyprus were given a secondary role, as collaborators with the British against EOKA. Even so, they were portrayed as more evil than the British. A map of Cyprus indicated places where atrocities had been committed against the Greeks during 1955–1959. British atrocities were marked by a polished boot; Turkish by an arm clenching a sharp curved knife in front of a fez. The British were soldiers who killed; the Turks were barbarians who butchered. In another room, a display presented butchers' knives, explaining that the Turks had used them to slaughter the Greeks. (I had seen the same knives in the Military Museum of Istanbul, used then by the Greeks of Cyprus to slaughter the Turks of Cyprus.) One display in Lefkosia's museum recorded an event that took place in 1958. Thirty Greeks from the village of Kontemenos who had been arrested by the British were deposited outside a Turkish village. The local Turks were notified and hunted down the unarmed Greeks, killing eight of them. This was a significant historical event in this museum; in the other it never happened.

EOKA was spelled out with the photos of dead heroes on one side, TMT on the other. Old guns EOKA fighters used were shown here to draw the contrast with the modern ones the British and their Turkish collaborators had access to; hand-made guns Turkish Cypriots used in contrast to real ones Greek Cypriots employed were shown in the other. Beyond their common name, the two museums echoed each other in other ways. History was always a history of war; of men; self-centred; our heroes, their terrorists; no mention of others' suffering; nothing about people killed by people of their own community; nothing about people also living well. Two desperate screams that never managed to reach the other side; a wall in the middle reflected them back. But the other museum did not exhume an air of abandonment and neglect like this. This now stood like a fossil from the past, since the political goal it commanded – ENOSIS – was no longer relevant.

MEMORY AND FORGETTING

Memory was revered on both sides. But if one looked at memory from both sides of the Dead Zone, it turned out to be as much about forgetting – about the past and about the future. The Turkish Cypriot WE WON'T FORGET legitimated a divided Cyprus in the future. The Greek Cypriot I DON'T FORGET expressed hope for the future return of Greek Cypriot refugees in a reunited island. No room was allowed in the Greek Cypriot I DON'T FORGET for Turkish Cypriots, for their refugees, suffering or pain. The Turkish Cypriot WE WON'T FORGET had nothing to say about the tragic experiences of Greek Cypriots. All those were to be discarded in the bin of social amnesia. Amnesiá, however, led to amnesty. No one was punished for the violence inflicted on the people of the other community, no one was held responsible.

Among Greek Cypriots, amnesty/amnesia was proposed by those who advocated forgetting but avoided the word 'forget'. DISY advocated that the coup should be forgotten and that the few Greek Cypriots whose only punishment for participating in the coup was that they lost their jobs in the public service should be reinstated in the name of amnesty. Amnesty was the road also chosen by Makarios for those who had turned against him. The argument was still that the Turkish threat left no time for self-accounting. It was decided that the notorious 'Cyprus File', the documents that might explain what happened and who was responsible, should remain closed forever. They were all forgiven and forgotten. But when it came to other evils, to evils committed by others, that could never be. Both sides spoke of justice and of the need to punish the culprits of violence, but only of those who inflicted violence upon them. And only those from the other side, never their own who inflicted violence upon their people. Both spoke of biased outsiders, of outside powers that had mingled in Cyprus and should be held responsible. Both sides asked *them* to acknowledge their responsibility.

Whatever happened to those who staged the coup? Who now remembered who they were? Some people did. Those who had been arrested and tortured could never forget them but their memories were neither written in schoolbooks, nor turned into material for the publications of the Public Information Office.

What happened to the coupists and their supporters? What happened to those Greek Cypriot student leaders in Athens who had passionately supported the junta? Could they have become noted academics, now pontificating on the evils of Turkish expansionism? What happened to the others in Cyprus? Could they have become important media moguls, owning newspapers and TV stations, using these to put forward their views? Could they one day become top administrators of the government department in charge of truth, memory and Enlightenment – the Public Information Office? Would they become respectable MPs, speaking the proud language of politics? Would such people one day accuse those meeting in the Dead Zone of being traitors? Would they one day threaten with expensive lawsuits those they had previously tortured whey they spoke out? No, such things were not possible. No, such things could never happen.

Injustice and pain could not be forgotten by those who had suffered. The wounds were still there. Trying to cover them up did not make them go away. It made them fester and turn deadly dangerous. This was what the crossings of the Dead Zone had taught me. But I felt that now it was too late for punishment. Evidence became harder to collect. Delayed justice could turn into injustice. Still, it could never be too late for acknowledgement, bearing up to the responsibility and asking for forgiveness.

BACK TO THE ZONE OF THE DEAD

My research on the Greek Cypriot side was almost over. Visiting the Zone of the Dead now felt like going back to the future, as each side projected into the past the version of history that led to the desired future.

Much of history then was about births. How births were chosen and how historical events came to life. How certain events were selected to live on, stand out and become part of history. Say a Greek Cypriot once offered a coffee to a Turkish Cypriot in a coffee shop. Later, this was elevated from oblivion to the status of a historical event in the Greek Cypriot story of coexistence. Suppose they later had a fight while playing cards. This was born as an all too meaningful historical fact in the Turkish Cypriot story of conflict. When I looked more closely at Greek Cypriot history, I began to understand the conditions of its birth. The conditions of birth were significant, as I had learnt from my own.

Greek Cypriot history did not always talk of a past of peaceful coexistence with their Turkish Cypriot brothers. This history only emerged after 1974. Before 1960, when ENOSIS was the goal and the British the real enemy, no attention was paid to Turkish Cypriots. They were just sad remains of a past conqueror. The British tried for a period to persuade Greek Cypriots that they were not Greek but Cypriot, an amorphous mixture of races and cultures. Greek Cypriots reacted by insisting that they were pure Greeks and nothing but Greeks. Similarly, the British initially supported the Islamists among Turkish Cypriots, those who disliked the emerging Turkish Cypriot followers of Ataturk preaching the new Turkish nation. As with Greek Cypriots, this had the opposite effect of turning Turkish Cypriots into zealous Turks.

But, after 1960, Greek Cypriot historians began to look more closely at the origins of those Turks who lived with them and voiced political demands. That was the time when Greek Cypriots still wanted ENOSIS, the period of inter-ethnic violence, the time when Turkish Cypriots demanded TAKSIM. Now, with the British out of the way they became the major obstacle. Greek Cypriot historians joyfully discovered that in fact there were no Turks in Cyprus. They were really descendants of 'Islamicized Greeks', though the poor things did not know it. So in essence, in blood, they were Greeks. And since all were Greeks, ENOSIS was totally justified. For their part, the Turks of Cyprus used blood sample studies to prove that the Rums living in Cyprus were not Greek, but had more affinities with the people of Anatolia. The history of self-affirmation went hand in hand with that of denying the other's existence and identity.

After 1974, the Greeks of Cyprus became Greek Cypriots, the others now Turkish Cypriots, and the history of Cyprus a story of coexistence. They were not Turks any more, especially given the need to distinguish them from real Turks from Turkey and the need to ask them to reunite as compatriots. Now they were Turkish *Cypriots*, having a great deal in common with Greek *Cypriots*. Turkish Cypriots too had gone through various rebirths of their own in their own histories: first as privileged Ottomans, later as Muslims, then Turks, finally as Turks of Cyprus in control of their own state, some now claiming they were Cypriots.

I had been choosing my births and ancestors too. I found out about a relative in Greece, a woman who had won a Greek-Turkish Peace Prize for a story she wrote about Greeks and Turks. This I considered highly significant. I had also become aware of the significance of my birthday. Being born of the events that gave birth to the Dead Zone had made us kind of kin. That was my own mother-fatherland.

Despite the enormous internal political differences, certain issues seemed to unite so much. Turkish expansionism, for example. It seemed that Greek Cypriots from all political persuasions endorsed this notion. It was so appealing because it provided such powerful, collective self-absolution, not just for the coupists, but for all that Turkish Cypriots suffered in the 1960s from Greek Cypriots. Turkish Cypriots held as tightly to their own version of accusation and blame condensed in one word: ENOSIS. That was their collective excuse and self-absolution. Greek Cypriots always wanted ENOSIS and still hoped one day to unite Cyprus with Greece. Even if such absolutions worked by attributing unchanging evil intentions to the others, they were true fears – fears based on past experiences and on past suffering. Both saw themselves as small and vulnerable. Turkish Cypriots compared themselves to Greek Cypriots, or Greek Cypriots and Greeks together. Greek Cypriots compared themselves with Turkish Cypriots and Turks together. The feeling of being weak minorities was multiplied by the notion that the whole world was always against them and on the side of the others.

The more Greek Cypriots feared Turkish expansionism, the more they leaned on Greece for help and security. The more they did this, the more Turkish Cypriots saw the threat of ENOSIS. The more Turkish Cypriots leaned on Turkey for help and support, giving Turkey more power in their own affairs, the more Greek Cypriots perceived this as Turkey taking over and as further proof of Turkish expansionism. Together they created the dangers they prophesied and the disasters they strove to prevent. The same worked with denial. The more the other peoples' pain was denied, the more the others insisted on it.

How were these images of the other side created? Who were the gatekeepers controlling the flow of information from one side to the other? One had become my Stepfather, against my will. (So fathers, like identities, were not always freely chosen.) He was a man who was a product of one of the darker sides of Greek society. He had his counterparts on the Greek Cypriot side. The handful of men in charge of disseminating the truth about the other side, the gatekeepers who knew the others' despised language, mostly came from the Greek minority of Turkey. In Greece too, some of the noted academic experts on the Turks also came from that oppressed, destitute minority. Their lives in those societies turned them into martyrs, preachers and prophets of the other's evils, all at once. They extracted their revenge daily through their professional calling. The sins of the mother-fatherlands had returned to haunt their children.

One injustice could never justify another. The 1960s could not justify 1974, as some Turkish Cypriots had insisted when I pressed them. That was the only justification they could come up with when I asked them to face Greek Cypriot pain. One injustice could not write off another. 1974 could not write off the 1960s, as some Greek Cypriots had argued when I pressed them with Turkish Cypriot pain. An injustice could neither erase nor justify another. The opposite was true. They created a circle of injustice leading to more injustices and pain. Injustices, sins, violence, however one chose to call them, eventually they came back to haunt us. They fed the Dead Zone, making it stronger as it stood there – lurking, waiting.

APHRODITE

What did the Goddess of Love bring forth into the world after all? By her lover, Ares the God of War, she had two children: Phobus and Deimus, Fear and Panic.

She never was just a goddess of love. She was a dreaded patron of war too, like her eastern ancestors. She was known as Enoplos (Arms Bearing) and as Androphonos (Slayer of Men). Some ancient writers suggested that the armed Aphrodites had their origins in Cyprus, due to the influence from her eastern ancestors. She was also known as Epitymbia (One of the Grave) and Melaina (Dark). She had many identities. In some statues she appeared as a young maiden, in others as a warrior, sometimes with a beard, or as a hermaphrodite. Even as a Goddess of Love, she was not what we took her to be. Plato had spoken of two Aphrodites, Ourania the Heavenly one, and Pandemos the popular, vulgar kind. These stood for two kinds of love, heavenly love and vulgar love. Pausanias explained the difference in Plato's *Symposium*. Vulgar love stood for the common love of the flesh by those who loved women and boys indiscriminately, those who loved the body more than the soul. Heavenly love he described as spiritual. This higher form of love could only be the love of the male, which was seen as naturally stronger and more spiritual. In the same dialogue Plato also gave another explanation for attraction between people. Once humans were physically joined together in pairs, two men, or two women, or a man with a woman, and were later separated. Ever since each had been trying to find again her or his 'other half'.

The British were as fond of Aphrodite as Greek Cypriots were, but made her speak in totally different ways. The autocratic British governor of Cyprus, Sir Richmond Palmer was clear:

> Seven thousand years ago a lady called Aphrodite landed in Cyprus, and the island has never recovered. The people of Cyprus made a luxury of discontent and always pretend they do not like to be ruled, and yet, like the lady I have mentioned as a prototype, they expect to be ruled, and, in fact, prefer it.

Other colonial authors stressed the eastern origins of Aphrodite to argue that the Cypriots were an oriental race in need of enlightened western guidance. They presented Cypriots as a degenerate people overcome by instincts of sexuality and cruelty, because they lived where Astarte had been worshipped. The mysteries of Astarte were described as rituals in which 'abominable lust, bloodshed and depravity reigned'.

The Greeks of Cyprus reacted by presenting their own purely Greek version of Aphrodite as proof of their pure Greek heritage and ancestry. If the British colonial masters had made her speak in support of colonialism, the Greeks of Cyprus made her speak for ENOSIS. They pointed to historical continuities transforming Aphrodite into the Virgin Mary as Panagia Aphroditissa, conclusive proof of the historical continuity of the Greek people in Cyprus. The British treated these ideas as further evidence of continuing primitiveness and degeneracy.

Even if my research in Cyprus was now over, it was incomplete. I needed to do more with Turkish Cypriots. I wanted to talk to those whose voices I had only heard in whispers. But the Turkish Cypriot side was out of bounds. Was there any way across? Only one, I learned, through an old, unused sewerage tunnel. This was a difficult journey. One would first have to negotiate his own side's underground dirt from the past, then the mess that the two sides created together, and last the hidden dirt created by the other side.

CHAPTER FIVE
ISTANBUL
JULY–SEPTEMBER 1992

WELCOME TO A FUTURE COMPATRIOT

When I arrived, my Turkish Cypriot roommates-to-be immediately welcomed me as a compatriot of a country-to-be by wearing the same T-shirt. I had just arrived in Istanbul for the first time. Previously, as a Greek, I had arrived in Constantinople. I managed to obtain a visa again but this time I wanted to spend my time with Turkish Cypriot students. I wanted to talk to the people who could only speak in whispers when I was in Lefkosha.

I had asked a Turkish Cypriot friend, a left-wing poet now living in London after having been officially designated as a traitor, to help me find someone to stay with. He arranged it all and I arrived at the flat to meet the students living there. They were close to my age. We were all a bit embarrassed in the beginning but soon we became close. With them I felt more comfortable than I had ever felt during my research. Word soon got round that a Greek Cypriot had been living with them and others came to visit. Any first-time visitor almost invariably wore a T-shirt with a map of Cyprus and *Eirini-Peace-Barish* written on it, the same word in Greek, English and Turkish. It was a greeting sign for me, and a statement of their views on Cyprus. They welcomed me warmly as a compatriot of a yet non-existent country, for the Cyprus shown on their T-shirts was one without a dividing line. A bunch of them together edited a youth magazine called *Young Cypriot*. The name reminded me of the Young Turks, who once created their own country. This time round the story was different: they were trying to create a country that was given to our parents, who rejected it and destroyed it.

'WILL THEY LIKE ME?'

Now I had the opportunity to see my old Turkish friends again. But when I invited Erkin, my Marxist friend, to visit me in the flat of my Turkish Cypriot friends he hesitated. I wanted him to meet my new friends. 'Are you sure they will want me there? Will they like me?' he asked. When Erkin asked this I realized that in the two weeks I had been in Istanbul I had never seen a Turk visit our flat or the flats of other Turkish Cypriots I had met. We had never gone out in the company of anyone from Turkey either. This was to be true for the whole three months I spent there, except once. And in that case, I thought there was a special reason of a linguistic nature.

'I'm asking you this,' Erkin explained, 'because I know Turkish Cypriots don't like us much. I'm in the university and I know many Turkish Cypriots there. I know how they feel about us Turks.' Erkin said that Turkish Cypriots preferred not to mingle with Turks and vice versa.

My Greek cousins had told me about something similar in Greece. Greek Cypriot students snubbed the Greeks and Greeks snubbed them in return, for driving expensive cars and because the Greek Cypriots snubbed them first. My cousin also explained that during the time of the junta, it was Greek Cypriot students who were the most supportive of the Generals, which made them very unpopular.

My Turkish Cypriot friends told me about the 'Zezes'. These were the well-off students from Turkey studying in Cyprus whose car license plates began with the letters ZZ for 'temporary residents'. So they earned the nickname 'Zezes' – rich, spoilt Turkish kids. Some Turkish students were upset at what they saw as a total lack of religion amongst Turkish Cypriots, while Turkish Cypriots regarded them as dangerous fanatics. Things like this, which were only whispered in Lefkosha, my friends were now able to tell me freely. Talking about problems with the Turks was treacherous according to the Turkish Cypriot authorities. A few weeks later, completely unexpectedly, I was made to sit down and hear a lot more on this, by a Turk.

QUESTIONS

Almost all my new friends were left-wing supporters of CTP. This time, I did not actively set out to meet people for my research but left it to others who so wished to come and meet me. Those who came were people interested in meeting a Greek Cypriot, people who wanted to talk to someone like me, and they all belonged to the left. In their company, I found a new sense of freedom. This was to be the most enjoyable research period of all because they wanted to learn from me as much as I did from them. From the start, I had real conversations rather than monologues where they spoke and I took notes. We felt that we could talk to each other freely, without stuttering and, if we felt like it, criticize our own sides without feeling fear. But they insisted that not everyone felt like them and that I should also talk to students who disagreed with them. Previously, people had often claimed that everyone thought just like them, that they spoke in the name of the whole community. My friends felt that they belonged to an important but politically sidelined group. They were people whose parents had trouble finding a good job, let alone a government job, in a society where nationalist right-wing credentials, especially if combined with the highest qualification – being an ex-TMT fighter – opened the doors. Diplomas, degrees, and qualifications did not count for much. With these people I finally became 'Yiannis'.

We also felt close for having many questions about each other. And for sharing a sense of uncertainty. They were not full of certainties about 'evil Greek Cypriots', but wanted to find out about ENOSIS, what it meant in the past, what it meant now, what Greek Cypriots thought about them, about the coup and if Greek Cypriots supported it, even about the effects of the division on Greek Cypriot refugees. We were able to share our shame for what we had done to each other, and what we were still doing. They were young people without a future and without a past. Their history had never been written and they had no flag.

But some questions created problems. When I asked what kinds of expressions Turkish Cypriots used about Greek Cypriots, I was met by an embarrassed silence. Fortunately, one was a real teaser of a woman who liked to taunt me with such expressions like *gavur tohumu* ('seed of an infidel'). They explained how 'seed of an infidel' had also been used in the past for Cretan Muslims who had moved to Turkey during the population exchanges between Greece and Turkey. It was sometimes used for Turkish Cypriots in Turkey, suggesting that their mothers had been Greek. Alternatively, they were sometimes called 'English bastards'. In return, I was able to explain how *tourkosporoi* ('seeds of Turks') had been used for those who moved the other way round, like my grandmother. They were pleased to let me know of another nasty expression Turkish Cypriots used about the Turks. *Karasakal* I already knew, but *fija* I didn't. They did not know it came from a Greek word meaning 'seaweed'.

WAR'S BIRTHDAY PARTY

'To War and many happy returns,' I said, proud of myself for having put in the first toast and for saying it in Turkish. 'No, no,' my Turkish Cypriot friends protested in mock horror. 'You should toast to peace instead.'

Savash ('War') was a student in Istanbul and we had all gone out to a restaurant in Kumkapi to celebrate his birthday. We were both born in 1964. When we spoke about names, they told me to read about another boy called War. This boy had become famous in the writings of a noted Turkish Cypriot psychiatrist. The boy was also famous because of the poems his father had written about him when he was born. He was born during the fighting of the 1960s. During the fighting, his father was separated from his mother when she was about to give birth. Not knowing if mother or child were alive, the father wrote several poems to his son War, including references to statues of Ataturk. Later, the psychiatrist was called to help the boy. He wrote about how War thought he had been marked by destiny. Because of his father's famous poems he felt that he had become a symbol. Once, War experienced a narrow escape when a Greek Cypriot bullet just missed him. Growing up amidst all the fighting, he gradually came to feel that he was a kind of living monument, a living statue. He identified himself with the statue of Ataturk and was afraid that if he scratched himself he might peel away as if made from plaster.

My friends had a name for themselves: *Barishji*, those for peace. Others called them by an ugly word: *Rumju*. A *Rumju* was a slimy person who liked Greek Cypriots and mingled with them, a traitor in short. When it was used, it catapulted a person onto the other side, by asserting that they belonged there. This was the other Dead Zone in Cyprus, the chasm between left and right. The other Dead Zone had its own paradoxes. One side – the two lefts – worked to diminish the Dead Zone; the other side – the two rights – deepened it, as they pulled Cyprus apart towards the two mother-fatherlands.

ARMY MEMORIES

> Those who fail in life become tramps, those who fail as tramps
> become army officers.
> – Greek Cypriot and Turkish Cypriot proverb

This and other military secrets were always whispered on the two sides.
We had been strongly cautioned that one should never, ever talk about
the army. Now, with my new friends we could even talk about that.
Cypriots of all kinds, I now realized, did not like the army. For Greek
Cypriots the most memorable day was the ritual burning of the army
uniform and boots after being dismissed. I served for the two years, two
months and 11 days. Everyone counted the days carefully. Some knew
from the first day exactly how many were left. Another pleasurable
tradition took place when countdown reached 100 days to dismissal.
Many then bought 'a metre', a soft measuring tape numbering 100
centimetres, normally used by tailors. In the absence of officers, it was
worn around our necks as a mock-tie. Its real function was to strike and
taunt anyone who was not yet able to wear one, the wretched beings
who still had more than 100 days to go. We did learn some useful skills,
though, like maths: 1 Greek = 10 Turks.

Who said that mathematics has no morals? The moral was that
Greeks had the indisputable strategic advantage over Turks. A moral
to raise morale. This reminded me of the annual army exercises on the
Greek Cypriot side, meant to test the army's effectiveness in real battle.
Would the army emerge victorious in such an eventuality? Just to be
on the safe side, the exercises were always named *Nikiforos* ('Bearer of
Victory') in advance.

I was not surprised to hear that the other side had the same proverb
and army maths. We had more sayings in common: 'Where the army
begins, logic ends.' This emerged from our similar experiences of the
army, senseless and chaotic beyond description. Nothing ever worked
to plan, except the immaculate parades and the exercises during which
the non-existent enemy was always triumphantly defeated. Perhaps it
was all the fault of the top brass, the Minister. Ministers of Defence all
had the same traits. Before their appointment, they spoke like ordinary
human beings. Once they became Minister of Defence, they only
spoke in bold underlined capitals. Every grand word loudly uttered
was underlined by vigorously shaking the hand with the index finger
pointing up.

During my army service I had been in charge of the storage, accounting and safekeeping of all material goods in the camp, from pins to army trucks. I had taken up the post when I was eighteen. The person who had been in charge was in a hurry to get out – no wonder – so foolishly I allowed myself to be rushed into signing a form to say that all the goods were there and that I had counted every single object, from thousands of bullets, to hundreds of belts to all kinds of tools for army trucks. Soon I realized that many soldiers had set up fully equipped mechanic's workshops at home. An enormous number of tools were missing. I had to find a way to replace them, so I developed an expertise in the scrap yards of Cyprus. I would buy broken tools from those who bought the broken ones dead cheap from the army as scrap iron, and return them to the Central Army Depot. There, once a broken tool was presented, a new one could be issued in its place, if I could persuade the person in charge that it had broken from natural use. Fortunately, the soldier in charge had been a schoolmate. Otherwise I might have had trouble claiming that fifty jacks had suddenly broken, all at the same time – though one could never know with the army. Mountains of jacks and screwdrivers were lying around at the scrap yards and I could buy these for next to nothing, at scrap metal prices. I spent long afternoons at the scrap yards sifting through hundreds of jacks, trying to find the makes that the army used. I exchanged them at the Army Depot for brand new ones. The people at the Depot would sell them back to the scrap yards, and if needed I could buy them back again and take them to the Depot for replacement. Within the army context, there was nothing strange about this. It was usual army life. Older officers who had done this themselves told me what to do.

If this was peace, what would war be like? It was all very well for generals to make their detailed plans and back-up plans with coloured crayons on tidy maps. I was sure the other generals on the other side had their own equally tidy plans. But what would the real thing be like? It could only be some kind of random slaughter. In the chaos of war, generals would confidently move their pawns about, only nothing would work. Who got killed and who lived would be a matter of chance.

I remembered having spoken with a couple of Greek Cypriot friends about the 1974 war. Panikkos had told me what it was like for him:

> When Turkey invaded, our camp had to quickly move to its designated location. Among a great deal of confusion, things and people were loaded and we finally set out. On the way trucks were

breaking down, the ones that managed to start I mean. Most did not even start. Out of twenty trucks only four managed to reach the area where we were going to fight. We had orders to attack by night. We were not sure where the enemy was and we had to walk slowly forward in the dark. This was war, the slightest noise could cost us our lives. Next to me there was this guy. You know the kind of guy who cares about nothing. He was walking forward smoking a cigarette, at night! He had his gun over his shoulder and then with the other hand he was holding a small radio and was listening to music. Listening to music! I still wonder if he was sane. Anyway, at some point they realized we were coming and there was exchange of gunshots. In the morning we ended up outside this house in the middle of nowhere and we could see them. The plan was that we would hit them with a missile from a bazooka and then attack. The guy who had the bazooka was summoned after much shouting, because our portable wireless was not working either. He came and took a shot with the bazooka, but the place there was full of sand and he raised a cloud of sand that clogged our guns and then we could not attack. Eventually, our officer told us to retreat. On the way we picked up the dead. What had they died for? I ask you this now. For nothing. All this big manoeuvre, from the army camp to the enemy position and we did nothing at all in the end.

Panikkos went on. 'After the war, I spent my time in the central headquarters at Nicosia. The officer in charge was the bitterest man I ever met. His main concern in life was our hair, that's *all* he was interested in. Everything was in chaos, and all he cared about was hair.'

One of the problems, as my new friends also confirmed, was that communists were often sent to the worst spots. That often meant right on the Dead Zone. Once there, they sometimes got to know the people opposite, and realizing that they too were leftists they sometimes became friends. But some of my Turkish Cypriot friends had not been to the army because unlike Greek Cypriots, who had to join right after high school, they had the option to join after university. Some had decided never to join, even if it meant never returning to Cyprus. Even if it meant living in Turkey. They were the first people I met from Cyprus who had chosen not to go to the army.

NOT WELCOMING A RETURNING HERO
I was sitting at the coffee shop table listening to the speakers in the

square at Dikili. Dikili was a seaside town where an annual festival for peace and workers' solidarity was held. The man sitting next to me suddenly spoke to me in Turkish: 'Why do they hate us in Cyprus so much?' He saw my surprise but continued: 'Yes, why do they hate us so much in Cyprus?' I thought there must be some misunderstanding. He was asking me, a Greek Cypriot, why we hated them? I began to explain that I was Greek Cypriot but he cut me short. 'No, I mean why do Turkish Cypriots hate us?'

I had gone to Dikili with my Turkish Cypriot friends who each year participated in the festival. Many left-wing politicians and activists from various countries were there, including the Turkish Cypriot leader of CTP and the leader of a small left-wing party, YKP, the notorious New Cyprus Party, the most outspoken in favour of Cypriots. The leaders of these parties had just finished their acid speeches against the Turkish Cypriot authorities and the authorities of Turkey. They accused them both of adopting oppressive measures against Turkish Cypriots. The man next to me had been listening silently. He drew on his cigarette and his eyes closed a little in his rough weather-beaten face:

> I was in the army in 1974. I come from a village near here and suddenly I found myself in the war in Cyprus. I couldn't believe my bad luck. Cyprus seemed so far away. We knew nothing about it. But once it happened, the officers started telling us what you... well not you, you were too young then, I mean what the Rums did to our Turks in Cyprus, to us. Yes to us, back then it was all 'us'. Before, I had never really thought of them but in those days it felt as if they had done something to my family. I'm talking about the mass graves, the killings, the rapes of our women. While we were fighting in Cyprus they were telling us that Rums were still killing Turkish Cypriots. And all about what the Greeks had done to us Turks in the past when they came to take our country. So I found myself in Cyprus, a soldier in the war. The things that happened in those days... How can one describe the war? We were filled with anger, with hatred, for what the Greeks had done and what they were still doing. We were young, you know, *delikanli* ['crazy-blooded']. But now I feel shame when I think of what we did. Some things I saw, some I heard...

He hesitated, wondering perhaps whether to describe what he saw. But he continued:

When it was over you should have seen how Turkish Cypriots received us, like heroes, like they had been living for a hundred years without air and we gave it to them. They treated us like kings. When I went back to my village there was a celebration and later people would point me out to their children and say, 'He is brave, he fought for Cyprus.' Well, after the army I tried working here but couldn't find anything. So I decided to try Cyprus. They were saying all kinds of things then: 'Go, they will give you a house, they will give you land, you are their heroes, you will find someone to marry there.' I was still single then. I thought of how they had treated me when I was there, of what we did for them, and so I went back. They gave me a house and some land at this village with other Turkish Cypriots, and there were some Turks there too. Of course the best houses and plots had already been taken. Now, five years after the war, everything had changed.

He drew a final puff, lit a new cigarette and offered me another.

Now it was as if we were criminals or carried some disease. In the village there were two coffee shops, one for them, one for us. We did not go to the coffee shop where Turkish Cypriots went and they did not come to ours. I sometimes heard a murmur when I went around: *karasakal*. It meant backward, religious peasants. Yes, we did build a mosque. Not myself, I'm not religious, other Turks built it and Turkish Cypriots didn't come. Others called us *Turkyeli*, the ones who come from Turkey, as if we were not all Turks. They said we took their jobs. As for a wife, no way. It was like I was a different person now, not the one who went there five years ago and fought for their freedom. I know you, the Rums, hate us. I can understand why. Now I'm not proud of what we did there. I try to forget some of the things I saw. But how can they hate us? So I came back here.

I couldn't help feel sorry for him. Then I regretted it. Should I feel sorry for someone who came to fight in Cyprus? Didn't he bear any responsibility? He was ordered to fight in a war, as all of us might be one day. Perhaps he was not responsible then. We all lived in societies where the most sacred duty demanded of us was to kill others in war when the state ordered us to. There seemed to be no choice. But my Turkish Cypriot friends had shown me that there was a choice, even if it came at a heavy cost. Then there was responsibility too. What would I have done if called to fight? In principle, I was against war. But I wasn't sure if I would have the courage to stand up for my beliefs if the time came.

ACTING PROBLEMS

Lale was now training as an actress in Istanbul. Her eyes were a striking deep blue, her hair short and nicely cut. One reason I liked her was that even though she was Turkish Cypriot she spoke Turkish in a way that sounded so polite and clear to my ears. I was still trying to improve my Turkish and she had a refined Istanbul accent. This was why many others disliked her.

'It's so difficult to become an actress in Turkey, I'll never make it,' she sighed with clouds in her blue eyes:

> It's like one step forward and two steps back. At the acting academy here as soon as I open my mouth, everyone knows I'm from Cyprus. My accent always gives me away, ever so slightly. I do pronunciation lessons and practise so much, but the problems really begin when I go back home. Here I have to learn to speak proper Turkish, so that no one can tell I am from Cyprus when I act. When I'm in Turkey I spend most of my time with Turks. Otherwise, I will never learn to speak properly. But when I go back home, there it's impossible to continue speaking like they do here. When I first tried it, people looked at me so angrily. I could read their thoughts. Well, sometimes I didn't even have to for they told me straight to my face. 'Who do you think you have become?' my own mother asked me. 'You go to Turkey to study and then you come back to the village speaking like this? Speaking like you are superior. Like we are all peasants while you have become something else?' You understand what's happening, don't you? They think I am being pretentious, when I talk like the Turks. They don't understand that I need to do this for my job. So whenever I go back to Cyprus for the summer, I speak Cypriot Turkish and when I come back I switch to Turkish Turkish again. Every time I come back I have to start from scratch.

Lale's problems reminded me of Greek Cypriot friends who had described similar problems in Athens. Greek Cypriots studying acting often failed the pronunciation exam. In films and TV productions made in Cyprus, the actors had to speak like the Greeks. Except in TV series showing village life, those series said to imitate the real Cyprus

– full of sheep, donkeys and goat's cheese, with women in their proper place, well covered and obedient. The accent had to be 'authentic'. This meant they spoke in a more rustic manner than was actually found in the villages. It was also difficult to find authentic settings. The problem with real Cyprus was that it was really difficult to find in Cyprus.

I only saw Lale once more, briefly, at the flat. She came with her boyfriend. That was the only time a Turk came there.

AMONG THE WOLVES

The three young men sitting opposite me, who had just turned eighteen, were wearing black, American, heavy metal T-shirts, their fingers adorned with silver rings bearing skulls. They were self-declared Grey Wolves. Well, Grey Cubs at least, I thought. The meeting had been arranged by my Turkish Cypriot flatmates, who insisted that I should talk to other young Turkish Cypriots with different views.

We were sitting outside, in the yard of a coffee shop sipping *chay*. Aktach came straight to the point:

> If there is a solution and we give away any soil, I myself will start shooting the Rums first. I have martyrs in my family whom you killed. All the time you wanted ENOSIS and you are not even real Greeks, you know. My father was a fighter in TMT and is writing a book about it all. I too read a lot about the Cyprus Problem and I know what I need to know. If Denktash ever tries to give away any of our soil, then an internal war will break out. You can't just give away soil for which so much Turkish blood was shed. We now have our side, you have yours and that's it. End of story. Each has our own state and that's how we must live in the future.

I pointed out the unanimous decision taken by the Turkish Cypriot assembly in support of a federal state in Cyprus. Did that not mean we would live in one state?

> I know what you are talking about and I disagreed with that decision from the first moment. Anyway, it does not express the genuine will of the Turkish people in Cyprus. That decision was taken under American pressure. We all want things to stay as they are. What if violence breaks out in the future, like in the past? Then what?

I didn't have much to say. There was nothing grey about their views. We soon said goodbye in mutual discomfort. I wasn't interested in meeting again and neither were they. I had heard them often enough before, on the Turkish Cypriot side, and their counterparts on the Greek Cypriot side.

BETRAYAL

'My father was a farmer. We were doing OK until 1963 when the killings broke out. I was only a boy then, feeling so afraid the Rums would kill us. The Green Line was drawn, the land was divided and my father's land, our fields, had become "the other side".' Jemal's eyes dampened as he spoke of how his father was killed. Jemal was in his late thirties, and he invited me to his house to talk and to meet his children:

> My father was a stubborn man. 'So what, I have been going there all my life, who will stop me now? Anyway, all the Rums around are my friends.' So he kept on going there. The TMT came to our house and told us that he should stop. The new 'law' was no working on the other side, no relations, no trade, no nothing with the Rums. And, of course, no speaking Greek among ourselves. But my father was stubborn like a donkey. He kept on going. One day a Rum friend of my father took him aside and cautioned him. 'Don't come here any more. It's too dangerous. I don't know if I can help you if anything goes wrong.' He said that his own son had taken arms and joined the groups fighting against us. My father would not listen. 'I only fear God, nothing else,' he said and kept on going. One day the TMT came to our house again. 'Hey Mustafa, come with us, we just want to talk,' they called and he went. Late in the night I heard my mother's screams, like a dog was being slaughtered. My father came back with his face all broken and bloody. 'It's nothing,' he said, 'I fell on a doorstep.' But later he told the family what had happened. I only found out after many years that they had beaten him with his head covered. One day five months later, my father did not come back from the fields. We started searching. First his dog was found, the one he used to take with him out in the fields. Then his body. The TMT came at once. 'You see, we told him not to go there.' They even told us the name of the killer. He was a Rum who drove a lorry. But later, when I was around sixteen perhaps, I began to hear things. That he was not killed by the Rums. That TMT killed him. But I refused to believe them. It was impossible to

believe them. I joined the TMT as soon as I was allowed to carry a
gun because I hated Rums so much. I don't know what made me
change later. I think it was two things, the university and the war
in 1974.

He went on:

In 1974 I understood what TMT really meant. When the Rums
attacked us and my friend right next to me was injured, none of
those brave TMT guys came to help. It was confusion in the war, the
Rums were attacking us in the village and we had explosives stored
all around us. I kept calling for help to carry them away, otherwise
we would all get blown up, but they just sat there talking or giving
orders. They were so scared they were going crazy, saying all kinds
of things that just came into their heads. Like one said: 'Let us dig
a big hole underground and hide the women and children there.'
You know Yianni, it's not impossible that some of the mass graves
of Turkish Cypriots from 1974 were created like that, by a lunacy
that someone like him came up with.

After the war I went to university. In Turkey I started to see things
differently and hear other things from Turkish Cypriot students
around me. And then one day I went back to our house. Now I
had to know. 'Why didn't you tell me that my father was killed by
the TMT? That so and so killed him?' It was like a bomb fell in the
house. Everybody froze. 'For us the issue is closed,' my uncle said.
'It's not good to talk about these things, it's not safe,' my mother
said. In the beginning they didn't want to talk about it, but when
they realized that I knew everything they told me what happened.
How a TMT man killed my father under orders, how other Turkish
Cypriots were killed by TMT and were later declared 'martyrs',
as if they had been killed by Rums. And how the TMT even came
to tell us the name of the killer, who was not the real killer. That
way they could kill two birds with one stone. Say that my father
was killed by a Rum and make us take revenge and create more
animosity. From then on I couldn't stand the TMT. I felt ashamed
for having been one of them, and for being so nationalist in the
past. Many people were killed by TMT but people still pretend that
they don't know, even though everyone does. The worst thing was
to grow up thinking that your father was killed by the Rums and
then find out. Can you understand how I felt, Yianni?

When Jemal's children returned to the house he called them over. As they were coming he told me that he had also invited me so that they could meet me. 'They never saw a Rum before and I don't want them to grow up thinking that you are monsters. I make an effort to help them grow up like they should. I don't want to betray them with lies too.' When Jemal asked them to come and meet 'a Rum' they did not seem surprised that I looked like a human being.

Later Jemal told me about the Museum of Barbarism. What he said was not written anywhere, he said, but he was convinced that it was the TMT who killed the woman and those children. 'At the time,' he said, 'Turkey did not want to get involved in Cyprus. So the TMT killed the wife and the children of a Turkish army officer in Cyprus in order to force Turkey to get involved.' I was not sure he was right, but the things he told me were disturbing. And they raised the some difficult questions about me.

As I was leaving, Jemal came to the door. He appeared anxious. 'Yianni, please tell me before you leave. It's not true those things they say that most Greek Cypriots are doubled-faced, that you are all fanatics, is it?' He needed reassurance and I gladly provided it. But after what he had told me I now needed it for myself.

OPEN SECRETS, CLOSED TRUTHS

How did the Dead Zone manage to divide the histories, the memories, the words, the names so powerfully? Who gave it the power to create such frightful chasms, allowing for no common ground? It was all based on four simple premises, shared in perfect symmetry by the two officialdoms and by the two rights. These premises allowed them to criticize those on the other side of the Dead Zone, as well as those on the other side of the other Dead Zone.

First premise: They have propaganda, we have enlightenment. They try to deceive others, we try to show them the truth.

The second was a bit more complicated: their propaganda has been more successful than our enlightenment. This was based on a sub-premise, itself a manifestation of the power of the Dead Zone: the rest of the world is with them. The world was split into those with us or against us. Nothing in between. Since no one was completely with us – as they should be since we were absolutely right – they were unfairly against us.

Then came the last two premises involving assertions and threats, but posing as understanding whispers of admission. 'This is a critical time for Cyprus. The discussions are in a critical phase. Let's not talk about our mistakes now.' This was an argument whose strength had not diminished after forty years of use. The main news headlines had been the same for more than forty years: 'THE CYPRUS PROBLEM IS IN A CRITICAL PHASE.'

And finally: 'You may be right, we did some bad things too. But we can't admit to these. Do they ever admit theirs? Do they ever criticize their side?' Those raising self-critical voices were swiftly catapulted across the Dead Zone. 'You speak just like Denktash.' Or: 'You are nothing but slimy Rum-lovers.' Put together, these four premises worked wonders. Those who used them claimed to be opposed but were in perfect cooperation.

NOMADS OF THE DEAD ZONES

Where were my new Turkish Cypriot friends now living? Where could they live? In no place really, none at all. They wanted to live in Cyprus but they knew that the economy there was in a shambles. Plus, being left-wing made things difficult for them job-wise. Turkey was another possibility but that was not where they wanted to be. This was another society with deep economic problems and human rights abuses, especially against people of the left. Their Turkish Cypriot passports were not recognized and so they had to get a Turkish passport to travel abroad. 'You see what this situation forces us to do?' they asked with a sense of bitterness also addressed towards Greek Cypriots. 'We have to get Turkish passports to travel anywhere. Or we are forced to live in Turkey.' Even with a Turkish passport, few countries in Europe would allow them to live there. Another option was to come and live on the more prosperous Greek Cypriot side. They knew that the Greek Cypriot authorities had to allow them since they claimed to be the government of all Cypriots. Whenever a Turkish Cypriot came from the north, it was triumphantly reported that 'yet another one who could not take the oppression chose to live with us'. But they also knew how hard it was for those who had tried it. They knew about the suspicion and discrimination they would encounter and how Greek Cypriots would publicize their move to score political points. This would make them traitors on the Turkish Cypriot side and their families would be stigmatized.

They were people without a flag. The flag of Turkey was proudly waved by the right as a symbol of gratitude to the mother-fatherland, turning any criticism of Turkey into an act of sacrilege, and as a loud statement of identity. The TRNC flag was triumphantly waved by the right as proof of the existence 'forever' of their state apart from Greek Cypriots. It also symbolized unity with Turkey, since it was exactly the same as the flag of Turkey in design but with the colours reversed, white for red and red for white, with the addition of two lines. They stood for the mother-fatherland on top and the babyland on the bottom.

They were left with no place to call home. Wherever they chose to live, they would be outsiders. All places had become Dead Zones for them because in Cyprus if one was not fully with one side or the other the only place left was the Dead Zone. That was why they worked towards creating a Cyprus without a Dead Zone.

Those who remembered described how initially they felt overjoyed with the arrival of the Turkish army in 1974. Their lives in the 1960s, when they were locked up in enclaves under constant fear, were not lives. In 1974, they were worried when Greek Cypriot extremists came to power with the coup, some of whom had become heroes by killing Turkish Cypriots in the 1960s. They thought their lives were over. The arrival of the Turkish army brought new hope and their own state with the promise of safety and liberation. But all the promises made that they would no longer be discriminated against, promises of freedom, democracy and prosperity, were betrayed. Now, they also wanted to tell me about their shame at having once been blind to the violence inflicted against Greek Cypriots.

In their presence I came to feel as if among my own people. I stopped being so afraid of the loud, threatening voices in Greek in my head. I also stopped hearing the fearful sound of my Stepfather's scissors when I wrote down certain things. But shame returned in a different form. When I saw the extent of their suffering, the dangers, and the price they paid for holding on to their beliefs, I felt that, in comparison, we gave in too easily to official directives, fears of media smear and the loud voices.

MEMORY AND FORGETTING

They were people without official flags and memories. Official commemorations, strongly supported by the right, were commemorations from the history of the mother-fatherland, or commemorations of gratitude to the mother-fatherland, or numerous commemorations of Greek Cypriot atrocities against Turkish Cypriots.

Left-wing parties, they now explained, sometimes grudgingly used the two flags and attended those commemorations.

They had only one commemoration of their own, the 'Commemoration of the Martyrs for Democracy'. This marked the deaths of two left-wing journalists killed during 1962 by the Turkish Cypriot right, which regarded them as traitors for working towards cooperation. On the same occasion, they commemorated the deaths of six left-wing Turkish Cypriot students in Turkish universities who died during student protests, killed by right-wing extremists of the Grey Wolves. This commemoration echoed in name and in logic one of the important commemorations organized by AKEL. This honoured the deaths of those who fell during the 'democratic resistance', killed during the fighting against the coup by Greek Cypriots of EOKA B and the Greeks who led the 1974 coup. Left-wing commemorations on both sides were commemorations of murders of leftists by their own right-wing extremists and by those of the mother-fatherland.

Many of my new friends were my age and had few memories of the events of the 1960s. All they could remember of their lives as children until 1974 were times of conflict and fear of Greek Cypriots. But their parents, who came from working-class backgrounds, made sure to tell them more. They had told them about the lives of people working together in the mines, of not caring then who was what, about neighbours and friends who happened to be Greek Cypriots back then. How life was also good once in their abandoned village in the south. How Greek Cypriots too suffered; and how Greek Cypriots too had been terrorized and killed by their own people. Plain things: that Greek Cypriots were not just murderers and fanatics. Things difficult to say in public, so all the more reason for them to be told in private. But the children, my friends, had also been creating their own memories as they asked to find out more about these things and by holding on to what they found out as their cherished secrets.

BACK INTO THE ZONE OF THE DEAD

This time the means to getting there were barred. There were no books written on Cyprus by Turkish Cypriot left-wing historians reflecting what I had been hearing. Their memories, experiences, and stories were only allowed to exist as rumours exchanged in whispers. There were additional reasons why it was difficult to get there. How could a history of ordinary, daily acts of cooperation be written? A history not based on heroes or martyrs, but on ordinary people? The kinds of histories we had become accustomed to called on heroes, politicians, and generals to speak about the past. This was a history of wars, spectacles, top political meetings, and changing dynasties. A history turning war into something so natural, that it appeared inevitable. A history presenting war as the motor of history. Its periods were defined according to the fates of rulers and changing dynasties. Ordinary acts by ordinary people were left out of the record. All those insignificant millions remained mute, unaccounted for, as if they were unimportant. Could one write a history where the mass of those silent people also had a say? A history saying something about the life of the largest part of the population? Did their lives really change from one dynasty to the next? Did the lives of half of the population, the women, really change as rulers changed? Often they did not, but the history books did not care. But it was possible to write this kind of history, and it had been done elsewhere.

Some people, so few, grew enormously after their death; others, millions of them, disappeared; and others were only allowed to live after their death in masquerade – killed by their own people, they were turned into martyrs killed by others. A five-metre-high bronze statue of Makarios portrayed him majestically erect, though not in a classical style. 'The Big Mak' was how UN soldiers joked about it. I remembered how years earlier I had stood in front of him in his real-life human size. That was when I visited Madame Tussaud's in London, the museum of life-size wax replicas of famous personalities. When I encountered him there I was taken aback. He looked so small that I thought this must be a British ploy to belittle him. Ataturk was another figure to make it into the museum. Apparently, many Turks who went to admire him were similarly displeased, finding his life-size statue disrespectfully small. We had all grown so used to their enormous depictions that anything realistic appeared small.

My Turkish and Turkish Cypriot friends told me various stories about Ataturk related to his size and masculinity. When he arrived in a town in Anatolia in order to meet the rough local fighters, they were shocked to discover how short he was. When he grandly addressed them in large words as politicians and generals did, but in a rather squeaky voice, they were exasperated. When he later asked for a 'very sweet' coffee – real men only drank plain bitter coffee – they despaired. Perhaps this was no more than a story. I was told that such stories were 'illegal' in Turkey. Certainly, they did not make it into history books or schoolbooks.

It was not easy to write history that included internal divisions and the killings of people by their 'own kind', where the murderer was not always someone from the other side. On the Greek Cypriot side, where there was less fear, where the left was stronger and more confident, where people were more affluent and less dependent on officialdom for their livelihood, it had become easier to write such histories. Some books appeared – roundly condemned for treachery, of course – about killings of Greek Cypriots of the left by EOKA. Such books coming from left-wing authors were also critical of the Greek Cypriot actions against Turkish Cypriots, critical even of the left itself for letting down Turkish Cypriots by wavering in favour of ENOSIS or choosing to remain silent. Even so, such books were extremely rare. Among Turkish Cypriots, another line had been taken, one less threatening. Some folklorists had begun to explore common folk customs of Greek Cypriots and Turkish Cypriots: dances, food, games, folk medicine, rituals. Even in a place as small as Cyprus, one where Turkish Cypriots once spoke well the Greek Cypriot dialect, one where people ate the same kinds of food and heard similar music, these had been treated as separated by national boundaries. Previously, Turkish Cypriot folklorists had only been interested in similarities with Turkey, never in comparisons and similarities with those they lived with in that small island. Except one. He had written a lot about Greek Cypriot folk culture. But, all his articles focused on what Greek Cypriots had taken from the Turks: words, food, expressions, names, etc. Never on any borrowing the other way round. In his writings, cultural influences turned into a one-way road, moving only in one direction from Turks to Greeks. The message was clear: Greek Cypriots should stop being so proud of their pure, authentic Hellenic culture, or blood for that matter, as he went on to show.

The kind of identity that my friends had been proposing, their version of what it meant to be Cypriot, was of a difficult kind. It was one they were still exploring, one they were unsure of, open, problematic. It had not been set in concrete or marble, it was not one informed by deep divisions from others. It had no flag, no anthem, no place of its own. It tried to be inclusive, to make room for the experiences of those on the other side, and those of their own side – dead or alive – who had been ostracized. It was an identity made by questioning and being questioned, rather than one formed of ready-made indisputable truths.

So why did I sometimes have this feeling of queasiness? At times I felt discomfort as we spoke about our island and our history. We had slowly, imperceptibly, begun to create our own Dead Zones around us by speaking so negatively about Turks and Greeks. To come together as Cypriots we were turning the Greeks and the Turks now into our opposites, our enemies even. I had felt the same when I wished to distance myself from Greeks. I was glad to note how often *kalamaras* was used and to collect stories of discord between Greek Cypriots and Greeks. But I had so many good Greek friends, even cousins, and I enjoyed Greek music and books. I gradually came to realize that there were many Greeces beyond the one I had encountered in our schoolbooks. That was the problem. I had mistaken the Greece we were taught at school for the only true Greece.

I was once as glad to hear nasty things said about *kalamarades* as to hear good things about Turkish Cypriots. My friends were glad to tell me about *karasakals*. Why did no Turks – except one, whose presence proved the point – come to the flat? There was another thing. In turning against the histories of animosity, we had been creating our own histories of cooperation: histories of the victimization and intimidation of those who strove to allow room for cooperation. Even if it was true that those stories had been erased from history, we spoke as if *our* history now *proved* that our desire for a united Cyprus was the only possible way ahead. History – our history – proved that… History, once more, commanded. Just like the official histories we so detested, whether ones of eternal conflict, or the others of peaceful coexistence. It was as if the dead dictated to the living what to do, and not the living that chose which of the dead could remain alive, who could speak, and what they were allowed to say.

Were we also turning what others said into outright lies? Our truth, their propaganda; just like them then? That was the question Jemal had posed to me. I did not believe that those atrocities had been a Turkish Cypriot fabrication. But I could see what made him say this. He had been lied to with such cruelty about the death of his father. How could he accept anything officials said after that? Did betrayal make me too go to this extreme?

Some facts of my own family history now seemed eerily relevant. Could there be a history of traitors there? My father's father had been awarded a title for his services to the British Crown while serving as the British consul in Rhodes. When I saw the MBE, Member of the Order of the British Empire, I noted that it was in my own name, since our names were exactly the same. More incriminatory facts lay deeper in the past. My 'queen' grandmother's uncle was the personal doctor of the last Ottoman sultan. His elderly daughter, whom I spoke to, remembered him coming home with a red velvet pouch full of gold coins after visiting the sultan. Later, he became a Turkish MP in the first parliament of Ataturk. Now, family members did not like to talk about him.

We all knew about the traitors meeting in the Dead Zone. Then again everyone was a traitor in Cyprus. According to the left, the right were traitors for not identifying with Cyprus but with the mother-fatherland, for having led most of the fighting against their own and those of the other community, and for dividing Cyprus. According to the right, the left were traitors for being communists, then for not identifying with the mother-fatherland but with Cyprus, and for not having participated in the armed struggles for independence. Being traitors was our only shared identity. Such was the bitter harvest of the other Dead Zones, the right-left divides.

Where could one stand to make sense of Cyprus? Where could one go, if one was only allowed to stand on one side or the other? Flying high above it all was not that easy. My friends had pointed me towards a new possibility. There was one place left where one could stand with one's feet on the ground, still inside the island, not on one side, nor on the other, yet in touch with both: the Dead Zone.

APHRODITE

Going back to meet Aphrodite was also getting to be more difficult. Not because it was prohibited, but because there now seemed to be so many of them. Was she the Goddess of Love at all?

That was how we knew her through our schoolbooks and lovely tourist posters, but that was not how the ancient Greeks saw her. They revered her as a goddess of uncontrollable sexuality, the goddess of irrational passion, a force far stronger than reason. She was a goddess of destruction. Homer had called her a seductress, a liar and devious. She was the goddess of subjectivity working against objective reason, causing love, hatred, rivalry and jealousy. She created states of mind that led to murders and wars between peoples. The ability of passion to rule over reason, to use reason and employ seemingly logical arguments for its own sake had turned Peitho, the goddess of Persuasion – propaganda, perhaps? – into Aphrodite's faithful companion. In Sappho's version, it was Aphrodite who bore Persuasion into the world, along with Panic and Fear. The version I preferred was Aphrodite as the most liminal Goddess, one situated between opposites – day and night, love and war, mortals and gods – demonstrating that there was common ground.

I was returning to her island again. By now I had spent more than a year doing research with Greek Cypriots, but only four months with Turkish Cypriots, one in Cyprus, the rest in Istanbul. I tried to get permission for more research on the Turkish Cypriot side. I failed but the Dead Zone captured me and made me settle there. It was finally time to go home.

CHAPTER SIX
PYLA/PILE
SEPTEMBER 1994–SEPTEMBER 1995

WELCOME TO A PROSPECTIVE SPY

I walked out of my home in the Dead Zone to buy eggs. This unique mixed village in Cyprus was a safe place, so I did not bother to close the front door. I waved good morning to the Turkish Cypriot woman opposite. She smiled back and I walked the few metres down to her neighbour, the Greek Cypriot woman who raised her own chickens. It took me less than five minutes to return and find two men in my study, examining my books and hovering suspiciously over my computer. Two pairs of dark sunglasses turned in my direction. This time I recognized them instantly.

Formal introductions were spared. 'What are you doing here?' the older man asked in Greek. I pretended I did not understand. 'I live here,' I answered innocently. I tried the best-defence-is-attack strategy. 'Who are you, coming like this, breaking into my house without permission?' I asked, as if I did not know. 'Listen, Mr-Yiannis-Papadakis-from-Lemesos. We are the ones doing the asking around here, got it? What are you doing here?' Joking time was clearly over. He lifted his sunglasses to look me straight in the eye. He let them down. 'Mr Yiannis, we want to know what you were doing last night at Ali's Bar in the company of three Turkish agents. And why have you come to stay here?' I explained that I had come to do research at this village where Greek Cypriots and Turkish Cypriots were living together. (Bored expressions, waiting for me to get to the point.) That I was working at an English university. (One eyebrow briefly emerged above a pair of sunglasses.) That I had gone to Ali's Bar the previous night for a drink and to see the place, with a man I had just met in the village and there we met two other men with whom we talked… (Cut short.) 'Mr Yiannis, we really want to know what you are doing here.' I repeated myself, adding that I had a research grant from the university. 'Fine, you have come to do research. So, you are paid by the English. OK, now tell us what exactly were you talking about with the three Turkish agents?' I explained that I had no idea whether they were agents, that what we were saying was our own business anyway and that I was not prepared to tell them what I discussed with anyone. 'Mr Yiannis, we are not journalists. We will not go about telling others what you tell us. We just want you to tell us what certain specific people told you. We will get back to you when we need to, you needn't look for us.' Evidently he thought the conversation was over. When I repeated that I would not tell him what he wanted to know, the big guns were brought out:

> Mr Yiannaki, are you refusing to cooperate with us on issues of national security? Are you refusing to help your country? You will do what we say, as any patriot would. Otherwise we will create problems for you, and your… research, or whatever you call what you are doing here, is over.

He placed a threatening hand on my computer. After they left, I walked out of the house, locked the door and ran to record our encounter on my portable computer and back up my files. I had already installed a security system before crossing to Lefkosha.

WATCHING

The two Greek Cypriot old ladies, a mother with her daughter, greeted me warmly when I walked over to them. My house was just behind the village square, theirs was right on the square, and we shared a common back wall, so three days after I arrived I went over to introduce myself. 'I am glad you are a Greek Cypriot,' the mother said:

> We were a bit worried our new neighbour could be a Turk. But you have good neighbours all around you. Opposite you is a young

family, Turks. Very good people, very quiet, and next to them live some more Turkish Cypriots. The old woman there, Zehra, often has her morning coffee with us. Wonderful woman, we have been friends as far back as I can remember. We have seen you many times and were wondering about you. Yesterday you bought vegetables from the Turkish grocer, then you bought a gas bottle from one of our grocers and then some fruit from our other grocer around the corner. Already we feel you will be a good neighbour. We have not heard any noise so far and you seem to get up early, at seven and go to bed early, at eleven.

We were sitting on the square, outside their front door. I remarked how nice it was to sit outside and just look around at passers-by. 'Yes, that's what we do in the summer. In the summer we sit outside and watch the square, in the winter when it's cold we sit inside and watch *The Bold and the Beautiful* on TV.'

On my left, Greek Cypriots sitting at the Greek Cypriot coffee shop were looking at the square and the Turkish Cypriot coffee shop, where Turkish Cypriots were sitting looking at the square and the Greek Cypriot coffee shop opposite. Above us, on the rooftop of the building next to the old ladies' house, the UN had a continuously manned watch-point, and on the hill right above the village I could see the permanently installed binoculars which the Turkish soldiers used to watch the village below. Secret policemen from both sides also came to the square to observe and – like it or not – be observed too.

I already knew a good deal about this village called Pile on the Turkish Cypriot side, Pyla on the other, from press cuttings I had been collecting during my earlier research in Nicosia. The media on both sides kept a close watch and so had I, when I had no idea that the Dead Zone would eventually draw me there.

When my request for further research on the Turkish Cypriot side was refused, I decided that my next best option would be this notorious village. It was located in the south-east of the island, right next to the Dhekelia British Sovereign Bases, near the coast of Larnaka. Pyla/Pile was the only mixed village inside the Dead Zone and had been under UN administration since 1974. There were around 800 Greek Cypriots and 400 Turkish Cypriots living there, their houses intermingling. How they managed to keep their village together ending up in the Dead Zone, belonging to neither or both, I did not know then. I went there because it was the only place in Cyprus where I could do more research with Turkish Cypriots, and it seemed like an interesting place.

By now I was married and had a baby daughter who lived with my wife in Nicosia, about thirty minutes away. We had agreed that, given the village's circumstances, they would not come to the village, and because they were more comfortable in our flat in Nicosia.

Pyla/Pile was the most watched place in Cyprus. Everyone – governments, police agents, local politicians, foreign diplomats, the Turkish Cypriot media, the Greek Cypriot and foreign media, plus this anthropologist to date – was watching this village. In the village, everyone was a spectator watching the others and an actor on stage being watched by the rest. And everyone there, as I would soon find out, was both a spy and a traitor. Because of its special status, a place belonging to neither side, or to both, it was said to be the centre spot for spying and smuggling. It was regarded as the gate through which unauthorized information and goods crossed between the two sides. It was a place beset with rumours and a place incessantly covered by the media. It was presented as a village of intrigue, mystery and danger, and *the* place for whiskey and king prawns. In contrast to Tahtakallas, that place next to the border, whose people were lionized as heroic *akrites*, the people here, living *inside* the border, were regarded as traitors.

Pyla was a gate in the Dead Zone between the two sides. By coincidence, its name in Greek meant just that: a gate. In ancient Greek, Pylos was the gate to Hades, the Zone of the Dead. Another coincidence?

COEXISTENCE AND CONFLICT
'Can the people of Cyprus ever live together again?' Everyone agreed that Pyla/Pile provided the answer. It was a symbol. It was living proof.

For the Turkish Cypriot authorities, Pile was a symbol of oppression: a place where Turkish Cypriots were once more oppressed by Greek Cypriots. A place where the West – the UN in charge of administering the village – sided yet again with Greek Cypriots. It was a place that proved that Turkish Cypriots and Greek Cypriots could not live together. It was living proof of a past of oppression and discrimination against Turkish Cypriots.

For the Greek Cypriot authorities, Pyla was a symbol of coexistence: a place where people lived peacefully and cooperated harmoniously, just like in the past. A place where the West – the UN – once more sided with Turkish Cypriots. It was living proof that Greek Cypriots and

Turkish Cypriots had lived together in harmony in the past, proving that they could live well in the future united Cyprus. Pyla/Pile was both the past and the future. And it was both damned and blessed.

For the people there who tried to make a life in the Dead Zone, it was something different again. It was where they had to live. Not an easy task. 'Living in Pile is like living on top of a powder keg,' was how the Turkish Cypriot grocer on the square put it during one of our first meetings. I had many chances to confirm this for myself. Every small event in this village had the potential to explode into a national issue, into a matter of supreme national honour. Pyla/Pile had the ability to amplify things tremendously. Not really the village itself, or its inhabitants per se, but rather those who watched it from outside, authorities and media alike. The smallest event would be reported in the two side's media in large headlines, ringing the alarm bells. It was the perfect source for news that could draw attention, frighten and alarm.

A FURTHER ACT OF AGGRESSION FROM THE OTHER SIDE IN PILE

WE ARE LOSING PYLA

THE UN ONCE MORE FACILITATE THE OTHER SIDE'S DARK PLANS TO TAKE OVER PYLA

According to the media, this was a place where no compromise could ever take place, where no ground could ever be lost. It was said to be the ultimate testing ground. Giving way just a little there prophesied national doom. The beginning of the end. But locals had very different concerns. These concerns, along with being constantly presented as smugglers and spies, were some of the reasons why they detested the media.

One day I was walking with a Greek Cypriot man when a Turkish Cypriot boy on a motorcycle almost ran him over. Mr Epaminondas screamed at the boy in Greek. 'Get out of here right now. Go, shoo. Get out of my sight and next time watch out.' The boy, who could understand Greek, was too young to be using a motorcycle and timidly drove away. Mr Epaminondas turned to me in exasperation:

You see? There is no police here, I mean no real police presence beyond the secret police. For the police to come in uniform there has to be a special reason and they have to get UN permission and accompaniment. So now you have all these underage kids speeding like mad on those motorbikes. Mind you, the same happened two days ago with one of our boys. I gave him a couple of slaps and let him go. But now, what could I do? The boy was theirs. I couldn't slap him because that could create real trouble. His father might come to ask for reasons and if there was a fight it could turn into a Greek-Turkish thing, and then you have the vultures of the media ready to blow it all up, always hovering over us ready to pick our bones.

On one occasion, some Greek Cypriots came to the village to eat. They drank quite a lot. Then they crossed the street to buy whiskey from the Turkish Cypriot grocer and tried to bargain with her. It was already very cheap and the grocer did not want to lower the price, so they pushed the woman, swore at her, grabbed the bottles and left. She reported this to the UN, and Turkish Cypriots became angry. Local Greek Cypriots were angrier. 'How dare they! Those bloody outsiders come and stir trouble here with the Turkish Cypriots, and then leave. And we have to clear the mess they left behind. We will all pay the price, us living here.'

People in the Dead Zone had to struggle to stay alive. They did this in myriad, small, daily ways. They had been at it for some time, even before the Dead Zone emerged in its current form. There were two stories that everyone wanted to tell me when I arrived and first picked up the courage to sit at the coffee shops on the square. They were about how the village managed to survive and hang together in the past. During 1964, right-wing Turkish Cypriots had come to attack the Greek Cypriots. They were stopped by local Turkish Cypriots. People openly admitted that this was to protect their co-villagers, as well as themselves, given the repercussions that were bound to follow from like-minded Greek Cypriots. Then – this was the second story – in 1974, Greek Cypriot right-wing extremists who came to attack the local Turkish Cypriots were stopped by local Greek Cypriots. They were stopped by local right-wing Greek Cypriots who supported the coupists, because they were the only ones able to stand up to their own kind. Turkish Cypriots repeated these stories as often as Greek Cypriots. (Later other sides to these stories were whispered to me.) These events, and the contingency that Pyla/Pile was close to the British bases were the reasons I was given why the village survived. In 1974, locals were able to move out to their fields, a few hundred metres away. There, they were in neutral ground, the British Base Area, from where they could always keep an eye on the village, and go back when things seemed quiet. The Turkish forces could not enter that neutral area and stopped short of the village.

The search for neutral ground was one of the challenges I faced. Even walking over from one coffee shop to the other turned out to be a problem. One had the Greek flag outside, small Greek flags criss-crossing the ceiling inside, photos of EOKA heroes, drawings of the Greek Revolution of 1821 showing battles with 'Turks', and a sticker with a Greek flag saying 'The true capital of Hellenism is not Athens but Constantinople'. In short, the standard decor of a Greek Cypriot right-wing coffee shop. A few metres across was the Turkish Cypriot coffee shop with mostly left-wing clients and no political decor, except a poster of a sumptuous blonde advertising Carlsberg beer sold by Greek Cypriots. No one ever walked from one to the other. No one would sit in the others' coffee shop. But I needed to make that walk in full view of everyone, making it the hardest twenty metres. Finally I found a solution of sorts, a cheat, but it took a couple of weeks to work out. And I only fooled myself really.

THE POWER OF DEAD ZONES

Borders were supposed to demarcate territory, determine what belonged to whom, and restore order. But who owned the border itself? This was the big issue in Pyla/Pile, where all three sides claimed some control over the village. Building permits inside the Dead Zone, for example, first had to be approved by the UN, based on a number of criteria. In areas of the village extending outside the Dead Zone they were under the jurisdiction of the respective authorities. Another major difficulty with borders was that it was impossible to define them beyond dispute. Even in the case of a thin line, one side could always claim part of the line itself. In this way boundaries acquired their power, as sites of dispute that could ignite and amplify conflict.

The problem over where exactly the border ended emerged in this village in a tragic manner. A Turkish Cypriot tried to build a shop to sell T-shirts at the southern edge of the village, towards the Greek Cypriot side. The Greek Cypriot authorities claimed that he was building outside the Dead Zone in the area controlled by the Republic of Cyprus. He argued that he was building just inside the UN-administered Dead Zone. This was a dispute about a few metres. When he tried to obtain electricity on his own by linking up to the nearest electricity pole, the Greek Cypriot electricity authority came to dismantle the connection.

He protested that his shop was inside the Dead Zone and they had no right to intervene there. The UN was called to adjudicate and decided that his shop was indeed on the Greek Cypriot side. The makeshift wiring was removed but this created friction between him and the UN. A few days later, during an encounter with two UN soldiers on a different issue, the Turkish Cypriot man was so enraged that he shot one of them. The injured man was able to return fire, killing the Turkish Cypriot.

LOOKS AND LANGUAGE

The Greek Cypriots living in the village could not cross to the Turkish Cypriot side north of the village. A Customs Office had been set up at the edge of the northern side of the Dead Zone mainly to demonstrate the existence of a separate state and turn the crossing into an inter-state border. The Turkish Cypriots living in Pile had – in theory at least – free access to the Greek Cypriot side since the Greek Cypriot authorities claimed to be the government of all Cypriots. Most Turkish Cypriots there worked on the Greek Cypriot side, because wages were as much as three to four times higher than on the other side. Since they also had free access to the Turkish Cypriot side, they could buy all their goods there, where things were much cheaper.

Whenever a Greek Cypriot friend visited me in Pyla, they expressed surprise, sometimes discomfort, at not being able to tell people apart. This caused problems, especially to local Turkish Cypriots. The village was close to the tourist area of Larnaka, where many Turkish Cypriots went to work or shop. Many Turkish Cypriots living there, who spoke the Greek Cypriot dialect fluently, had the same bitter complaint. 'I was waiting for the bus in Larnaka when a Greek Cypriot man started talking in Greek. He asked me where I came from and I said I was from Pyla. "So how do you get along with those Turkish dogs? Do you get along well with them?" he asked.' Once Greek Cypriots realized their blunder, if the Turkish Cypriot chose to reveal it, they were embarrassed. Turkish Cypriots also found themselves in a tough spot. If they did not explain, the Greek Cypriot might continue ranting and the situation would only get worse. If they explained, they sometimes heard comments behind their backs as they were leaving. 'My God, see how well he speaks Greek? No way you can tell he is a Turk. Could he be a spy then? Should we notify our police?'

KING PRAWNS, WHISKEY AND ADIDAS

By 1994, when I arrived there, the village restaurants and bars were closing. The village's Happy Hour in the grand scheme of History had finished. The shops selling cheap drinks, cigarettes and clothes were now abandoned. Most restaurants had also been forced to close. Up to 1989, hundreds of people, locals and tourists, came to visit from the Greek Cypriot side. Pyla was known as the cheapest place to eat fish. The fish was 'smuggled' from the Turkish Cypriot side according to Greek Cypriot officials, and so was everything else that was sold cheaply there. Buying anything constituted 'an act of illegal smuggling and national treachery': this was the official line. Even so, Greek Cypriots flocked to the village in their hundreds. 'In Pyla you eat twelve king prawns for four pounds.' That was the line that mattered. On top of that were the whiskey, the cigarettes, the leather jackets and the prestige brands such as Adidas or Gucci. They all came dead cheap from the Turkish Cypriot side. The whiskey and cigarettes were good, but the clothes were fakes. Greek Cypriots bought them knowing they were fakes and that they would fall apart, but they could always pass them on as expensive gifts to others who didn't. The whiskey they kept for themselves.

A rewarding division of labour was soon established. Greek Cypriots ran the fish restaurants, Turkish Cypriots ran the shops. Strategies were devised to keep things running as smoothly and cheaply as possible. Turkish Cypriots delivered the fish to the Greek Cypriot restaurateurs. Some restaurant owners employed both Turkish Cypriot and Greek Cypriot waiters for a good reason. If a fight broke out due to heavy drinking – who would drink anything but whiskey there? – say, between two Turkish Cypriot tables, then a Turkish Cypriot waiter would rush to calm things down. Had a Greek Cypriot tried to do this, issues could have exploded into national dimensions. Or if two tables, one Turkish Cypriot the other Greek Cypriot, brawled then a Turkish Cypriot waiter would rush to cool the Turkish Cypriots down, a Greek Cypriot to the others.

Turkish Cypriots in Pile refused to pay for services such as electricity, water and garbage collection to the Greek Cypriot authorities, claiming that doing so would mean that they recognized their authority. But when it came to obtaining scores of other official documents of the Republic, such as identity cards, social insurance documents or documents for government subsidies for farmers, when it came to receiving benefits in other words, Turkish Cypriots had no qualms. They applied for whatever they were entitled to, confident that they would get them. If the did not, they could accuse the Greek Cypriot authorities of blatant discrimination. Greek Cypriots were as quick to take advantage of Pyla's peculiarities. Those who owned restaurants installed a line to their closest Turkish Cypriot neighbour and received all their electricity from them free of charge.

Locals were fairly pleased with this situation, unlike the authorities. For the Greek Cypriot authorities, Pyla became a headache due to the issue of the trade embargo. Greek Cypriots had for years been arguing that other countries should not trade with Turkish Cypriots because the goods came from a state that did not legally exist and exploited occupied Greek Cypriot property. They were successful in enforcing an embargo internationally. But inside Cyprus, a situation emerged in Pyla where Greek Cypriots and tourists daily came to buy Turkish Cypriot goods. This caused uproar in the Greek Cypriot newspapers, which constantly accused the local Greek Cypriots of smuggling and profiting through unpatriotic means. Behind the accusations of treachery and smuggling lay a fair amount of resentment and jealousy of the villagers who were getting rich. The Turkish Cypriot authorities were pleased that all those goods had an outlet on the Greek Cypriot side and that their side could benefit financially, especially given the trade embargo. But they had concerns too, given their claims that the two peoples could never live together or cooperate. Pile became a glaring example of Turkish Cypriots cooperating with Greek Cypriots, and – adding insult to injury – a place where local Turkish Cypriots became richer than Turkish Cypriots in the north. Turkish Cypriots living in the north envied and resented the villagers for earning many times what they earned. Turkish Cypriot newspapers were quick to express the general feeling, rushing to condemn locals for unpatriotically cooperating with Greek Cypriots and 'selling out their national soul for money'.

Thankfully there were trade-offs, even for officials. Greek Cypriots were ecstatic to point out that in Pyla where people cooperated, Turkish Cypriots were much better off. Turkish Cypriot officials had their own reasons to be happy with Pile. After the Greek Cypriot authorities placed a police control outside the village to the south, leading to the suffocation of village trade, their political claims were proven right beyond any doubt: 'Another example of the inhuman Greek Cypriot trade embargo against Turkish Cypriots, like the 1960s, and the one currently imposed against us internationally, can now be seen taking place in Pile.'

FISHY DEALS

Mihalis came over to me from 'Macedonia'. He was angry. I was sitting at the 'Happy Nest Pub' on the village square, my own precious refuge. This was a Greek Cypriot snack-bar, also used by Turkish Cypriots because it was not loaded with Greek national symbols, and had chosen a neutral name in English, in contrast to 'Macedonia', as the Greek Cypriot right-wing coffee shop had recently been named. The Happy Nest Pub was ideal for those who wanted to sit on the square but preferred not to sit either at the Greek Cypriot or the Turkish Cypriot coffee shop, acts which might be regarded as taking sides. The locally based Irish UN soldiers, chosen in the hope that their own political problems might enable them to better handle a place like this, often went there for a drink. For me it provided a heaven-sent diversion from having to walk straight from one coffee shop to the other. Instead, I could spend a few minutes in the Happy Nest Pub and then go on to the other. Because the two coffee shops on the square were segregated, I was worried that people would think I was a spy telling those in one coffee shop what I overheard in the other. The fear of being taken for a spy followed me even in Pyla/Pile where everyone was said to be one. Many villagers of both communities said so to my face. *They* didn't think I was one, but *others* thought so.

Mihalis sat next to me. 'Did you see what happened over there in Macedonia?' I hadn't. The old coffee shop was newly baptized after the violent conflicts in the Balkans. A dispute had taken place regarding the ownership of the name Macedonia between Greece and the newly created state that wanted to call itself Macedonia. Greeks protested that the name was Greek and only Greek, that only they had the historic right to use it, and that calling the new state Macedonia might encourage the others' expansionist plans to take over part of the area in Greece called Macedonia. Right-wingers in Pyla decided to name their coffee shop Macedonia, adding a Greek flag next to the name, as an act of solidarity with their Greek brothers. This was in violation of the strict UN rules determining the use of flags in the village.

'There you have it,' Mihalis went on:

> A smuggling deal right in front of your very eyes. Didn't you see? That man sitting there who called over to the Turkish Cypriot man walking by has the largest fish restaurant on the coast. The other is the biggest trader of fish here, the biggest smuggler I should say. He called the Turkish Cypriot to arrange a time to drop by his home,

where he keeps all the fish, and buy what he needs for his restaurant. He even arranged for cheap whiskey to be available so as to get both in one go. Do you understand what has happened here in Pyla now? You know about this checkpoint that our police imposed on us to suffocate the village. They said that our government put it there to stop the smuggling. But what really happened is this. All those restaurant owners on the coast were losing out bad from all the tourists and our people who come to Pyla. So they complained to the government about smuggling in Pyla, they got newspapers to publish articles about Pyla all the time, until they managed to get a police control at the entrance, close the village down and ruin us. And then, they, the same people, come to the village, buy their fish and whiskey here and leave the village through the other road passing through the British Bases. Now that road is out of bounds for our police so they can take the fish to their restaurants down the coast in total safety.

I had heard about this before from angry Greek Cypriot and Turkish Cypriot villagers. Apparently, all the professional smugglers used this other road. The ones caught unaware by the Greek Cypriot police at the checkpoint were those who did not know about it, people who just came to the village and bought a couple of bottles of whiskey to take home. They were arrested, prosecuted and became headlines in the papers, creating an atmosphere of fear and illegality around Pyla. After hundreds of such widely publicized arrests, eventually almost no one dared to visit. Everyone who was in the real business knew the right way, as did all the villagers, and the police of course.

The Greek Cypriot secret policemen often sat on the square to check illicit transactions. They sat at the Greek Cypriot restaurant on the square, one of the few that still had some customers. The secret police were its most regular customers, sitting there day in and day out, and perhaps the main reason it managed to survive. My house was right behind it and I walked past its back yard to get to the square. It was Mihalis first, and many others later, who told me why the fence behind the restaurant was broken. I had walked past many times but never noticed. It was broken because that was where the Turkish Cypriot fish trader went to deliver the crate of fish, at the back of the restaurant unseen by prying eyes on the square. Meanwhile, the secret policemen sat in the front eating the fish as they vigilantly watched the square.

CHEATING

The people at the front of the crowd around the Greek Cypriot Chief Humanitarian Officer were deadly serious. The other Greek Cypriots at the back, where he could not see them, were having a good laugh at the answer he had just received. He asked the usual question. 'So do you get along well with the Turkish Cypriots here?' He was sitting on the balcony of Macedonia surrounded by Greek Cypriot villagers who were, as usual, trying to use the opportunity to voice complaints and make demands on the government. Predictably, at some point, a couple of locals sounded the standard alarm bells by telling the officer that the Turks were really gaining ground in Pyla. The tone was one of urgency and fear, one I had never heard during our own conversations. Others in the back had already begun to smile, knowing where this would lead: to demands for government money in order to enable the local Greek Cypriots to remain strong in Pyla. As the demands were fired, the officer began to get upset and tried to change the topic by asking the usual question. A man in the front, earnest-faced and serious, immediately gave the appropriate reply, as the others in the back were laughing. 'We get along very well of course. Look, they even come to our coffee shop all the time. See inside, that man playing cards right now? He is Turkish Cypriot.'

They were not laughing because the man in front had lied about the man inside being Turkish Cypriot. That was true. They laughed because Ibrahim was the only Turkish Cypriot who ever went there and he did this for a specific reason, as everyone there knew, except for the Humanitarian Officer. He went there to play cards with the Greek Cypriots. He was a likeable man and everyone knew his passion for gambling. 'He is ill with gambling, really hooked, addicted. He is a bit light in the head, poor Ibrahim.' As they all knew, no real gambling was involved. It was daylight robbery. A Greek Cypriot always sat behind him, ostensibly watching the game, signalling Ibrahim's hand to the other Greek Cypriots.

The local gambling war had been decisively won by Greek Cypriots. In the early years after 1974, the heavy gambling took place across the street in the Turkish Cypriot coffee shop where devotees from both sides, not just locals, flocked. The police could not do much about it given their limited authority. The Greek Cypriot police were particularly worried that losses might place people in compromising situations where they might be persuaded to spy in return for writing off debts. They threatened some of the habitual Greek Cypriot gamblers, took others to the Greek Cypriot police station outside the village for interrogation and finally one night they beat four of them, stripped them naked and let them find their way home in that miserable state. That way gambling died out in the Turkish Cypriot coffee shop. Instead, it now took place in Macedonia, which was why Ibrahim went there. It was finally brought under control and was closely monitored, since the secret policemen often joined in the game.

Some Greek Cypriots were still suspicious. They took me aside, pointing to Ibrahim:

> See there, this Ibrahim? See how he comes to our coffee shop in order to play cards? Everyone thinks he is kind of stupid. Well, I don't think so. He is probably a spy, using the pretext of gambling to come and listen to what we say. Why else would he come here day after day if he always loses? You know, looking stupid is the best cover for real spies.

Their comments upset me. I was not upset by the suspicion, which was as prevalent as the air in the village and included everyone. I was more upset because if this was what Greek Cypriots said about someone like Ibrahim, what would Turkish Cypriots say of me when I went to their coffee shop? Or, come to think of it, what were Greek Cypriots saying? I heard people were saying things about me like 'Well, if he spends so much time here away from his family, surely he must have a higher purpose.'

THE TURKISH CYPRIOT COFFEE SHOP

Before going there, I knew how suspicious my presence would appear. I had to make sure I was well introduced. A Greek Cypriot friend introduced me to two local Greek Cypriot families who in turn introduced me to others. 'Let me call our village headman myself,' said the wife of the first family. 'Don't go to see him out of the blue otherwise he is sure to take you for a spy.' How about Turkish Cypriots? In the end, it wasn't so difficult. The other Dead Zone worked in my favour.

Left-wing Turkish Cypriot friends living in the south, in Lefkosia, called up their friends in Pile and told them I was going. Their friends introduced me to the owner of the Turkish Cypriot coffee shop in the square, who was himself left-wing. He was kind and when I explained my plans and asked for his permission to sit in his coffee shop he made me feel welcome. From that day on I would sit there, sometimes alone in the morning reading newspapers, usually with other Turkish Cypriots, most from the left, who tried to make me feel comfortable and help me understand that elusive village. Often, they would lean forward and whisper in my ear. Most people were kind, polite at least, except some younger men of the right. From the first day to the last, they gave me nasty looks and avoided me.

When I first started going to the coffee house, an old man said I had no right to be there. I was sitting with some other retired men, struggling to explain the reasons for my presence there – always an effort. The old man hit his cane on the floor, as his face turned red with anger. 'How dare you come here to our coffee shop? You are a Greek Cypriot spy, coming here to hear what we say and then tell your people. Get out, right now.' I prepared to leave but a firm hand on my back made me stay. Ersen, one of my friends' friends, intervened and told the old man off for showing such a lack of hospitality and manners. He then spoke close to me. 'Stay here, Yiannaki, it's him who should leave our coffee shop. That bloody fascist.'

Right-wing Turkish Cypriots often talked to me, even if some of the younger ones made fun of me and tried to confuse me. They talked to me in order to make sure that the others' views, those of Greek Cypriots and left-wing Turkish Cypriots, did not prevail. I only began to feel comfortable there a few months later when, in the course of the same day, I was allowed to pay for the coffees for the first time and was called a spy, not behind my back as usual, but right to my face.

'TROUBLESOME HOJA CAUSES DISTURBANCE IN PYLA'

The headline of the DISY-aligned Greek Cypriot newspaper was disturbing. How come there was a *hoja* here causing such a racket and I, the resident anthropologist, had not even noticed? This article, followed by another the next day, described how Greek Cypriots in Pyla were deeply disturbed by the recent arrival of a *hoja*, the Muslim religious functionary, who made the call to prayer from the minaret. The minaret was right on the square, only a few metres away from my house, and I had heard nothing. Whereas the reporter, who did not live there and I had not seen in the village, knew all the details.

That afternoon I paid close attention and indeed a *hoja* climbed the minaret and made the call to prayer. He called without a loudspeaker, in his own barely audible voice. That was why I had not heard him. Neither had anyone else, it appeared. I immediately walked over to Macedonia, while he was still calling, to see the reaction of Greek Cypriots. There was nothing to see. No one paid any attention. I waited for a comment that was not forthcoming, then I tried the direct approach. I nonchalantly pointed out the *hoja* and waited for a reaction. People did not seem to care. Only an old man made a comment. 'Well, their *hoja* is there now. So what? We have our church bells ringing, they have their *hoja* calling. We have our religion, they have theirs and that's it.'

But the journalist was right – in a way. The *hoja* did cause trouble. In the evening I went to the Turkish Cypriot coffee shop. It was a cold winter night. Only three men were sitting outside in the cold, two old locals with the *hoja*. The others inside were laughing. My left-wing friends found this particularly amusing:

> So, these two old men brought the *hoja* to the village. You know we don't care about religion here. Not like those Turks from Turkey. Anyway, they brought the poor old man who has just finished the prayer in an empty mosque. They were embarrassed and tried to at least appear hospitable so they invited him to the coffee shop. But now they are ashamed to bring him inside after the empty mosque, to see that the place is full and everyone is drinking brandy. So they kept the poor old man outside in the cold.

ELECTIONS

At around ten in the morning I took a break from writing up my notes to buy yogurt. I put two empty clay pots in a plastic bag and walked towards the square. I was surprised by the commotion. It was full of Turkish and Turkish Cypriot flags criss-crossing the square. Large, dark cars were parked outside the Turkish Cypriot coffee shop. Everyone was there. The square was full of Greek Cypriots watching the Turkish Cypriots in their coffee shop. I knew the election campaign was on. I was embarrassed for not having picked up on any of this going on only a few metres from my house, and sheepishly entered the Turkish Cypriot coffee shop, still carrying the shabby plastic bag with the two yogurt containers. Suddenly I came face to face with the Turkish Cypriot leader, Denktash. He was about to sit down and speak. I edged towards his local party representative, who I knew, and asked if I could stay. He whispered to Denktash who turned, looked at me and nodded that it was fine.

He spoke for fifteen minutes about the usual things in front of a small audience of old men and women, the latter having made their way there for the first time. They were so few because it was early and all the men were at work. When Denktash finished, his local man thanked him, pointing out that this was a wonderful opportunity for everyone to personally ask their leader anything they wanted. An embarrassed silence followed, the kind that made people suddenly interested in their shoes. He repeated the invitation. He fiddled with the knot of his tie, loosening it a bit, and looked around. The few old people sitting around appeared too embarrassed to address the living legend leader of theirs. I was rather maliciously enjoying the scene and the feeling of embarrassment. People shifted uncomfortably in their seats, but help came. Denktash spoke. 'So where is this Greek Cypriot?' I stood up and introduced myself in various shades of pink, aware that everyone, including all the Greek Cypriots standing in the square, was watching me. 'Your Turkish is not bad, well done,' he commented and asked if my previous research about which he had heard good words – yes, that's what he said, 'good words' – was to be published soon. I was glad no Greek Cypriots were present. I replied that I still needed to do more research with Turkish Cypriots and had requested to spend more time on their side, but had been turned down. So it looked like I might never publish it, I ruefully explained. He replied that had he known he would have personally given instructions for the permit to be issued. If I wanted I could apply and he guaranteed that I would be allowed. I replied that now I was getting really interested in Pile, plus I had recently got married, so now even if he gave permission, there were higher authorities than him upon which things hinged. We kept on talking, though he occasionally stopped to see if any locals wanted to address him. But no one else spoke, so he kept turning back to me. A few minutes later he left.

Local Turkish Cypriots immediately ran to take down all the flags and posters, because the UN had protested, as an armada of Greek Cypriot journalists rushed into the square, tyres screeching, all leaping out of the cars with cameras ready to catch Denktash. They caught me instead, still carrying the plastic bag, as I was quietly trying to leave through the back door in order to avoid them. No other Greek Cypriot had been present in the coffee shop and no journalist had made it in time. The first Turkish Cypriot they tried to talk to pointed me out trying to avoid the camera. They all turned to me with the same question. 'Did Denktash say that Pyla is Turkish?' I replied that he did not and that I did not want to talk more and left. Immediately, the Greek Cypriot villagers gathered around me with the same question. 'Did Denktash say that Pyla is Turkish?'

'DENKTASH CAUSES PROVOCATION IN PYLA BY CLAIMING IT IS TURKISH'

Next day, Pyla was front news in all the Greek Cypriot papers, with the same headline, the anticipated answer to the burning question. Left-wing Turkish Cypriots immediately noticed the distortion in the Greek Cypriot press and were quick to point it out disdainfully, even if they disliked Denktash and would not be surprised if he had said that. Overall, they were delighted with Denktash's visit and the way things had been turning out. Two days earlier two other men, high up in the largest Turkish Cypriot right-wing party, also visited the village for the elections. As usual they went to the coffee shop but this time they made the mistake of going there in the afternoon when, as usual, it was full. As usual it was full of leftists, who snubbed them. But I was interested in the campaign, and so I introduced myself and asked if we could talk for a bit. The bit dragged into a long talk and they invited me to eat in the local Turkish Cypriot restaurant. We had a long dinner, after which they left. After the visit of Denktash, a joke began to circulate among leftists:

> They come, no Turkish Cypriots talk to them, who do they end up talking with? Yiannaki. Denktash then comes, no one talks to him, who does he end up talking with? Yiannaki!

They had a chance to rejoice more when I recounted a blunder an official from another right-wing party made. Once more they went to the coffee shop, at midday this time, and a few right-wingers joined them, along with myself. An old man, evidently a respected party official, opened the show with a poem. 'On my way here I made up a poem about your village,' he said. 'Please allow me to honourably offer it to you.' The poem recounted the joy of people for finally having their own state and living peacefully under the shadow of the Turkish flag, the village in unison with the state, the state in unison with the motherland. The poem reached a crescendo in the last line:

> *Living in beautiful Beyarmudu, how proud you should be.*

He smiled in anticipation of the clapping. None came, as people once again looked at their shoes. Beyarmudu was the name of the nearby Turkish Cypriot village. After an angry nudge from the party leader and some hurried whispering, the last line was repeated:

> Ummm... yes... *Living in beautiful Pile, how proud you should be.*

A few days after Denktash's visit, I was allowed for the first time to buy rounds in the Turkish Cypriot coffee shop, as a gesture of their appreciation for my role in the elections. Allowing me to buy rounds was a sign of acceptance. I was no longer just a guest and an outsider. That evening the leader of CTP arrived, a man I had met during my research in Lefkosha. The place was packed and the few young right-wing Turkish Cypriots who were there departed contemptuously as he entered. He recognized me, smiled, came forward and we started talking. The local CTP man, whom I had come to know well, smiled and came forward too. 'Oh, I see you know Yiannaki, our famous secret local spy,' he said loudly as they all laughed.

SOCCER AND DEAD ZONES

The local UN officer argued that if they agreed to the Greek Cypriot demand for a permit to build a soccer field, the field should be used by both communities. This was the directive he had received from UN headquarters in New York. I explained that Turkish Cypriots had made it plain to me that they were not at all interested in using the Greek Cypriot soccer field even for practice. They wanted their own field. The officer agreed that if this was the case it was pointless to insist on bi-communal use. Greek Cypriots made their own pitch, and so did Turkish Cypriots eventually.

Once the local soccer team was mixed. I found out from a couple of very old Greek Cypriots that in the late 1930s the village's mixed team was called 'Balkans'. They showed me some old photos of the team. When I asked how come it was mixed then and had taken that name, I was told that that was the period of the 'Ataturk-Venizelos Friendship Treaty' signed by Greece and Turkey. That was also the time of the Balkan Entente, agreed amidst widespread and enthusiastic talk of Balkan unity and solidarity, only to be dissolved with the onset of the Second World War. During the 1950s, when ENOSIS and TAKSIM clashed, the team ceased to be mixed and two separate village teams were formed.

On evenings when European League football games were on, the men watched in the coffee shops on the square. Greek Cypriots watched a Greek team and Turkish Cypriots the Turkish team. The Dead Zone had come to separate soccer watching. What was interesting was how the other Dead Zone emerged through soccer watching.

A couple of Turkish Cypriot friends took me aside in their coffee shop one evening when a Turkish team was to play against an Italian side. I was feeling a bit concerned as to what Greek Cypriots would think, given that I was watching the Turkish team rather than the Greek one with them. The two left-wing Turkish Cypriot friends spoke softly. 'Just sit tight and watch what we are going to do to them,' they said with much winking and laughing. 'We'll drive them nuts tonight.' The game started. Each time a Turkish player made a bad pass or a mistake they roared. 'LOOK AT THEM. BLOODY IDIOTS. THEY DON'T EVEN KNOW HOW TO PLAY SOCCER THESE TURKS.' A bit later: 'USELESS. BLOODY USELESS. THEY CAN'T EVEN ORGANIZE A SOCCER TEAM AND WE EXPECT THEM TO RUN A COUNTRY.' The Italians scored a goal, the ball passing through the legs of the Turkish goalkeeper as he rushed towards the attacker. 'WHOAAA... SEE THAT? HE OPENED HIS LEGS LIKE A WHORE AND THE BALL WENT RIGHT THROUGH. WAIT. THEY ARE GOING TO REPEAT IT. WHOAAA... SEE THAT AGAIN? JUST LIKE A WHORE. WAIT, WAIT, THEY WILL SHOW IT ONCE MORE...' After the game they explained their political strategy. 'You see all these right-wingers coming here to our coffee shop to support the glorious motherland team. We don't want them around, but how can we get rid of them? So, when a Turkish team plays we just shred their nerves to pieces with our comments. See how they turn red but can't say anything? Anyway, the Turkish team always loses. Of course they lose, they're bloody hopeless that's why.'

The men usually left the two coffee shops on the square together as the games finished at the same time. They had each heard the others' screams and shouts. Usually both teams had lost and they could take some consolation in that. Someone would pose the question. 'So how did you do tonight? Oh, so you lost too? Well, better luck next time then.' The wish would be reciprocated, as they made their way home through the darkness, relieved in the knowledge of their joint failure.

LIVING IN THE MIDDLE

The singer in the fish tavern began his song in Turkish, switched to Greek in the middle and finished in Greek. Then he sang a Turkish song, as the Greek Cypriots sitting around, who knew it well, mouthed the words in Greek. Then he switched to a Greek one, and the Turkish Cypriots sitting around sang the words in Turkish. These songs were hits in Greece and Turkey, and popular on each side of Cyprus. The unauthorized trade in music between Greece and Turkey, which many people in Greece and Turkey were unaware of, was clear for all to see in this village. It made no sense to call the music or food people enjoyed either Greek or Turkish. It had not been possible to separate the food, music and dances that people enjoyed. Sharing, not difference, prevailed in that unique fish restaurant in Pyla/Pile.

In a departure from the established tradition, this was a Turkish Cypriot fish restaurant. Through his choice of performer, the owner had been able to turn his restaurant into a popular joint for all villagers. He prospered by exploiting the lack of Dead Zones around food, music and dance.

The Dead Zones around language were not clear either. People there, especially Turkish Cypriots, easily switched between Greek and Turkish, beginning one sentence in one dialect, ending it in another. In Pyla/Pile, people often greeted each other in the other's dialect first. A Greek Cypriot would say 'good morning' in Turkish to a Turkish Cypriot and she would reply in Greek. The two dialects, which had not yet been as rigidly divided as the two 'standard' languages, provided a common ground for people living in the middle.

COVERING PYLA/PILE

The same right-wing newspaper that had reported the *hoja* incident later reported another disgraceful non-event regarding a concert that took place in Pyla. Fedon, a singer famous in Turkey who came from the Greek minority there, gave a concert in the village. Some Greek Cypriot friends active in the bi-communal peace movement came to watch it with me. At some point, some people embraced Fedon and a small commotion ensued. I briefly saw a flag produced and then put away but couldn't tell what happened. Two days later I found out from the Greek Cypriot newspaper, in an article featuring a photo taken from a Turkish Cypriot newspaper's previous day's coverage of the concert. It was clear that the photograph was taken from a Turkish Cypriot newspaper because the headline in Turkish was still visible under the photo. The photo showed Fedon half covered with a flag of the TRNC. The Greek Cypriot article explained how some peace activists had gone to Pyla to admire and applaud Fedon, who danced covered with a flag of the pseudo-state. The implication was clear: they were traitors and so was Fedon. But the Turkish headline under the photo, that Greek Cypriots were not able to understand, and evidently the reporter did not either, said something different. 'FEDON FINDS HIMSELF IN A

DIFFICULT SITUATION.' From the headline, and as I found out from the original article, it was clear that something different had transpired. Fedon got into trouble when someone tried to cover him with a TRNC flag as he was singing. He did not like this and immediately removed the flag as the photograph showed him doing.

Pyla/Pile was the place some newspapers loved to hate. The village had to be defended at all costs from the encroaching others, otherwise who knew where they would stop. At the same time, the villagers were presented by right-wing newspapers on both sides as unpatriotic lawbreaking smugglers, or as spies and traitors. Pyla/Pile demonstrated to all – and it did this due to the enormous coverage it received – that the notion of natural loyalty to one's nation or state was not self-evident.

The locals saw the inflammatory media reports as direct affronts to the delicate balances they worked so hard to achieve in order to continue living there. They understood that Pile/Pyla was an anomaly in nationalist ideology, one that it would happily do without. They experienced the coverage of the media as constant incitement towards violence. Locally non-existent issues, or issues that they would rather deal with on their own, were inflated into alarming headlines leading to all kinds of interferences by outsiders and the authorities. In turn, hot-headed villagers who wanted to create trouble there, or say someone who held a grudge against a villager of the other community, found it all too easy to cloak their actions under the glittering mantle of national honour.

Living there provided daily access to both sides' newspapers, allowing me to examine how each side's press covered the other. Many newspapers had daily sections of significant events or articles from the other side. In the Greek Cypriot press, three issues regarding the other side were constantly highlighted. First, the issue of recognition. News of other states possibly offering recognition, but more commonly of refusing to do so, was always reported. Second was the issue of armaments and military exercises. Third was the issue of crime. All crime was welcome as a sign of social breakdown, but crime involving Turkish settlers was cherished. The overall image of the other side emerging through such objective reporting – 'Hey, it's not us who say this, they say it in their own press' – was of a society ridden by crime, continually arming itself and staging provocative military manoeuvres. The Turkish Cypriots also liked crime, corruption, armaments and military manoeuvres on the Greek Cypriot side. Somewhat predictably, the overall picture was of a society ridden by crime, continually arming itself and staging provocative military exercises.

But there were significant differences regarding the sources favoured on each side. Turkish Cypriots translated a lot of material from extreme right-wing Greek Cypriot newspapers, even if they had low circulation. There they could find all kinds of Revealing and Representative inflammatory statements. Greek Cypriots by contrast often favoured left-wing newspapers critical of the right-wing government. These were presented as Revealing and Representative, proving once more that Turkish Cypriots were displeased and wanted to join with Greek Cypriots.

It was also interesting to see how little either covered events outside Cyprus. In newspaper coverage, Cyprus was the earth around which the universe of politics revolved. Even when international events were covered, it was Cyprus that was really discussed.

ON BROTHERS' BROTHERS AND ENEMIES' ENEMIES

The events related to the collapse of the Soviet Union and the subsequent conflict in Bosnia had repercussions in Cyprus. The macabre term 'ethnic cleansing' came into vogue in the media worldwide and now everyone was keen to use it. Turkish Cypriots pointed to the 1960s, saying that 'Greek Cypriots had invented ethnic cleansing well before the destruction of Yugoslavia.' Greek Cypriots used the term for 1974 to talk about the division into two ethnically homogeneous areas resulting from the Turkish invasion, 'a blatant case of ethnic cleansing well before the destruction of Yugoslavia'. The two sides were united in castigating the role of the West in the Yugoslav conflict. Both saw this as indisputable evidence of western bias against them. Turkish Cypriots lamented western inaction during the onslaught by the Serbs against Bosnian Muslims: 'Yet more proof of the deep historical western Christian bias against Muslims. See how they just stand by and watch the Bosnians being slaughtered, like they stood by when Turkish Cypriots were being slaughtered in the 1960s.' Greek Cypriots saw the western anti-Serbian stance as further proof of long established historical Catholic bias against the Orthodox, 'just as the West has historically sided with the Turks against us Orthodox Greeks'.

Why did Turkish Cypriots side with Bosnian Muslims? Because they were Muslims would be the easy answer. But being Muslim did not matter much to Turkish Cypriots, nor to many Turks. When a foreign reporter asked at the Turkish Cypriot coffee shop if they ate pork or drank wine the reply was angry: 'Are you crazy? Of course. Have you ever tried the traditional way of eating pork in wine with coriander?' A better answer as to why these alliances developed could have been that Turkey sided with the Bosnian Muslims and Greece with the Serbs by simultaneously applying the rule that 'our enemies' enemies are our friends'.

This time a rare and, to my eyes, disturbing consensus emerged among Greek Cypriots. All were in favour of the Serbs, left and right alike. The left, the communists who were – at least in theory – atheists and against Greek nationalism still supported the Serbs. They supported the Serbs through the application of the opposite rule: 'our brothers' brothers are our friends.' The Serbs were supported by the Russians and so the communists readily adopted their brothers' brothers as their own. Plus, it gave them another opportunity to rant against the biased USA.

That Greek Cypriots reached a consensus on this of all issues was unbearable. Given the Serbs actions – 'pure western propaganda' according to the Greek Cypriot media – and given what Greek Cypriots had suffered, it was hard to understand how they readily sided with those inflicting such pain. A cynic might say that this was politics after all and that politics had little to do with fairness, rights or principles. But Greek Cypriots always complained about everyone else's unprincipled stance each time they employed for themselves the language of rights and principles to seek international support. Turkish Cypriots, who spoke the language of rights and principles with equal fervour, did not seem to support the Bosnian Muslims primarily on the basis of this either. One day, as we sat in the Turkish Cypriot coffee shop watching the news describing Bosnian Muslims' suffering, a left-wing Turkish Cypriot commented in exasperation: 'What is all this business now about our Bosnian brothers this, our Bosnian brothers that? Two months ago no one knew what Bosnian meant, no one had ever heard of them and now they are our lost brothers that we suddenly care so much about?'

Turkish Cypriots in Pile, right and left, often came up to me with a bitter complaint regarding the Greek Cypriot stance towards the Yugoslav conflict. 'Yiannaki, how can we ever trust the Greek Cypriots when you side with the Serbs?' I could only look down and they shook their heads. (I disagreed, so why feel ashamed? I disagreed, but did not say anything.) Left-wing Turkish Cypriots were especially hurt. 'You are hurting us, Yiannaki. How can we ever persuade our people to trust you when you support the Serbs? You are destroying us and building up Denktash. You've become his best ally.'

The spirits of those who were being killed in that bloody conflict were unceremoniously brought back and hurled about in the local political arena between Greek Cypriots and Turkish Cypriots, Greeks and Turks. There were further repercussions of a most welcome nature related to the conflict in Eastern Europe and the collapse of the Soviet Union. The sexual fantasies of men, Greek Cypriots and Turkish Cypriots alike, could now be fulfilled. Striking young women, tall, blonde with blue eyes, were all of a sudden seen to accompany men on both sides of the island of Aphrodite. In this case, it was not about religion or politics but art of course. Their official Greek Cypriot job description was 'artistes'. In their case, it was possible both to have sex with them and proudly display them. Previously, when it came to the Filipinas who worked as 'artistes' this was not possible. Sex was fine, but taking them out was out of the question. They did not fit the ideal standards of beauty. With the influx of whiter, more blonde women, the Filipinas were displaced from sex slaves into the domestic sphere, becoming domestic slaves. As in their previous work – strictly speaking they were never workers to be accorded workers' rights; previously *artistes*, now 'domestic *helpers*' – the human rights abuses involved were enormous, yet invisible. Cyprus was beginning to look more and more like a real western country, where darker people were employed to perform menial jobs. When it came to female slavery, Dead Zones no longer mattered. In both sides, within left and right alike, all were in agreement that principles or human rights had nothing to do with this whatsoever.

RIGHT AND LEFT

In this village things often worked in unexpected ways. Borders were anyhow sites of the paradoxical. I expected leftists to cooperate more and express a strong sense of fraternity but that was not always obvious. I expected those of the right to keep their distance, even act maliciously, but this was not clear either. It was, after all, partly due to preventive action taken by Turkish Cypriots of the right in 1964, and then Greek Cypriots of the right in 1974, that the village was not attacked and survived. Things there were more jumbled, more confusing, more like real life perhaps. Ideas and ideologies did not operate as consistently when judged by the actions of ordinary daily life.

Right-wing Greek Cypriots were as likely as leftists to buy 'smuggled' fish from the Turkish Cypriot seller. People would gossip about each other, degrade others or praise them irrespective, from what I saw, of ethnic descent or party side. Even the secret policemen from the two sides, who one would expect to detest each other and keep their distance, would often lock themselves in the restaurant on the square, close the windows and confer together. The old people found comfort from their loneliness with other lonely elders, irrespective. The women would read their coffee cups together in the morning and sometimes accuse the other of being some kind of witch in the afternoon. People would cooperate for work without regard for ethnic sides and political views, even if at the same time they would not go to each other's coffee shops.

The Dead Zone separating the coffee shops spoke to me of Ethnic Segregation. Turkish Cypriots did not even frequent the other Greek Cypriot coffee shop of the left, just behind the square. I thought that if people mingled, there would be more tolerance, more understanding, and less cause for conflict. One day the old Turkish Cypriot grocer told me why this was perhaps for the best:

> You see Yiannaki, the coffee shop is the place where people talk about politics all the time. It is the place where they like to behave freely, to shout and swear at others or make fun of them. Now imagine if I went there and a young Greek Cypriot who did not know me said something nasty about the Turks in my presence. I would get upset and there could be trouble. Or else people might not talk freely. They might think I was a spy. That is why I prefer not to go there, for all our safety's sake, to make sure none of us gets in trouble.

MEMORY AND FORGETTING

Everyone was keen to remember the story about how during July 1974 local right-wing Greek Cypriots stopped others from attacking Turkish Cypriots, or 'the village' as it was often put. Left-wing Greek Cypriots had things to add. 'Yes, it's true, that's what they did but do you know what the coupists did to us?' demanded Mr Akis. 'They came and took me by force from my house. Same with other AKEL people. In front of my wife. They tortured us. Our wives didn't know if we were alive then. I'll never forget those days. I'll never forgive them for this.'

I heard more about this when a Greek Cypriot man died in an accident. He was among the supporters of the coupists. Whispers were soon heard among left-wing Greek Cypriots. 'That was his payment perhaps for what he did.' But they were not referring to themselves. They were talking about one of the commonly known local secrets from the 1960s. A group of those Greek Cypriots had stopped a bus heading for Famagusta full of Turkish Cypriots, killed them and buried them near Pyla.

I was sure I would hear more on this from Turkish Cypriots, but nothing came. After a while, I tried to ask but people were evasive. It was not denied but it seemed that they did not want to talk about such things. After a while I dropped it, even though I heard it again from other left-wing Greek Cypriots. I only found out more when I returned the following year for a brief visit. As we were talking with two left-wing Turkish Cypriots about my research, I expressed surprise at having heard that story from left-wing Greek Cypriots but none of the Turkish Cypriots. The two men looked at each other. Each seemed to wait for the other to say something. 'Maybe we can tell you now, Yiannaki,' one of them said, looking at the other for approval, and receiving it with a pensive nod:

> I know about this because I had relatives on that bus. None of the people killed were from Pile, but those who did it were. But you see we don't want to talk about this any more. It's over and it will do us no good, especially here in this place, to talk about these things all the time. Some things are better forgotten.

This was in stark contrast to the official Turkish Cypriot view of what people should remember. 'PYLA: A VILLAGE OF UNPEACEFUL COEXISTENCE' was the title of a forty-one-page booklet about Pile produced by the Turkish Cypriot authorities in English. Out of the forty-one pages, twenty-seven did not refer to Pile at all, but to events of Turkish Cypriot victimization elsewhere during 1963 to 1974. The pamphlet responded to a comment in a UN publication presenting the village as an example of coexistence, and it explained how the UN and other western diplomats had been duped, as usual, by Greek Cypriot propaganda. It took up the task of setting the record straight. The smaller section of the pamphlet dealing with the village presented various instances of discrimination against local Turkish Cypriots. The term 'ethnic cleansing' was abundantly used in the pamphlet to describe Greek Cypriot actions. By showing case after case of Greek Cypriot aggression against Turkish Cypriots in the past elsewhere, the reader was invited to consider Pile in the context of a persistent history of 'ethnic cleansing'. But the kinds of memories that officials insisted upon seemed to be those that the locals, who were trying to make a life there, preferred to forget.

BACK TO THE ZONE OF THE DEAD

> Aphrodite the Cyprian, is not only Cyprian, but has many names.
> She is Hades, she is immortal life, she is raving madness, she is
> unmixed desire, she is lamentation… All the plans of mortals and
> of Gods are cut short by the Cyprian. – Sophocles

> The complexity of Aphrodite is such that it so pleases and so
> saddens the mortals. – Euripides

Why should one go back there in the first place? Why was the Zone of
the Dead such an important place to us all?

Should we really bow down and respectfully obey the words reaching
us from the Zone of the Dead? Whose words were they anyway? And
from which Zone of the Dead? Which Ataturk should one choose?
Which Aphrodite? Didn't the living have a say at all? I had encountered
many heroes, sometimes looking at me sadly, sometimes accusingly. I
had encountered many histories. Once I thought that was a problem;
that ideally there should be only one history. And one identity. But I
was wrong. A society with only one story of the past, with only one
vision of the future, with only one identity would be a terrifying place:
a nightmare of a totalitarian society, devoid of arguments, differences
and competing visions. The problem was not the presence of many
histories and identities, but that they were so divided by Dead Zones,
with little possibility of dialogue between them.

We always tried to listen attentively to the past, to hear the murmurs
reaching us from so far away. Our desires were so strong that what
we heard were our own thoughts echoed in those indistinct murmurs.
We forced heroes to speak on our behalf, pretending that they were
speaking of their own volition. Was this respect? Was it respect to dye
Ataturk's hair after his death? To bring the heroes back to fight again
and again, battles so different from the ones they had fought in their
lifetimes? To recruit others dying elsewhere for our causes? Perhaps the
dead should be allowed to rest in peace; perhaps it was time to bandage
the open wounds of the statues.

Suppose there was this one God, this extraordinary being who could
see everything and was accepted by everyone as the ultimate judge.
Suppose she was invited to reach a final verdict on the past. What if one
could weigh all the past and reach the verdict that it was one of conflict?
Or one of coexistence? Did that determine the future? Could the living

not decide the future for themselves? There was no doubt that they did, that we all did this as we gave birth to our ancestors and as we re-conceptualized the past in line with the desired future.

There was still that brush with destiny to figure out: my birthday and the Dead Zone, how I came to work at the area that had caused my birth and that of the Dead Zone, the names of the Dead Zone through history, the name of Pyla and so much more. Was my preoccupation with the Dead Zone a mere coincidence? Could there be something more? Deep inside, I sometimes felt there was. Then again every place was symbolic or hid a memory, every date had some meaning, we had so many flags, histories, and commemorations. 'It is the magic of nationalism to turn chance into destiny,' I read in what I thought was the best book on nationalism, *Imagined Communities*. We also turned history into destiny by making it seem that there was only one way forward. But nothing was preordained and there was no such thing as destiny, much as we sometimes believed, or wanted to believe, in it. We chose the past – the ancestors, the dates, the events, the anniversaries – that made the present appear inevitable and the future preordained.

So who was to blame? I had no clear answer. After all those years I still could not come up with an answer. Because now I thought that it was the wrong question; that sometimes the question of blame was not the right one, especially when societies were caught in a circle of violence and counter-violence.

> OK, yes we can accept some of what you say, that they suffered too, but surely not as much as we did in 1974. Not even close. So who suffered most? Tell us. Just check the numbers. Can't you even answer that? Are you afraid to take a stance? Where do you stand?

> We suffered so much in the 1960s from you all the way to 1974. Check the numbers and you will see. You still make us suffer. OK, OK, so you suffered too in 1974. But look at you now, look at how well you live.

I was never able to give a straight answer, but I did not want to either. The one thing I was certain of was that we had caused each other unbearable suffering; that we bore heavy responsibilities for what we had done to others and our own. I also wanted to add that now we were displaying tremendous cruelty to people weaker than us living among us. We demanded absolute justice, but there was none absolutely just among us. We demanded unconditional respect of all our human rights when we never respected those of others.

But were things that simple? Was it ever possible for people who were still in pain from those festering wounds to feel the others' pain? I had often been in the company of right-wing nationalists who refused to even consider such things. They were responsible for many of the terrible things that had taken place. But they were in part the creation of the other side's cruelty too, the others' atrocities and lack of acknowledgment of their own record of blood. And they became each other's excuse.

I was still trying to shake off the weight of responsibility. I, who was born in 1964, born of and with the Green Line, I, who never did anything, surely I was not responsible. We, the young, had nothing to do with it. We bore no responsibility. But there were many kinds of responsibility. Responsibility for committing acts of violence was only one. Perpetrating atrocities only became possible under conditions that, if not encouraged, at least allowed them to happen. This was the responsibility of indifference and inaction. The largest atrocities had often been committed by a few who lived in a society that did not care. A society that did not want to know, one that did not care enough about the victims to bother to know. We still refused to assume any responsibility for the pain and misery we had inflicted upon each other. This only left the wounds festering until acknowledgement and forgiveness was offered. Sadly, even that did not always work.

What about outsiders' responsibilities? Britain, the USA, the mother-fatherlands. They had serious responsibilities without doubt. But I came to believe that more than enough had been said in Cyprus about their roles, though not enough in the countries themselves. In Cyprus we always spoke of others' responsibilities and so little about our own. They had been turned into our alibis. There was yet another alibi. 'It's all the politicians' fault.' But who voted for them and then put microphones in front of them to amplify their voices? And we even had some responsibility for the other side's politicians.

I remembered how relieved I was to get to know the left-wing Turkish Cypriots living in Istanbul. Now, I felt I had a right to criticize my own side, because that was what they did with theirs. Why should it be so? What about that thing we called principles? Why always wait for them to go first, as they also waited for us? And another thing. Beginnings. The original sin. We always argued that someone else started it all, that someone else was responsible for all the evil. 'The other side', 'the foreigners', 'a woman'. And one more thing: I was no longer interested in who had borrowed from whom. The question of authentic culture and origins, as if this was an issue of national ownership – coffee was originally Arabic, or Turkish, and others later 'borrowed' it – was no longer relevant.

The Dead Zone was a place of fear and hope. It was one of the most militarized places on earth; a void pulling us into protests and confrontations. The Dead Zone was always alive – lurking, waiting, pulling us all towards the Zone of the Dead. The more we fed it with our blood, the hungrier it became. It was also the place drawing the peace activists. Pyla/Pile too was a mixed place, one of conflict and cooperation, the past and the future, a life continuously threatened and one that wished to persist. So was Cyprus. It was a place of danger for Greece and Turkey, one that brought them so close to wars. But it could also become a place of hope for them too, one that could bring them together into a more peaceful future; one that could offer them new ideas, new ways of thinking about their own sad records. The two countries could also provide models for Cyprus. New historians there were writing thoughtful critiques of the histories of the two countries, and calling for changes in schoolbooks. There were many kinds of Greece and Turkey, those diverse societies with complex cultures, despite those who claimed that they only came in sealed, pure, homogeneous packages, with nothing in common. For much of the twentieth century, western archaeologists who also tried to keep the 'West' well apart from the 'East' had presented Cyprus as the buffer separating the two.

POSTSCRIPT

A month and a half after all hope for a solution was lost, I was suddenly pushed across the Buffer Zone, as the UN called the Dead Zone. The other Greek Cypriots who were also pushed across the Dead Zone were as surprised. When the first Greek Cypriot man was formally allowed by the Turkish Cypriot authorities to cross, we were carried along with the crowd of journalists and TV crews rushing to memorialize the event. Turkish Cypriots waiting to cross the other way round welcomed him with loud claps and cheers. This was being transmitted live and the whole world knew at once: people were now crossing the Dead Zone of Cyprus in both directions.

I walked forward a few steps. Then a few more metres. No one had noticed. No one seemed bothered. I was free to go anywhere I wanted. Impossible. So, I turned back, crossed the barricade and went back to stand in line at the Turkish Cypriot checkpoint in order to formally cross. The other Greek Cypriots who had also been pushed through were already standing in line. We had all gone to the Turkish Cypriot checkpoint after hearing conflicting reports that the Turkish Cypriot authorities might on that morning of 23 April 2003 open the border. And they did. The moment the news became public, thousands of people from both sides began joyfully walking towards the Dead Zone.

About a month and a half earlier, only a handful of people were converging on the Dead Zone from the two sides. Their stride was heavy but purposeful, knowing they were heading there to offer their blood, this time for an unusual cause. The Dead Zone was coming alive again. This was 10 March 2003, a bleak Monday morning, when news had just reached Cyprus from the Hague that the negotiations between the two sides to reach a solution based on a UN-proposed plan had failed. 'There was no middle ground' was the BBC's headline. There had been much hope that this time round the negotiations would succeed. The stakes were enormous. Failure would mean that only the Greek Cypriot side would enter the EU, rather than the whole island. That would have meant that Turkey's entry would subsequently face a possible obstruction by Greek Cypriots. Yet, once again the talks had failed.

The Turkish Cypriots had staged the largest demonstrations ever, in support of the jointly negotiated, UN-brokered plan that came to be known as the Annan Plan, after the UN's Secretary General. The demonstrators also expressed their desire for EU entry, and dislike of their leader Denktash. But he managed to stand rock-firm, unyielding under the wave of protests. The -tash in his name, meant precisely that: a rock. A rock that would sink not only the Turkish Cypriots but the future of Turkey too.

Greek Cypriots publicly demonstrated against the Annan Plan. One of the bishops, another Golden-Mouthed, declared that he was praying for Denktash, who was ill at the time of the previous negotiations, to get well because he would surely reject the plan. Eventually, whether due to the bishop's efforts or not, the Greek Cypriot leadership was indeed able to hide behind Denktash's recovery and rejection.

A few days before the March negotiations failed Greek Cypriots elected a new president, Papadopoulos. He was the leader of the centre-right DIKO, one of the least compromising Greek Cypriot parties. Some of his party's MPs had led the demonstrations against the Annan Plan, calling it the 'Satanan Plan'. His law firm had been accused in a number of international press articles of being implicated in the violation of the UN sanctions against the Milosevic regime by registering and offering various services to Yugoslav companies involved in money-laundering for Milosevic. His party was the single significant Greek Cypriot party that had generally avoided participating in bi-communal events. Now, however, he had the support of the left-wing AKEL, and had to drastically change his image. AKEL dug up and published a single decades-old photograph of him at a bi-communal meeting, claiming that he had always been in support of such events. He had undergone such severe photographic surgery on his campaign posters that when

I first saw them I thought that it was someone else with an uncanny resemblance to him. It took a while to realize that it *was* him, with wrinkles removed and a drastic nose job. For AKEL, the lure of power had proved more powerful than principles. The other Dead Zone, the divide between the Greek Cypriot left and right, had proved more powerful than the Dead Zone itself, making it impossible for AKEL to support Clerides, the ex-DISY leader and ousted President, who had shown a desire for compromise during the negotiations. Gradually, AKEL would express more scepticism about the proposed Plan, while DISY would support it. During the final countdown at the Hague, the new Greek Cypriot leadership was left in no doubt that Denktash, who had called the plan backed by the UN Secretary General 'a crime against humanity', would reject it. So Papadopoulos conditionally accepted the plan, leaving Denktash to take all the blame.

I had been bitterly proved twice wrong in all this. Naively, I had expected AKEL to stand for its principles rather than power, as I had also expected it to adopt the more compromising stance and support the Plan. Given the stakes and the benefits of a solution to all involved, I had also expected that the Plan would be accepted. The negotiations had been lengthy and arduous. Newspaper headlines sometimes described them as 'a dialogue of the deaf'. In the meantime, people who were deaf had begun their own bi-communal meetings in Pile/Pyla.

The eventual failure of the March 2003 negotiations meant that, as things stood, only the Greek Cypriot side would enter into the EU, Turkish Cypriots remaining in isolation. The visit of the President of the European Council, at the time the Greek Prime Minister, was wildly celebrated on the Greek Cypriot side, despite the inconvenience of pouring rain, as Turkish Cypriots watched in despair. For Greek Cypriots this was a sign of finally becoming western. No one noticed that on that symbolic day, the island was covered by a thin layer of African soil, as Africa gave us a physical sign of its proximity. The rain carried with it African desert sand giving everything an orange hue. (Actually someone did. 'You see this dust,' the owner of the car-wash remarked, noting the long queue of waiting cars. 'For us it's gold-dust falling from the sky.') I feared that the common desire to lift the wall in Cyprus so that all Cypriots could become European, carried with it a disturbing vision of Cyprus as a whole turning into another wall, the outer wall of 'Fortress Europe'.

The stakes were particularly high for Turkey too. The Cyprus Problem had turned into a major obstacle for Turkey's EU aspirations. Greece, under the influence of new visionary leaders, became a supporter of Turkey's application and Turkey's efforts towards democratic reform, arguing that a stable and democratic Turkey within the EU would be to everyone's benefit. A new government came to power in Turkey before the crucial negotiations on Cyprus. It was a party with an Islamic background, whose leaders sometimes used the term 'Islamic-Democrat' to describe it in English. This party regarded Turkey's entry into the EU as a means to develop a more open and tolerant society, including more tolerance towards religion. The newly elected government wavered wildly on the Cyprus issue. At the last moment, it came to the support of Denktash and the talks failed. Soon I would be proved wrong yet again, but this would be the happiest occasion.

Despite the news of the diplomatic failure at the Hague, or perhaps because of it, some people from both sides began a steady walk towards the Dead Zone the morning the news arrived. They were meeting there to give blood samples in order to find a suitable bone-marrow transplant for Jale, a five-year-old Turkish Cypriot girl suffering from leukaemia. This was the second such drive since February 2000, when a bi-communal group had organized a campaign where thousands of people gave blood in order to save two boys, one Greek Cypriot the other Turkish Cypriot. The public's participation was so enthusiastic that in no time the island gained the largest donor registry per capita in the world.

A few weeks after the Hague, the unexpected happened, and the initiative came from the most unlikely source. Denktash announced the opening of the borders. The man who had always obstructed contacts, insisting that Turkish Cypriots would be 'massacred once again' if people got together in numbers, allowed the opening of the border both ways. His motives were wildly disputed. Was this due to pressure from the Turkish Cypriots' demonstrations? Did he expect violence to ensue that would prove him right?

Given the opportunity, people immediately took things into their own hands, crossing in their thousands to the surprise, and initial dismay, of both government leaderships. But on the first morning things were still uncertain. Many people from both sides went to Ledra Palace on 23 April, unsure that they could cross. Unbelievably, in a few minutes with few formalities, we were on the other side, 150 metres down the same street. This place that until yesterday was so far away, further than any other country in the world; this place of lost memories and homes for some, of complete mystery for the young.

Many Greek Cypriots went straight to their old homes, towns and villages. Some found their old homes where Turkish Cypriots or Turks now lived. They knocked and were let in, were offered coffee and sat unable to know how to act. The Greek Cypriots felt they were finally back in their home, but they saw this was home to their host too. In some cases, as Greek Cypriots left, the Turkish people or Turkish Cypriots living there took out an album of photographs the Greek Cypriots had left behind and returned it. Turkish Cypriots too went to see their places in the south. Those who were younger said that the next day they would bring their elderly parents to see their homes. But they would have to prepare them well, they cautiously added. Things were no longer as the parents would remember and expect. Others went to find old friends. Sometimes the disappointment was enormous: their friends had died. When they did find friends they had not seen for more than thirty years, they saw in their faces how much they themselves had aged. When Turkish Cypriots returned the old photographs, the Greek Cypriots were able to reunite with their old selves after so long. Others immediately began to talk money. Greek Cypriots searched for potential employees, Turkish Cypriots for employers, others for partnerships. Prices were compared in detail, including those for Russian prostitutes. Greek Cypriots marvelled at the natural beauty of the north; Turkish Cypriots gaped at the flashy shopping malls in the south. Greek Cypriots rushed to the casinos in the north, Turkish Cypriots to the horse-races in the south.

On Thursday, one day later, divided Nicosia became a mixed city once again. Streets were full of people from the other side, the others' language was heard everywhere. Old people stumbled as they tried to speak a language they had not spoken for more than thirty years. In a few minutes they spoke comfortably, smiling as they said how good it felt to speak it once more. People spoke their language loudly and without fear while on the other side. They seemed to want to let others know they were there, and when the others understood they immediately welcomed them. In many cases, they acted as their guide and host for the whole day, taking them around, always insisting on paying. Then they arranged a date on the other side the next day: the host would in turn become guest on the other side, and the guest would become host and guide. Many of the younger people were shocked to realize they could not tell who was who.

I was all too pleasantly surprised at the way things were working out. It seemed like a festival of goodwill that people were determined to express towards each other.

But, on the first morning I also saw some Greek Cypriots standing paralysed at the Ledra Palace checkpoint. They stood still watching others crossing, with tears flowing down their cheeks. Perhaps it was difficult for them to believe this was happening. Perhaps they wanted to go too but felt it was not politically right. Perhaps they did not dare visit their old home in case it was not there. Maybe they worried about their own reaction if someone else now lived there. Or perhaps they were not ready yet for the encounter between their memories and the current reality.

'This was the day I had been waiting for so long, thirty years,' Mr Antonis told me. He was in his early thirties when he left with his wife and small children:

> I drove to my village alone. My wife said she was not sure yet, if she wanted to come. On the way, I noticed that some houses were no longer there. It had all changed so much. When I turned the corner, I saw mine. It was such a relief. Still there, as it was before. But when I saw it, I understood someone was living in it. What should I do? I had to go in. How can I explain the moment when my hand touched the front gate. How long I had waited for this moment. Now I saw that some things had changed. I wanted to go around the garden, to first see it all but was ashamed. I knocked on the front door. This middle-aged woman opened the door. I told her I used to live here and she was still so nice. She asked me in and in the living room I saw the photos of the whole family, with the children and her husband. Thankfully, she was Turkish Cypriot. She seemed pleased to see me and told me I could go around the house. 'Can I, really?' I asked. 'Please, it was your home,' she said, but she looked down when she said it. We stood up but I didn't know if I should wait for her to go first. I think she didn't either. I went ahead and she came behind me. 'This is our son's room,' she said when I entered one of the bedrooms full of posters. 'Sorry, it's untidy.' At some point, when I came to the garden I started crying – it was too much, to see it again, my home, but now others living there, everything also different – she turned away with her eyes wet and left me alone. 'I will wait inside,' she said. She must have called her husband to come from work. When I came back to the living room they wanted me to sit down for a while. I asked her where she came from. 'We are refugees too,' she said. They told me how they left theirs behind in 1974. 'We won't go back to Paphos,

but we want to see it again.' I felt sorry for them. They wanted me to have lunch with them and to meet their children, but all I wanted was to be alone in my car and drive away. But it felt like an insult to refuse them. They really wanted me to stay. I promised I would return with my wife and children, and we soon did. In the car, everything swirled in my head. The pain, the relief, finding my home, others living there – sometimes I was angry at them, then I also felt sorry for them, and then they saved my home because they lived there. All my life I wanted to go back. Now I'm not sure any more. It's not the same and now they live there. When I spoke to my wife, at first she became angry at me. 'How can you keep on calling her 'the house-lady'?' she demanded.

Neyir Hanim, a Turkish Cypriot woman, now living in a house where Greek Cypriots lived before 1974, told me about the Greek Cypriot family's visit:

We too wanted to go and see our old places in the south, but we waited. We knew soon the Greek Cypriots would come and we wanted to be there when they did. We did not want them to come after thirty years, and find the house closed. All around our neighbourhood Greek Cypriots began coming. But ours took so long – almost three weeks. The wait was the worst. Waiting, waiting, keeping the house tidy, preparing nice food to offer them, next day the same again, jumping every time the door knocked. And then you were afraid – how would they react, what kind of people would they be, what should you tell them? So when they came and they stayed with us to eat, and we saw they were good people it was such a relief. It was not easy. With them around you felt strange in your home.

Many people wanted to go back and thousands tried it. Instead, many came to understand this could not be, because they were not the people who left – they were not the same people, nor were the places the same. They found it difficult to talk when reporters eagerly asked how it felt to be back. All they were able to explain was their confusion: knocking on the door of their home to be allowed in, often welcomed and treated as guests, almost relatives, allowed to walk through every room and check the trees in the garden. They met the family now living there, understanding how this was now their home too; what it would mean to them too, if they had to leave. Greek Cypriots understood that those living in their house must have been refugees too. The divided experiences of dislocation were now put together. Previously they hated the idea that someone else might live in their home. Now they felt almost thankful someone did and looked after it, allowing it to be a living home instead of ruins. Even if the current owners were Turkish settlers, they now encountered a living family, not an abstract idea. Some, though, chose not to go back. They said that they would only go back when the home was theirs. Why go back to be treated like visitors in their own home, and then leave?

Did Greek Cypriots really want to return? That would mean leaving another life behind to begin all over again, and asking someone else to leave theirs behind once more. The trees they had planted after 1974 were now fully grown. I wondered if people were greeting their old homes, or if some were saying goodbye. Saying goodbye in their own way, now that they were able to return and spend time there. Before they had fled in panic. The younger generations thought that they were going back home, but found themselves getting to know the place for the first time.

People seemed to go out of their way to make the owners-visitors feel comfortable. Many seemed embarrassed, guilty even, for intruding into someone else's home – or for living in another's house. Despite the difficulties, shock and anger, the absence of incidents was as remarkable as the tact and goodwill that people expressed towards each other. I would never have anticipated that things could work out as they did. Perhaps it was the combination of confusion, embarrassment and guilt that created the humility necessary to behave humanely.

The lack of incidents was as remarkable at the once fearful Ledra Palace checkpoints that marked each side of the Dead Zone. In a few weeks, crossing became a routine. One policeman's job was to draw a line every time someone crossed. Four lines were then crossed with a fifth, and so on, to make counting easier. Usually a few more bored policemen lingered around sitting together and smoking, doing nothing obvious. Mornings around seven became very busy with hundreds of Turkish Cypriots crossing to work on the Greek Cypriot side. Afterwards, things got very quiet, except minor incidents when people expressed resentment at having to present documents while crossing. The most serious incident on the Dead Zone took place one bright November afternoon.

When the Turkish Cypriot policeman at the Ledra Palace checkpoint looked up from his booth into the large sad eyes and long ears of a passport-bearing donkey demanding to cross, he was not caught by surprise. He was required to check one unusually furry visitor from the south with a fake passport. Under the name it wrote 'Mr Cyprus' and under occupation 'porter'. This was part of a stunt-protest demanding free movement and the lifting of all crossing restrictions by both sides, organized by bi-communal groups. The protesters held banners writing 'We Demand the Freedom of Movement of the Donkeys of Cyprus'. A Turkish Cypriot donkey was to cross the other way but it failed to appear. Events took an unexpected turn when the Turkish Cypriot authorities allowed the Greek Cypriot old man leading the Greek Cypriot donkey to proceed. The Greek Cypriot donkey stood in front of the police booth. The Turkish Cypriot policeman examined its passport. He looked at the photo and then back at the donkey. Even though the photo did not match, and the passport identified the donkey as male while it was in fact female – and pregnant as it embarrassingly transpired – it was ushered through without further formalities. Lurking Turkish Cypriot plain-clothed policemen grabbed the old man with his donkey and pushed them to an unmarked police car. They arrested them along with another Greek Cypriot and a Turkish Cypriot. The donkey initially walked unperturbed in front of the car, until another policeman took over and led it to the police station.

Wild speculation ensued. Would the Greek Cypriot donkey also appear in court? Under what charges? Were they going to photograph the donkey in the standard convict photo, profile with a hanging number? How about fingerprints? In fact, the donkey was not taken to court the next afternoon, only the three men who were released on bail after being charged for disrespect towards the Turkish Cypriot state and for causing a disturbance.

Political donkey-protests have had a long history in this island that was once renowned for its donkeys, when they were a rare and valuable asset, until they were replaced by pick-up trucks. In the late 1950s, the British governor of Cyprus issued an ultimatum for EOKA fighters to surrender. A donkey displaying 'I surrender' was left to roam the streets, until it was taken in by the British police. The recent protest played upon a long discussion on the Turkish Cypriot side sparked by a statement from the Turkish Cypriot leader, Denktash. He said that there was no Cypriot nation and the only true Cypriots were the Cypriot donkeys. Denktash explained that there were no Cypriots, only Greeks and Turks in Cyprus. The left-wing Turkish Cypriot opposition immediately reacted with headlines like 'Of course, we are donkeys, otherwise how could we bear the heavy burden of our leadership', or suggesting Cyprus should be called *Eshekistan* ('Donkeystan'). One of the most outspoken critics of Denktash's statements was a radical journalist, Shener Bey. When the Turkish Cypriot authorities later closed down his newspaper *Avrupa* ('Europe'), he reopened it and called it *Afrika*, presumably to suggest that the authorities behaved like African-style autocrats. Shener Bey faced dozens of charges and was a regular visitor at the Lefkosha court. His latest case was heard just before that of the three men of the donkey incident, where they all met. *Afrika* came up with the best headline: '2 Greeks, 1 Turk and 1 True Cypriot Were Arrested!'

After the border openings, people could enjoy the unprecedented, previously unimaginable, luxury of coming together for ordinary outings and parties. Rather ominously, though this was not apparent then, on Friday the 13th (February 2004) we organized an impromptu party with Turkish and Greek Cypriot friends, all supporters of the UN Plan. The occasion was to celebrate the solution of the Cyprus Problem! We thought then that this was The End. The two leaders had agreed in yet another round of talks in New York to renegotiate, but in this case, whatever the outcome, the Plan would be put to a referendum on both sides.

This time round, Denktash did not give room for Greek Cypriots to hide. The recent Turkish Cypriot elections had given a majority to the pro-solution, pro-Annan Plan forces, headed by a new Prime Minister, Mr Talat, leader of the left-wing CTP, putting even more pressure on Denktash. The Turkish government no longer wanted to be stigmatized with Cyprus and strongly urged Denktash to acquiesce. Under twin pressures, he reluctantly agreed, hoping perhaps that Papadopoulos would now refuse. Papadopoulos was caught off-guard but, no longer able to hide behind Denktash, he too reluctantly acquiesced. Countdown began to 24 April 2004, Referendum Day.

Our optimism at the party was based on our understanding that the YES was fairly certain on the Turkish Cypriot side. On the Greek Cypriot side, the leadership of DISY had indicated a strong YES spirit, though there were doubts as to whether its supporters would follow its lead. AKEL had been reserved, at times negative, but surely now it would strongly emerge in support of the Plan, given its role as the champion of compromise and rapprochement. Together, the two parties commanded almost seventy per cent of the electorate.

But the mood was different on each side. The stakes were different, after Greek Cypriots had secured entry into the EU, given the failure of a previous round of talks in March 2003 due to Denktash. (Was that the end after all?) Turkish Cypriots saw the solution as an opening to the rest of the world along with automatic entry into the EU, after decades of economic and political isolation. These worked as powerful incentives towards accepting a compromise, enabling them to go through a political revolution with the Turkish Cypriot left in the lead. Greek Cypriots, having secured EU entry, were much more reluctant. Polls indicated a strong NO lead, even as more than eighty per cent of Greek Cypriots asked said they had not actually read the Plan. DISY's leadership made the difficult YES choice, much to the credit of its leadership who was aware of the large risk of a NO result. AKEL would waver until the last moment.

The two head negotiators whose mandate was to negotiate a solution led the NO campaigns. Denktash and Papadopoulos staged spectacular performances, both with live tears recorded on camera. Denktash's tears were rejected as of the crocodile variety; his talk of a 'diabolical Plan' was dismissed. Papadopoulos' tears were welcomed, as those of an honest leader. One of the Greek Cypriot Bishops warned YES supporters in no uncertain terms that 'they would loose the Kingdom of Heaven', meaning that they would go to hell. The most frustrating aspect of the Greek Cypriot NO campaigners' argument was their patronizing insistence that they supported the NO having 'Turkish Cypriots' best interests in mind too'.

There were also unexpected developments. In the only open rally in support of YES, I saw the very man, the proud Hellene who had verbally attacked me in the past. We smugly smiled at each other. The last hope, the big question was: Which way will AKEL go? AKEL proved to be full of surprises, perhaps not so surprising in retrospect. It appeared that sensing the strength of the NO campaign, and not wishing to relinquish its position in government, AKEL eventually came up with the convoluted position that it was in principle in support of the Plan but that the referendum should be postponed in order to work towards a YES and that guarantees were needed to ensure the implementation of the Plan. If these were not offered, it would call for a NO. At that point, a few days before the referendum, both demands were unrealistic. So, AKEL, still in principle in support of the Plan, eventually announced its final NO, adding in a memorable phrase, that 'we say NO in order to cement the YES', meaning in another referendum.

AKEL's ability to discipline its members was phenomenal. I wish I had never been to see a man high in AKEL's hierarchy, widely admired for his integrity and courage and known for his pro-YES views, arrive amid enthusiastic applause to a bi-communal YES meeting, only to turn himself into the sad spectacle of a muted man. AKEL's choice to write the darkest page in its history at this most critical juncture was distressing to many of us who had for years pinned our hopes on the left of both sides. Turkish Cypriot friends, who had spent arduous sleepless months away from their jobs engaged in the YES campaign, sometimes under threats and right-wing media-smearing, called in tears unable to believe AKEL's position. I never felt so disorientated – a loss of direction and hope, a sense of betrayal from those I too had lain my ultimate hopes upon.

RESULT: seventy-six per cent NO on the Greek Cypriot side, sixty-five per cent YES on the Turkish Cypriot side.

Turkish Cypriots celebrating the YES vote on their side carried placards accusing AKEL of treachery and urging 'Denktash to the South' to join the NO supporters there. A Greek Cypriot friend who went to the doctor complaining of various pains, was surprised when the first thing he was asked was if he had voted YES. Indeed so, and the doctor, who had also voted YES, said that many of his patients had indicated similar political symptoms.

One week later, on a fine Saturday morning, Greek Cypriots, having slept in this island uncertainly placed between Asia, Africa and Europe, finally woke up in Europe. This was 1 May 2004, when Cyprus officially joined the EU 'forever', as Papadopoulos pointed out. Among spectacular fireworks and celebrations Cyprus triumphantly became the ninth and two thirds new country of the EU. It failed to become the tenth, since only Greek Cypriots were in, despite the YES vote on the Turkish Cypriot side. The Greek Cypriot leader, Papadopoulos, was welcomed into the EU with caustic remarks by top EU officials that he had cheated them, soon to be repeated in more diplomatic language by the UN Secretary General himself. Cyprus immediately became a headache for the EU, due to the Cyprus Problem and the unclear status of the Dead Zone that now became the EU's uncertain border. Greek Cypriot politicians who led the NO campaign spoke with a new European sense of pride and achievement: 'We have now managed to turn the Cyprus Problem into a European Union Problem as well.' As well as a UN, Greek-Turkish, NATO, occasionally American-Russian problem – among others, they meant.

'The Cypriots know they cannot become a World Power; but they have succeeded in becoming a World Nuisance, which is almost as good,' commented a humorist. And this was back in 1965. Could this change? If a reunited federal Cyprus does eventually join the EU, it will become the first EU Muslim-Christian federation. Cyprus, for a change, could become a beacon – well, a candle at least – of hope in this post-9/11 era that has witnessed boundaries turning into iron lines of division, as dangerous and difficult to cross as our own barbed wire line.

Or will the Dead Zone keep haunting us? 'History is a nightmare from which I am trying to awake,' mused Joyce's protagonist.

MAIN SOURCES AND SUGGESTIONS FOR FURTHER READING

This selection includes works that were of key importance for this research intended as suggestions for further reading, rather than providing an exhaustive bibliography. For further information and references on specific topics, the reader may consult the list of my publications below.

GENERAL

On East and West, Edward Said, *Orientalism* (New York: Vintage, 1979) has become the classic text. On nationalism, see Ernest Gellner's *Nations and Nationalism* (London: Blackwell, 1983), Benedict Anderson's *Imagined Communities: Reflections on the Origin and Spread of Nationalism* (London: Verso, 1983), Eric Hobsbawm's *Nations and Nationalism Since 1780* (Cambridge: Cambridge University Press, 1992).

On social memory, the work of Paul Connerton, *How Societies Remember* (Cambridge: Cambridge University Press, 1989) provides a good discussion. On the use and abuse of history David Lowenthal, *The Past is a Foreign Country* (Cambridge: Cambridge University Press, 1985) provides a magisterial survey. On narrative and the question of historiography, see Hayden White, *The Content of the Form* (Baltimore: Johns Hopkins University Press, 1990). On issues of responsibility, acknowledgement and blame: Zygmunt Bauman's *Modernity and the Holocaust* (Cambridge: Polity, 2000), Stanley Cohen's *States of Denial* (Cambridge: Polity, 2001) and Michael Ignatieff's, *The Warrior's Honour* (London: Vintage, 1999). On Aphrodite: Stass Paraskos, *The Mythology of Cyprus* (Nicosia: Georgiades, 1981), Bruce Thorton, *Eros* (Colorado: Westview Press, 1997), Paul Friedrich, *The Meaning of Aphrodite* (Chicago: University of Chicago Press, 1978), Diane Bolger and Nancy Sherwint (eds.), *Engendering Aphrodite* (Boston: American Schools of Oriental Research, 2002). Two key literary influences for this work were Salman Rushdie's *Midnight's Children* and Gabriel Garcia Marquez's *100 Years of Solitude*. The excerpt from the poem at the beginning is taken from *St Suniti and the Dragon* by Suniti Namjoshi (Melbourne: Spinifex Press, 1993), which I first encountered in Marina Warner's fascinating *Managing Monsters* (London: Vintage, 1994).

CHAPTER 1

Bernard Lewis' *The Emergence of Modern Turkey* (London: Oxford University Press, 1968) is the standard introduction to the history of Turkey. Hugh Poulton, *Top Hat, Grey Wolf and Crescent* (London: C. Hurst and Co., 1997) provides an overview of the development of Turkish nationalism. A thorough biography of Ataturk is Andrew Mango's *Atatürk* (New York: Woodstock, 2000). On Turkish historiography, see Halil Berktay, 'The "Other Feudalism"' (Unpublished Ph.D. thesis, University of Birmingham, 1990). On Greek perceptions of the Turks and vice versa in history, popular culture and beyond, I am indebted to and was inspired by the unique work of Herkul Millas, *Tencere Dibin Kara...* (Istanbul: Amaç, 1989). On the Greek minority in Turkey, see Alexis Alexandris, *The Greek Minority of Istanbul and Greek-Turkish Relations, 1918–1974* (Athens: Centre for Asia Minor Studies, 1992).

CHAPTER 2

The standard history of Greece is Richard Clogg, *A Short History of Modern Greece* (Cambridge: Cambridge University Press, 1986). For the influence of the West and the changes in Greek historiography, see Konstantinos Dimaras, *Ellinikos Romantismos* (Athens: Ermis, 1985) and Elli Skopetea, *To Protypo Vasilio kai i Megali Idea* (Athens: Politipo,

1988). On Greek identity and folklore, see Michael Herzfeld, *Ours Once More* (Austin: University of Texas Press, 1982) and Alki Kiriakidou-Nestoros, *I Theoria tis Ellinikis Laografias* (Athens: Etairia Spoudon Neoellinikou Politismou, 1978). On Greek nationalism, see the special issue of *European History Quarterly*, vol. 19, no. 2 (1989), especially the article by Kitromilides. The standard Greek Cypriot school textbook is Katia Hadtzidimitriou, *Istoria tis Kyprou* (Nicosia: 1987). On the Greek Cypriot historical outlook regarding 'past peaceful coexistence', see Costas Kyrris, *Peaceful Coexistence in Cyprus Under British Rule (1878–1959) and After Independence* (Nicosia: Public Information Office, 1977). A very useful overview of the Cyprus Problem by a Greek Cypriot author is Michael Attalides, *Cyprus: Nationalism and International Politics* (New York: St Martin's Press, 1979). On the plight of Greek Cypriot refugees in 1974, see Peter Loizos, *The Heart Grown Bitter* (Cambridge: Cambridge University Press, 1981). For an official Greek Cypriot view of the Cyprus conflict, see the publications of the Greek Cypriot Public Information Office, or the relevant web-page (http://www.pio.gov.cy/).

CHAPTER 3

The standard history of Cyprus in Turkish is Şükrü Gürel, *Kıbrıs Tarihi* (Istanbul: Kaynak Yayınları, 1985). The standard Turkish Cypriot school textbook on the history of Cyprus is Vehbi Serter *Kıbrıs Tarihi* (Nicosia: Kema Ofset, 1990). On the 1960s conflict, the most detailed study is Richard Patrick, *Political Geography and the Cyprus Conflict* (Ontario: Department of Geography Publication Series, 1976). For an interesting view by a Turkish Cypriot psychiatrist on the Turkish Cypriot experiences of the 1960s and 1970s, see Vamik Volkan, *Cyprus: War and Adaptation* (Virginia: Virginia University Press, 1978). An overview of the events of the 1960s up to 1974 from the perspective of Turkish Cypriots is provided by Pierre Oberling, *The Road to Bellapais* (Boulder: Social Science Monographs, 1982). For an overview of the Cyprus Problem by a Turkish Cypriot author, see Metin Tamkoç, *The Turkish Cypriot State* (London: Rustem, 1988). For the official Turkish Cypriot view on the Cyprus Problem, see the publications of the Turkish Cypriot Public Information Office, or the relevant web-page (http://www.trncpresidency.org/).

ECHOES FROM THE DEAD ZONE

CHAPTER 4

For an early courageous attempt by a Greek Cypriot author to move beyond one-sided views of the Cyprus Problem, see Zenon Stavrinides, *The Cyprus Conflict* (Nicosia: 1975). An excellent collection of articles from various disciplines and viewpoints is Vangelis Calotychos (ed.), *Cyprus and Its People: Nation, Identity and Experience in an Unimaginable Community* (Colorado: Westview Press, 1998). A fascinating account of the opposed views on the history of Cyprus presented by the British and the Greek Cypriots is provided by Michael Given in the first chapter of *Symbols, Power and the Construction of Identity in the City Kingdoms of Ancient Cyprus* (Unpublished Ph.D. Thesis, Cambridge University, 1991). On inter-ethnic killing in Cyprus see Peter Loizos, 'Intercommunal Killing in Cyprus', *Man*, no. 23 (1988). On the Greek Cypriot left and Turkish Cypriots, see Loukas Kakoullis, *I Aristera kai oi Tourkokyprioi* (Nicosia: Kasoulides, 1990). A recent interdisciplinary overview of the Cyprus Problem inclusive of all the views of those involved is Alexis Heraclides, *Kypriako: Sigkrousi kai Epilisi* (Athens: Sideris, 2002). The most exhaustive and balanced internet source of academic writings on the Cyprus Problem is http://www.cyprus-conflict.net/.

CHAPTER 5

The standard left-wing Greek Cypriot account of the history of Cyprus is Kostas Graikos, *Kypriaki Istoria*, vols. 1–2 (Nicosia: 1980–1982). On Turkish Cypriot folklore, see HAS-DER *Halkbilim Sempozyumları* (Istanbul: Gümüş, 1986).

CHAPTER 6

No published academic research on Pyla beyond that mentioned below exists.

AUTHOR'S ACADEMIC PUBLICATIONS FOR FURTHER REFERENCE

For a general discussion on the historiography of Cyprus, see Yiannis Papadakis, *Perceptions of History and Collective Identity: A Study of Contemporary Greek Cypriot and Turkish Cypriot Nationalism* (Ph.D. Thesis, University of Cambridge, 1993), Chapter 2. On language and dialect in the two sides, see 'On Linguistic Bea(u)tification and Embarrassment',

Modern Greek Studies Yearbook (2004). For a comparison of the two National Struggle Museums in Nicosia, see 'The National Struggle Museums of a Divided City', *Ethnic and Racial Studies*, 17:3 (1994). On memory, forgetting and commemorations, see 'The Politics of Memory and Forgetting in Cyprus', *Journal of Mediterranean Studies*, 3:1 (1993) and 'Nation, Narrative and Commemoration: Political Ritual in Divided Cyprus', *History and Anthropology*, 14:3 (2003). On a comparison of folklore studies on the two sides, see Bekir Azgin and Yiannis Papadakis, 'Folklore', in K. Grothusen, W. Steffani, P. Zervakis (eds.), *Zypern* (Gottingen: Vandenhoeck and Ruprecht, 1998). On divided Nicosia, see V. Calotychos, P. Hocknell, Y. Papadakis (eds.), 'Divisive Cities, Divided Cities: Nicosia', *Journal of Mediterranean Studies*, 8:2 (1998). On the Greek Cypriot left and right, see Yiannis Papadakis, 'Greek Cypriot Narratives of History and Collective Identity: Nationalism as a Contested Process', *American Ethnologist*, 25:2 (1998). On the bi-communal peace movement and the issue of recognition, see Costas Constantinou and Yiannis Papadakis, 'The Cypriot State(s) *in Situ*: Cross-Ethnic Contact and the Discourse of Recognition', *Global Society*, 15:2 (2001). On how Turkish Cypriots employ the notion of 'Enosis' and Greek Cypriots that of 'Turkish Expansionism', see Yiannis Papadakis, 'Enosis and Turkish Expansionism: Real Myths or Mythical Realities?', in V. Calotychos (ed.), *Cyprus and its People* (Colorado: Westview Press, 1998). On Pyla, see: 'Pyla: A Mixed Borderline Village Under U.N. Supervision in Cyprus', *International Journal on Minority and Groups Rights*, 4: 3–4 (1997); 'The Social Mapping of the Unknown: Managing Uncertainty in a Mixed Borderline Cypriot Village', *Anthropological Journal on European Cultures*, 9:2 (2000); and 'Discourses of "the Balkans" in Cyprus: Tactics, Strategies and Constructions of "Others"', *History and Anthropology*, 15:1 (2004).